Harper Lee's
To Kill a Mockingbird

Harper Lee's
To Kill a
Mockingbird

New Essays

EDITED BY MICHAEL J. MEYER

THE SCARECROW PRESS, INC.
Lanham • Toronto • Plymouth, UK
2010

Published by Scarecrow Press, Inc.
A wholly owned subsidiary of The Rowman & Littlefield Publishing Group, Inc.
4501 Forbes Boulevard, Suite 200, Lanham, Maryland 20706
http://www.scarecrowpress.com

Estover Road, Plymouth PL6 7PY, United Kingdom

British Library Cataloguing in Publication Information Available

Library of Congress Cataloging-in-Publication Data

Harper Lee's To kill a mockingbird : new essays / edited by Michael J. Meyer.
    p. cm.
  Includes bibliographical references and index.
  ISBN 978-0-8108-7722-1 (hardcover : alk. paper) — ISBN 978-0-8108-7723-8 (ebook)
  1. Lee, Harper. To kill a mockingbird. I. Meyer, Michael J., 1943–
PS3562.E353T63375 2010
813'.54—dc22   2010020634

∞™ The paper used in this publication meets the minimum requirements of American National Standard for Information Sciences—Permanence of Paper for Printed Library Materials, ANSI/NISO Z39.48-1992.

Printed in the United States of America

For the cast members of *Raisin in the Sun* produced at Walther High School, Melrose Park, Illinois, in 1977—Sean, Donald, Carlotta, Cheryl, Paul, Greg, Claudette, and Jeff. You helped me realize how important black equality is and how much untapped talent was beneath the surface of your personalities. There was so much injustice then, and producing a play with an all-black cast was a risk in a school with a majority of whites, but we broke barriers that will never be put back up. Thank you for sharing your talents with me. I share this book with you now as a symbol of how far we've come and with a recognition of how far we have yet to go.

Contents

Foreword

Maggie Seligman

I first encountered Harper Lee's *To Kill a Mockingbird* in 1962, as a student at the New Lincoln School in New York City, previously a lab school at Columbia University and one founded on what Jem calls the "Dewey Decimal System" (*TKAM* 18). Unlike Miss Caroline, who tries to enforce on the white first graders of Maycomb an awkward and misguided interpretation of John Dewey's ideas regarding democracy and education, New Lincoln embodied the democratic and diverse demographic and pedagogical approaches that Dewey advocated. Indeed, I always felt sorry for Miss Caroline, since her own preconceived notions and prejudices interfered with her ability to integrate Dewey's ideas about progressive education into her classroom, and the all-white population she taught—while economically diverse—did not truly represent what Dewey had in mind. The teary tyro teacher, whose first day of school is no better for her than it is for her outspoken, academically talented student Scout, offers a touching irony and serves to introduce us early in the novel to the perils and intransigence of early socialization and education, a point which the novel investigates by relating the experiences of the citizens of Maycomb in the context of a trial that shakes the foundations upon which their society and culture are built. Indeed, as the characters discover, it is difficult to uproot a tree whose roots run deep, and while one can perhaps loosen its grip in the soil or hack off a few branches, it will take more than the martyrdom of one man, Tom Robinson, to cut the taproot.

My first reading of *To Kill a Mockingbird* in a classroom that was balanced by gender and populated by an array of children from a variety of racial, ethnic, religious, and social backgrounds made for interesting discussions. But what stands out for me as that young reader was the moment when I read Bob Ewell's accusation of Tom Robinson: "I seen that black nigger yonder ruttin' on my Mayella!" (*TKAM* 196). How could I not be shocked by Ewell's language and its inherent hatred and violence? Indeed, that accusation plunges any reader right into that crowded, sweltering courtroom. And for good reason, as parsing out Ewell's accusation reveals that his words embody many of the thematic concerns addressed in Lee's novel as well as the critical attention the text has received. In fact, Bob Ewell's declaration may have been responsible in large part for the widespread censorship of the novel, often on the basis of racial prejudice but also for its use of "questionable" or "immoral" language.

Ewell perjures himself immediately because he admits to seeing the act of rape in progress. He calls Tom a "black nigger," using a racial epithet reflective of the attitudes of many Maycomb citizens who represent a wide range of age and economic status. More significantly, Ewell uses the word "black" as a way to underscore Tom's skin color and, in so doing, emphasizes the converse, the color of the white community of Maycomb and the white jurors who will decide the case. In fact, given Ewell's economic and educational deprivations, whiteness is all he has, the only quality that raises him above the level of the African Americans in his community and elsewhere in his cultural geography. Therefore, Bob Ewell's accusation underscores the problems of racism that the novel addresses in complex and kaleidoscopic ways.

Next, Ewell uses the word "ruttin'"—a word that, by definition, describes the mating of animals. This word dehumanizes Tom. In fact, by using the words he does to describe the ravishment of his daughter Mayella, Ewell channels Iago's words to Desdemona's father, Brabantio, when Iago informs him that Desdemona is eloping with the Moor, Othello, also a man of color: "I am one, sir, that comes to tell you your daughter and the Moor are now making the beast with two backs" (*Othello*, I.i.115–116). Iago's intent is to destroy Othello, just as Ewell's intention is to destroy Tom Robinson. But surely this destruction becomes an easier task psychologically speaking when the alleged perpetrator is no longer considered a human being in the mind of the antagonist and is, instead, transformed into an animal. Even more interesting, by comparing Tom to an animal, Ewell seems to reveal that he views Mayella as somewhat of a beast herself for attempting to seduce Tom. As Iago tells Brabantio, "You'll have coursers for cousins, and gennets for germans," (*Othello*, I.i.112–113), as if the offspring of a white woman and a man of color could be nothing but inhuman. Quite ironically, in his testimony, Tom Robinson states that Mayella told him "'what her papa do to her don't count'" (*TKAM* 221), implying that Ewell himself is engaging in unnatural acts with Mayella—and the genetic consequences for the offspring of incest are well-known.

Moreover, by describing Tom—and Mayella—in animalistic terms, Ewell highlights the fact that throughout *Mockingbird*, characters that Maycomb society deems "the other" are dehumanized, ostracized, or isolated. These characters include Arthur Radley, who becomes a ghost with a ghostly name, not a human one; Tom and Helen Robinson, Calpurnia, and the African Americans citizens of Maycomb County in general; the Mrunas in Africa, whom the missionary ladies want to save, lifting their poor benighted souls by enlightening them with Christianity; the Ewells themselves, Mayella Ewell in particular; and finally, the tomboy Scout. "Otherness" is also an issue for the Radley family, who sever themselves from the quotidian social world of Maycomb; for Mrs. Dubose, a relic of another age, symbolized by the pistol she allegedly keeps hidden in her lap in case she needs to shoot at Yankees or anyone else attempting to pillage the Southern way of life; for Miss Maudie, whose magnificent garden subjects her to threats and warnings from the fundamentalist "religious right" of Maycomb County and whose protection of her flowers leads to a fire that destroys her entire house and possessions, a loss she rises from like a phoenix, connecting her with the bird imagery in the novel; to Dolphus Raymond, who, as Scout observes, "deliberately perpetrated fraud against himself" (*TKAM* 228), because he chooses to engage in culturally forbidden love; and to Dill, "who preferred his own twilight world" (163), using his imagination to cushion himself from the emotional pain of feeling unloved and unwanted. Indeed, a large number of the characters in *Mockingbird* are nonconformists who live by their own lights, to the extent that they can do so, surviving within the microcosm of Maycomb and the macrocosm of the South in the 1930s, a region just sixty-eight years removed from secession from the Union and from the resentment and resistance to Reconstruction that followed the Civil War.

The words of Bob Ewell's accusation also spotlight the violence that permeates the novel and the way in which all the violence in *To Kill a Mockingbird* is perpetrated by men. First there is the home imprisonment of Arthur Radley. He is not chained to the bed, as Jem imagines, but, as Atticus explains, "There are other ways of making people into ghosts" (*TKAM* 12), namely, to destroy them psychologically, a form of murder perpetrated upon Boo by his father. (It seems worthy of note that like Bob Ewell, Mr. Radley abuses his own child.) The ensuing acts of violence, both real and threatened—among them, the alleged rape, Mayella's beating, Burris Ewell's threats to Miss Caroline, Tom's murder, the scene at the jail with the Cunningham lynch mob, the "chunking" and ugly language aimed at Helen Robinson as she walks to and from work, the threats to Atticus, the cut screen at Judge Taylor's house—all culminate in the attack on Jem and Scout by Bob Ewell and Ewell's murder at the hands of Boo Radley on Halloween night. Indeed, only when Boo is "spared" the consequences of the murder of Bob Ewell is the chain of violence broken.

Victimization because of race or gender, another theme that is central to the novel, is also inherent to Bob Ewell's words. When Scout observes that she feels the "starched walls of a pink cotton penitentiary closing in on [her]" (*TKAM* 155), she is recognizing the limitations of a patriarchal, paternalistic society that, in the Southern world of Maycomb County, is, ironically, perpetrated by its matriarchs—Aunt Alexandra being the most leviathan of these figures. The paternalism that dictates how Scout and other Maycomb ladies must behave is, by extension, the same sort of paternalism that rationalized the "peculiar institution" of slavery. At their core, therefore, Ewell's words clarify for readers that in the world of Maycomb County and places like it, women and those placed in socially inferior positions, such as people of color, Jews, Catholics, or the socially or economically disadvantaged, are vulnerable to becoming victimized or marginalized. As a side note, it is interesting that Mayella, both disadvantaged and marginalized, is, unlike Scout, willing to breach the social and gender codes that confine her, though with disastrous results. Clearly, Harper Lee invites readers to consider gender roles, gender codes, and sexism as well as social roles, social and religious codes, and racism.

Harper Lee wrote her novel shortly after some of the early skirmishes in the civil rights movement, in essence the Civil War of the twentieth century, and when Bob Ewell refers to his daughter as "*my* [emphasis mine] Mayella" (*TKAM* 196) in his raw description of her alleged rape by Tom Robinson, Ewell seems to be speaking of himself and, by extension, any whites who felt that their way of life and economic status were in danger of being usurped or plundered by African Americans and other people of color. Such an interpretation not only allows readers a retrospective glance at the Fugitive Slave Law, Dred Scott decision, states rights, secession, and the Civil War but also highlights the ways in which diversity or changes in the social order that might threaten the status quo are central concerns of Lee's novel.

One thing that remains somewhat of a puzzle is why Bob Ewell brought what was a private and, to him, humiliating matter into the public eye. Why didn't he attempt to save what he had of his reputation and protect himself and his daughter from public embarrassment and scrutiny? Surely Tom Robinson was not going to speak of what happened, given the social codes of the time, and Mayella's beating at the hands of her irate father would go a long way toward keeping her from doing such a thing again. It appears that what Bob Ewell hopes to gain is what all American citizens hope for—equality. The courts are "the great levelers" (*TKAM* 233), as Atticus reminds the jury in aid of Tom Robinson's defense. But if this is true for Tom, it is true for Bob and Mayella Ewell as well, no matter how despicable readers may find them. In contemporary times, ones that are in some ways not so different from the 1930s, American citizens continue to suffer from racism, economic deprivation and the stigmas that accompany it, sexism, and prejudice or marginalization on the basis of disability, religion, or sexual orientation. Consequently, these times seem ripe for a reevaluation of *To Kill a Mockingbird*. Indeed, this present volume, in commemoration of the fiftieth anniversary of the publication of the novel, offers its readers an opportunity to discover new ways of seeing its themes, imagery, characters, controversies, and structure, while also providing ideas for its use in the classroom. Issues of pedagogy and pedagogical approaches to the text are addressed by Christian Z. Goering and Cindy M. Williams, who offer a fresh and contemporary way to make the novel more accessible and relevant to today's middle and high school readers and writers. In the Soundtrack of the Novel assignment that they have devised, readers establish connections to the text by associating aspects of it with songs, describing and explaining the connections they perceive and collecting the songs. In contrast to focusing on the learner, James B. Kelley employs grounded theory to determine three main patterns or unifying concepts that reveal the ways in which teachers are talking to their students about the novel. His findings suggest that teachers do a fine job with text-based approaches but need to do a far better job with teaching critical literacy and the theories that can take readers beyond initial, predetermined readings of the text.

Racism and the novel are examined in this present collection by Angela Shaw-Thornburg, who considers the ways in which African Americans might feel marginalized by the text and concludes that it can nevertheless be taught today as a way to open up discussions of white identity and social stereotyping in the South and in the country as a whole, a new perspective indeed. Katie Rose Guest Pryal argues forcefully that there is a failure of cross-cultural racial empathy in the novel and suggests that whites cannot truly empathize with blacks because of "fear of revelation"—that is, a fear of what it will show them about themselves.

The novel's portrayal of the legal system and analysis of Atticus through the lens of the law form the basis for another series of discussions. Jeffrey B. Wood proposes that the real protagonist in the novel is the law and that "bending the law" for the sake of a higher purpose is a necessary and moral act. Ann Engar provides a detailed examination of the ways in which Atticus has been a model of what a lawyer should be and how his character has influenced the legal profession and shaped some individuals' choice to become lawyers. Malcolm Gladwell takes an opposing view regarding Atticus' courtroom performance and legal judgment, finding him not to be a reformer but someone who perpetuates the status quo. Gladwell also compares Atticus to "Big Jim" Folsom, the governor of Alabama during the time Harper Lee was writing the novel.

The presence of "the other" in the novel is examined herein, most notably by Hugh McElaney, whose study suggests that the novel addresses differences as forms of disability and that in Maycomb, fear of exposure to these differences leads to the creation of boundaries that are not to be transgressed. Careful investigation of related issues, such as the stigmas arising from disabilities and the connections among eugenics, racism, and social groups, enhances this comprehensive discussion. A performance analysis of the novel is offered by Lisa Detweiler Miller, who argues that Boo Radley and Tom Robinson, as representatives of the medical and minority models of disability, should be read not for their metaphorical significance as disabled bodies but as figures that move the narrative of social progress forward by inviting performances that subvert cultural norms.

Themes and imagery in the novel receive considerable attention as well. Michael J. Meyer presents a detailed and artfully woven exploration of the images of fear and darkness that permeate the novel and leads readers to a deeper understanding of the ways in which the text demonstrates that to overcome fears, whether they be childhood fears, fear of the unknown or differences, or fear of the dark—including "dark" people of color—one must see beneath the protective "masks" the characters wear and see beyond the surface of such things as skin color. Carl F. Miller breaks new ground in his consideration of the sporting culture of the South and provides a heretofore unexamined look at the way in which Lee uses sports to establish the identities of some of the characters. Moreover, his consideration of the balance between progress and tradition in sports reflects the tension between tradition and progress that is present in Maycomb society. Other significant attention to themes and imagery in the novel is offered by Jochem Riesthuis, who discusses three episodes that contribute to Scout's development and that seem to form touchstones for the development of themes and symbols within the novel. Finally, in a particularly insightful discussion, Robert C. Evans presents a very close reading of the text and by illuminating the strong parallels that exist between Boo Radley and Bob Ewell, as well as other characters, maintains that the novel achieves its cohesion and aesthetic plan from these paired characters. The collection is rounded out by contributions from Alec Gilmore and from Derek Blair and Cecilia Donohue.

In "To Catch a Mockingbird," Cathy Newman reports that each year the Heritage Museums of Harper Lee's native Monroe County, Alabama, produce a two-act dramatic adaptation of the novel, enacted by local people, and that this performance, in addition to the Old Monroe County courtroom where the trial was filmed, attracts upwards of thirty thousand visitors who seek a connection with Harper Lee and *To Kill a Mockingbird*. (Interestingly enough, Harper Lee herself has never seen the play.) Without a doubt, just like the knothole that Boo fills with treasured objects intended to pique the interest, curiosity, and amusement of Jem and Scout, *To Kill a Mockingbird* is full of an abundance of treasures intended for its readers. Perhaps Harper Lee, like Boo, gave the reader everything she had, and thereafter retreated back into the private quiet of her daily life as he did.

Finally, regardless of the reader's feelings or views of the book and despite the criticism and censorship it has faced, *To Kill a Mockingbird* has endured. It is hoped that the essays herein can act as intellectual keys and guidebooks to a novel that continues to leave such an indelible mark on the literature and ethos of the United States.

Works Cited

Lee, Harper. *To Kill a Mockingbird*. New York: Harper Perennial Modern Classic, 2006.

Newman, Cathy. "To Catch a Mockingbird." *National Geographic*, January 2006, 114–122.

Shakespeare, William. *Othello*. Ed. Gerald Eades Bentley. Pelican Shakespeare Edition. New York and London: Penguin Books, 1970; 1986.

Preface

> The most important things are the hardest to say because words diminish them.
>
> —Stephen King, *On Writing*

As a teacher of literature for over forty years and as a professor of American literature for the last twenty, I have been passionate about adding to my extensive library. My finished basement, in fact, boasts eight large bookcases that are completely filled with a very eclectic mix of volumes: the works gathered there range from Stephen King to John Steinbeck, from Michael Crichton to F. Scott Fitzgerald, from Garrison Keillor to Robert Penn Warren. Yet despite the number of volumes on the shelves, there are far fewer books that I actually "own," that I claim as texts that are "part of me," that have touched my soul and whose characters I identify with and know intimately. Such ownership on my part suggests that an author has somehow developed a very unique relationship with me, a reader. *To Kill a Mockingbird* by Harper Lee is one of those texts that has literally "come alive" for me; indeed, her fictional construct has taken root in my consciousness.

Charles Shields, in his biography of Lee entitled *I Am Scout*, draws his readers' attention to all the "real" elements in *Mockingbird*. Maycomb, Alabama, is based on Lee's hometown, Monroeville, located in the same state; Atticus Finch is based on Lee's father, Amasa Coleman Lee; Charles Baker Harris, also known as Dill, represents Truman Capote, Lee's childhood and lifelong friend; and, of course, Lee's child heroine, Jean Louise Finch, is grounded on the author herself. Moreover, real historical parallels are also evident in the story setting of the historical 1930s—an era notorious for Jim Crow laws and for racial injustices evident in such trials as that of the Scottsboro boys (1931), during which nine black men were convicted of raping a white woman and whose sentence of death for that crime parallels the fate of Lee's Tom Robinson. Mention is also made of economic deprivations during the Depression, FDR's first inaugural address, and the developing Nazi movement in Germany, highlighting the racial discrimination and persecution practiced by Hitler's Third Reich.

Yet what I wish to suggest in this preface to my collection of essays on *To Kill a Mockingbird* is that it is of little interest to readers if Harper Lee is Scout or if there is actual fact behind the fiction. What matters is that Lee has created a novel wherein her readers can create an empathetic connection between the written word and their lives, can find the ownership I spoke of previously. Thus, as I read Lee's words, *I* become Tom Robinson, *I* become Boo Radley, *I* become Scout, *I* become Atticus Finch, *I* become Bob Ewell. Though I may not be black or emotionally unsettled, am not a six-year-old child, am not a lawyer or an illiterate living on the fringe of society, I am Lee's characters because I genuinely identify pieces of myself in her work. That, of course, is a rare talent for an author to possess. To be able to transform readers into a gossipy old woman like Miss Stephanie Crawford, into a pretentious and overbearing aunt like Alexandra, into a repressive father like Mr. Radley, or into a nurturing black housekeeper like Calpurnia takes skill indeed.

Since the bulk of my work has primarily been as a Steinbeck scholar, I cannot resist relating an experience that occurred some twenty years ago at a 1989 conference held in Tuscaloosa at the University of Alabama and entitled "The Steinbeck Question." As one of my first academic experiences as a recent PhD, the event remains an important one precisely because it helped me learn about the fragility of an author's reputation. I discovered somewhat belatedly that the conference had been originally motivated by an apparent decline in Steinbeck's reputation in tertiary academia. When I arrived at the first session, it was clear that several of the audience members were not convinced that Steinbeck's writing was still worth reading and, in fact, were quite hostile toward the author for what they perceived as inaccurate even derogatory portrayals of the "lower" class and the poor. The session on *Of Mice and Men* was one of the most controversial I attended as one member of the audience made it clear she felt the text was not only inferior literature but also morally objectionable. When several of the conference participants questioned this quintessential "Southern lady" about her feelings, she sheepishly admitted she had never actually read Steinbeck's novel. Her objections were based on rumor and hearsay rather than actual interaction with the text. When we asked her to return the following day—the conference was a three-day affair—after having actually read the brief 108-page novel, she agreed. As promised, she returned, but her opinion of *Mice* and Steinbeck had clearly changed. In fact, when we asked for her honest reaction after she had read Steinbeck's very concise masterpiece, she replied, "Why, them's my people!"

Harper Lee's characters are just as much my people. I find Lee's honesty amazing and engaging; I appreciate her ear for a child's voice; I consider her imagery complex and well planned; and I find myself returning to the text again and again to rediscover its nuances and to further plumb its plot and themes. While like Steinbeck, Lee has often been relegated to a middle school or high school curriculum, *To Kill a Mockingbird* is far more crafted than has previously been imagined, as the essays included here give evidence. Unfortunately, the novel continues to be seen as adolescent rather than adult fiction, and over the fifty years since its publication, only a few serious literary studies have given credence to the contention that it is a literary masterpiece—no matter that it is the author's only production—one that even mature readers can return to with pleasure, continuing to cull genuine insights into life's numerous lessons as well as to discover historical economic conflicts in the 1930s, to probe continuing discrimination against the African American race in America, and to learn about gentrified Southern customs and how upper-class value systems might differ from those of the lower class. Such historical emphases, however, do not make *To Kill a Mockingbird* a dated artifact, precisely because the prejudice against those who are "different" or who are "othered" remains quite evident even in 2010; such prejudice is reflected in the attempt of a dominant class to assert its influence and power over the less competent or the less powerful, in the persistent prejudicial treatment of gender differences, and in the treatment of differently abled individuals as inferior souls, practices that persist some fifty years after the novel's publication. Even today, readers are still called to "walk in another's shoes" in an attempt to understand those who seem to be "strange" and whom we fear out of ignorance rather than any concrete proof that they are threatening or "scary" individuals.

Hopefully, this volume will serve as encouragement for yet further in-depth study of Lee's American classic and recognition that it is hardly a child's novel, a fictional construct intended for preadolescents that features a naïve and immature narrator whose appeal is limited at best. Finely tuned by a woman whose literary talent never again reached the printed page, *To Kill a Mockingbird* remains a classic text. Despite complaints about its so-called moralistic preachiness, its "inconsistent" shift between and adult and prepubescent narrator, and its "over-sentimentalized" prose style, I believe the novel will continue to find still more readers who will "own" its characters, embrace its themes, and recommend it to another generation. I am convinced that decades from now, Scout, Jem, Dill, Atticus, Calpurnia, Tom, Boo, Mayella, and Bob will continue to live in the imagination of new readers who will own them, just as I do now.

Acknowledgments

There are so many people that have contributed to making this book a reality. Once again I need to thank David Kellam Brown for his cover illustration. His talent is incredible, and I am happy to have him participate once again in an important volume of literary criticism. Spot art was provided by Claire Walsh, and I owe her a debt of thanks as well. Without Maggie Seligman, who contributed the foreword and close readings of all the essays, I am sure that the accuracy of details and references would be less meticulous. As a person who has taught *Mockingbird* many times, Maggie was able to find numerous errors and to help contributors be confident of their accuracy both in quotes and in specific details they recorded from Lee's plotline. I am grateful for her feedback and for her willingness to spend extra time in writing the foreword to this collection. To my production editor at Scarecrow Press, Jayme Bartles Reed, I once again offer gratitude. Her sharp proofreading skills and clear editing made this second book for Scarecrow much easier than the first. To the contributors, with their various skills, I send my warm congratulations for a job well done. Deadlines were met, revisions were prompt, and the responses to suggested changes were warm and friendly. That makes an editor's job pleasant indeed. On this fiftieth anniversary of Lee's novel, I believe all readers should pause to reassess the complexity and greatness of this novel. While it is true that more has been written about *Mockingbird* in law reviews than in literary criticism, I hope this volume will mark a change in that pattern, and the opinion that *Mockingbird* is merely a children's book will become a critical assessment of the past and one that will not resurface in the future.

Editor's Note

In order to facilitate easy location of the quotes from *To Kill a Mockingbird*, I have changed all references to the novel to a standard edition: Harper Lee, *To Kill a Mockingbird* (New York: Harper Perennial Modern Classics, 2006). Please consult this version for all quotes. The title *To Kill a Mockingbird* is shortened to *TKAM* in text citations.

Part 1

EDUCATIONAL APPROACHES

CHAPTER 1

What Teachers (Don't) Say: A Grounded Theory Approach to Online Discussions of *To Kill a Mockingbird*

James B. Kelley

Online forums for talking about creative literature—which include the commercial Internet sites eNotes.com, SparkNotes.com, Amazon.com, and Oprah. com—are often ignored by contemporary literary critics, if not dismissed outright as unreliable or even undesirable resources for persons wishing to explore meaning in a given literary work. These popular and ever-growing online forums, however, are heavily trafficked by contemporary readers and thus present a unique opportunity to explore how a popular novel is being read and discussed today. By December 3, 2009, for example, the "Question & Answer" section at eNotes.com on Lee's novel *To Kill a Mockingbird* contained 2,124 postings, with each posting consisting of one question and one or more answers to that question. Nearly all of the posted questions come from middle school and high school students, and most of the posted answers come from teachers at the middle school, high school, and first-year college level. *To Kill a Mockingbird* is the most widely discussed work at eNotes.com. The Question & Answer section on Lee's novel not only attests to the novel's popularity in school curricula today but also presents an opportunity to explore how teachers tend to explain *To Kill a Mockingbird* to students.

Perhaps the main obstacle in analyzing these online forums, aside from a possible perceived triviality of the postings, is the literary critic's lack of familiarity with a method for making sense of such massive amounts of data. In the case of the novel *To Kill a Mockingbird*, there are thousands of postings at eNotes. com that contain answers written by hundreds of different teachers, and each answer often measures only one to three paragraphs in length. This essay employs a widely used method in qualitative studies in the social sciences, a method called grounded theory, to explore what teachers say and do not say about Lee's novel. This study uses a simplified grounded theory approach to review a sample of the postings at eNotes.com; uncover recurring themes in the teachers' answers to students' questions; and draw conclusions about how teachers working in middle school, high school, and first-year college classrooms tend to talk to students about Lee's novel.[1] In the final sections, this essay explores the extent to which recent trends in critical literacy are present (or are not present) in the teachers' answers to student questions about *To Kill a Mockingbird*.

Defining Grounded Theory

Grounded theory is an approach that views generalizations as necessarily built from the ground up, from a wide range of specific incidents in concrete, real-world data. Researchers using grounded theory begin with an initial, open-ended question. In this study, the initial question is how middle school, high school, and first-year university teachers talk to students about Lee's novel. To explore the question of what teachers say and do not say about Lee's novel, the researcher using grounded theory needs to collect and evaluate a large number of statements from teachers to students about the novel and, through both close engagement with each statement and constant comparison among different statements, begin to identify the larger and broader categories of statements (or "concepts" and "emerging themes," as they are called later in this essay) that slowly begin to manifest. Whether performed manually or with the aid of computer software, grounded theory is both rigorous and creative. Grounded theory is rigorous in that the researcher must read and code the entire sample of data (usually more than once, as recommended by Robert C. Bogdan and Sari K. Biklen) and must constantly reconsider the significance of individual pieces of data as the researcher moves back and forth through the sample; this process of ongoing reconsideration is part of what is called the constant comparative method. Grounded theory is creative in that the researcher needs to ask innovative questions and develop unique approaches to the material with the goal of "creat[ing] new order out of the old" (Strauss and Corbin 27). Grounded theory is also necessarily subjective. In order to avoid forcing the data to fit some preconceived notion, for example, the researcher should consider all data and ideas that are encountered in the study and reject nothing outright. The researcher should also reflect on her or his own biases and remain willing to reconsider the manner in which she or he has been organizing and interpreting the data.

Grounded theory is not as alien to the literary critic as it may first seem. In a sense, grounded theory is literary criticism (or, more precisely, a mix of New Criticism and structuralism) writ large. This approach has its roots in the humanities and, like New Criticism, concerns itself with close, repeated readings of the "data" (the term for the prose passages to be examined here) in order to uncover one or more core ideas, or concepts. Like structuralism, grounded theory then seeks to uncover larger, unifying patterns (or emerging themes) that show how the separate narratives under examination collectively make sense of the problem or situation being discussed.

Sampling, Coding, and Grouping the Data

To read, code, and group well over two thousand items—even if each item averages only one to three paragraphs in length—is a daunting task. Thus, a sample of the most recent postings to the Question & Answer section at eNotes.com on Lee's novel *To Kill a Mockingbird* has been retrieved and carefully examined in this study. The sampling process used here can be characterized as systematic and non-purposeful. The sampling is systematic in that two postings—the top posting and the bottom posting—have been retrieved from every "page" (with each page containing fifty postings) of the first thirty pages in the Question & Answer section, beginning with the most recent posting (dated December 2, 2009) and working backward to the earliest posting in the sample (dated August 30, 2008). The sampling is non-purposeful in that samples have not been selected or rejected on the basis of criteria such as the length of the answer, the relative success of the answer in replying to the initial question, or the rating of the answer by readers of the thread. This method of systematic, non-purposeful sampling has been used to preserve a high level of generalizability; in other words, any general statements growing out of this study of the sampled answers should hold true of all of the Question & Answer postings on Lee's novel at eNotes.com from the last year or so.

Each of the retrieved postings consists of one question, usually asked by a student, and one or more answers, usually posted by a teacher or a number of teachers. The purpose of this study is not to explore how well the teachers have answered the students' questions but rather to explore what the teachers have had to say to students when asked about the novel. Thus, the questions have been removed from the working sample. (It bears noting, however, that the questions themselves, taken as a whole, read very much like homework assignments given out by teachers to their students. A number of questions end in tell-tale phrases such as "Justify your answer" or in statements that sound even more specific to a particular classroom setting, such as "Make reference to the use [or avoidance] of the poetic elements covered in the unit." If many of the questions themselves have indeed been written by teachers for students, the Question & Answer section at eNotes.com may be seen as a particularly trustworthy source of data for this line of inquiry, as an echo chamber of sorts for teachers' thoughts and statements about Lee's novel.) Also deleted from the working sample are all individual answers that have not been written by self-identified teachers at the level of the middle school, high school, and first-year college classroom. The initial retrieved sample of ninety-three answers (in sixty postings) has thus been reduced to a working sample of seventy answers. The seventy answers making up the working sample have then been coded, compared, and grouped by emerging themes.

Even when using a simplified method of coding rather than a highly complex one, researchers find coding to be a time-consuming process.[2] Each item of data (in this case, each answer from a teacher) is read line by line in order to identify what are often called "incidents"; in this study, incidents may be seen as any number of notable key words, phrases, and small ideas. In even the shortest of the posted answers examined in this study, multiple incidents can often be identified. One short answer reads,

> Scout's observations at the end of the novel about protecting Boo Radley from suffering shows how much she has grown up. Scout makes the connection between Boo and the mockingbirds Atticus had forbidden Jem to kill because she has come to understand the value of innocence and goodness and the evil of cruelty. This passage shows that Scout has adopted her father's values. It also serves to emphasize the major themes of the novel.

In the passage, multiple key words and phrases stand out, including "Scout's observation," "at the end of the novel," "protecting," "suffering," "grown up," "makes the connection," "forbidden . . . to kill," "come to understand," "innocence," "goodness," "evil," "cruelty," "adopted . . . father's values," and "major themes." From the incidents in this answer and in any number of the other answers in the working sample, more general and abstract terms—sometimes called concepts—can be identified; these concepts need to be specific yet broad enough to contain a grouping of incidents. Thus, the phrase "at the end of the novel" can be grouped, along with a set of related incidents appearing in other answers, under the concept *story structure*, and "protecting" can be grouped— again, along with a set of related incidents appearing in other answers—under the concept *sense of duty*. As in this case in this answer, multiple key words and phrases within one answer can sometimes be grouped under the same, single concept. Three of the incidents identified here—"grown up," "makes the connection," and "come to understand"—can be grouped under the concept *education* or *development* or *life lessons*, for example, and four of the incidents in this same answer—"innocence," "goodness," "evil," and "cruelty"—can be grouped under the concept *morality* or *values*. Of course, coding is not limited to the words actually used. A second short answer reads,

tough wording by example

> Like the intellectual southern gentleman that he is, Atticus treats the ladies of his neighborhood with a degree of kindness and respect that is typical of this era: Men and boys were expected to treat all women and girls with near-reverence, standing when women entered a room, offering seats to them when none were available, opening and holding doors as they entered buildings, addressing them with the formal title "ma'am," and basically showing courtesy and politeness that was above and beyond today's standards. Atticus exemplifies the expected male treatment of women in the south of the 1930s.

This answer contains a string of incidents—from the concrete word "kindness" to the unnamed notion of chivalry—that can be grouped under the previously established concept *morality* or *values*. Even a negative or implied incident can be noted. For example, the slip in terminology from "gentleman" and "ladies" in the opening sentence to "male" and "women" in the final sentence suggests that the idea of *social class* is operating in the answer, even if it remains unstated. Alongside the unstated idea of social class are incidents of a particular place ("southern" and "south") and a particular time ("this era," "today," and "the 1930s"); these three incidents can all be grouped meaningfully under the concept of *setting* or *context*.

The exact phrasing of each concept is unimportant. What is important is that these concepts are grounded in the data itself; they are not imposed from above by the person who interprets the data. A concept that contains multiple incidents across multiple answers is a good candidate for promotion to the status of "emerging theme"; emerging themes are statements of the central topics, concerns, and approaches of the answers as a whole. Through this grounded theory approach to the Question & Answer postings, three emerging themes have been identified: *Moral Character, Life Lessons,* and *Text and Context.*

An understanding of these three emerging themes has been refined through a process called "theoretical sampling." Key words, phrases, and ideas related to each emerging theme (e.g., "good," "right," "innocent," "evil," "bad," "wrong," "guilty," and names of specific characters in the novel for the emerging theme Moral Character) have been entered into text searches of the entire collection of postings (not the much smaller working sample) as an informal test of the generalizability of the conclusions about the sampled answers to the collection of answers as a whole. This theoretical sampling of the entire collection has also served as a means to explore the possibility of a wider range of ways in which teachers talk about Lee's novel.

Discussing Three Emerging Themes

A simplified grounded theory approach to the Question & Answer postings on *To Kill a Mockingbird* reveals three emerging themes in the ways that teachers talk to students about the novel: Moral Character, Life Lessons, and Text and Context.

MORAL CHARACTER

When talking to students about fictional characters in Lee's novel, particularly when talking about Atticus Finch and Bob Ewell, the teachers frequently move from character analysis to explicit and implicit statements of morality. Describing the fictional characters in the novel becomes a way of talking about moral character in the world.

One teacher calls Atticus Finch the "conscience" of Maycomb County and of the novel as a whole. In a second answer by the same teacher, also included in the working sample, Atticus is elevated above the other characters in the novel:

> Atticus's empathetic nature stands above all others, and this genu-
> inely honest and humanitarian aspect actually works to his disadvan-
> tage at times. . . . Atticus even tries to understand Bob Ewell after
> being spit upon: "Jem, see if you can stand in Bob Ewell's shoes a
> minute. I destroyed his last shred of credibility. So, if spitting in
> my face and threatening me saved Mayella Ewell one beating, that's
> something I'll gladly take."

Other answers in the working sample that talk about the moral character of Atticus Finch and Bob Ewell offer a similar interpretation. One teacher, for example, contrasts Atticus' "solid principles" and unchanging "sense of moral-ity" with the "despicable" and "evil" nature of the other man. In their descrip-tions of the two characters, many of the answers outside of the working sample likewise reproduce this opposition of "the good" and "the evil," as manifested in the two characters: Atticus Finch is "professional" and Bob Ewell is "low liv-ing," the former "courageous" and the latter "cowardly," the former "empathic" and the latter "hateful," the former "defending" and the latter "threatening," the former "not retaliate[ing]" and the latter "seek[ing] revenge," and so forth. Eight answers outside the working sample liken Atticus Finch to the very centers or arbiters of moral values for many people today, the figure of Jesus Christ and the God of Christianity. Theoretical sampling shows no similar parallel between

Bob Ewell and Satan but reveals an overwhelmingly strong pattern (in thirty-four answers, within and outside the working sample) in identifying Ewell with evil. One source outside the working sample even points out the sound similarities between Bob Ewell's last name and the word "evil."

Two posts in the working sample challenge the widespread characterization of the Finch family, headed by Atticus Finch, as good and the Ewell family, headed by Bob Ewell, as evil. The student posted a question that included the characterization of the Ewell daughter as "disgusting" (i.e., "Why is the Ewell daughter both pathetic and disgusting?") and the teacher, in replying to that question, challenged the characterization (i.e., "I don't agree at all that she's disgusting. Instead, I have strong sympathy for the character"). A second teacher's answer perceives Atticus' treatment of the Ewells to reveal a flaw, not a virtue, of his character:

> Atticus' view of Bob Ewell is perhaps the only chink in his armor. We are supposed to like Atticus; he's the moral center of the story, and is a sympathetic and likeable character. However, he does refer to Bob Ewell as "trash," and while his characterization may be accurate, it does not sound like a statement from a man who is supposed to be so tolerant and compassionate. However, one could also argue that Atticus has sympathy for those who he feels deserve it, like Mayella, but not for those who do not, like Bob.

A theoretical sampling of the full collection of answers has failed to locate further instances of challenges to the dominant view of Atticus Finch and Bob Ewell as embodiments of good and evil.

LIFE LESSONS

When talking to students about the experiences and changes of the younger characters in the novel, particularly when talking about Scout and Jem Finch, the teachers frequently move in their answers toward explicit and implicit discussions of influence, identity development, intellectual and social development, loss of innocence, growing awareness of hypocrisy and evil in the world, and other topics related to adolescence. The teachers' emphasis on education and the development of youth in the novel is understandable, given their occupations and their audiences of middle school, high school, and first-year college students.

A number of answers in the working sample explicitly address the idea of education. The longest answer discusses four main ideas of the novel, all relating to the emerging theme of Life Lessons. Even as one teacher writes that "Harper repeatedly mocks the various deficiencies in modern education," the teacher tracks the maturation of several young people in the story through lived experiences outside of school and explains how the novel gives the reader a lesson in the importance of being tolerant and being free of prejudice. Several answers in the working sample similarly point to the hypocrisy of the schoolteachers in the novel, who do not live by their own lessons, and one answer in the working sample argues that the children's true growth occurs when they step outside of the confines of formal education: the children "are attacked by Bob Ewell [i.e., they encounter real evil] after leaving the school." One answer in the working sample focuses more specifically on Scout's education in gender identity or performance. The teacher writes,

> Because Scout is motherless, Atticus knows that she must have a feminine influence and leaves that task to several women whom he trusts. . . . From Calpurnia, Scout learns that Southern ladies are tenacious and protective . . . [and] what it means to show hospitality as a Southern woman. . . . Scout learns from [Aunt Alexandra] what it means to be a gracious lady even when people make distasteful comments in one's home . . . [and] that even the most stubborn, set-in-their-ways Southern women can change. . . . Scout learns from Miss Maudie that sometimes Southern ladies need to be bold, especially in defense of their friends and family. . . . Scout also learns from Miss Maudie that true Southern ladies don't gossip or prejudge others.

Two answers in the working sample suggest that reading the novel can itself be an educative act. One teacher writes that reading the novel gives a student the opportunity to "analyze the themes of racial intolerance and prejudice in your own life." Another teacher writes,

> Ultimately, *To Kill A Mockingbird* is the story of humanity learning to understand each other. As a reader, we see the world through the eyes of all children, who enter this world as the most pure of human beings. The realization of life's hard lessons is taught through Scout and Jem Finch as they watch their father and community struggle with the Depression, racism, and the justice system of the Old South. We see the remnants of the old stereotypes toward blacks, women, and anyone who is considered to be an "outsider" (Boo Radley). It is a great book to teach young people about how NOT to be.

The answers outside of the working sample similarly contain explicit and implicit references to learning, influence, maturation, the loss of innocence, and life lessons.

TEXT AND CONTEXT

When talking to students about the novel's setting and publication date, the teachers frequently touch on past and present organizations of race, class, and gender. The novel's setting often receives detailed treatment in the teachers' answers, whereas the treatment of the social situation in the early 1930s and in the late 1950s is often brief and undeveloped.

No fewer than six answers in the working sample address the divisions, hierarchies, and economies within the novel's population. These answers tend to follow the promptings of the text and cluster around three scenes: Walter Cunningham's behavior on the first day of school, Walter Cunningham's behavior at the Finches' dinner table, and Jem Finch's analysis of the four classes of people in town. The working sample answers that move past a literal and text-based discussion often contain undeveloped references to Alabama in the 1930s. Atticus' kindness toward and respect for women is "typical of this era," one teacher writes: "Atticus exemplifies the expected male treatment of women in the south in the 1930s." Another answer contains a glancing reference to limits on behavior of a "black man . . . in the 1930s South." A third answer contains a series of vague references to mannerisms and dress that are typical for a certain time ("this era") and a certain place ("the area"), but neither the time nor place are specified. Part of the answer reads,

> [Atticus] wears glasses, normally wears a suit and tie, and speaks nearly flawless English, as is the custom for professionals of this era. When Atticus is at home, he "dresses down" or becomes more casual, as is the standard for men of this era. Jem . . . is your average pre-teen southern boy: his dress and manner reflect the geography and culture of the area. Typically, he dresses in pants or short pants, the average shirt, and depending on the weather, he and Scout may run barefoot.

A theoretical sampling of the full set of postings shows that teachers are highly attuned to the fictional world created in the novel. One or more teachers even ask students to draw a map of the town of Maycomb based on details given throughout the novel. Theoretical sampling also shows that answers in the full set of postings in the Question & Answer section on Lee's novel are only slightly more contextualized than those in the working sample. The full set of posts contains many glancing references to the Depression, the civil rights era, and Martin Luther King but few specific references to landmarks in the struggle for African American civil rights, including no references to the Montgomery bus boycott, one reference to *Brown v. Board of Education*, one reference to the murder of Emmett Till, and three references to the rape trial of the Scottsboro boys.

The emerging tendency in the teachers' answers to explore the presentation and transmission of unchanging and universal "truths," particularly the central idea of learning to distinguish between good and evil—coupled with the emerging tendency among the teachers' answers to discuss the novel without solid grounding in the period in which the story is set and/or the novel is first published—may have the effect of transforming the complex novel *To Kill a Mockingbird* into a simple and timeless morality tale. Such an approach runs counter to trends in critical literacy and literary theory, which seek to question, reevaluate, and contextualize a work rather than transform it into something universal and removed from the world in which it is produced, circulated, and read. The final sections of this essay define the term "critical literacy," review the working sample of teachers' statements about Lee's novel for evidence of critical engagement with the novel and with the students to whom the answers are largely addressed, and finally draw several conclusions and make several recommendations about how teachers talk to students about *To Kill a Mockingbird*.

Defining Critical Literacy

"Critical literacy" is a recent theoretical term that is used mostly in the context of secondary education—see, for example, the cited essays by Margaret C. Hagood and by Maureen McLaughlin and Glenn De Voogd—to describe the skills needed to read any given "text" (whether it be a printed novel or television advertisement) in more ways than one and to explore how the meanings of texts are constructed. In developing critical literacy in the middle school, high school, and first-year college classroom, teachers are to guide their students past an initial decoding and comprehension of the text's surface content toward a fuller understanding of how dominant and alternate readings may be performed on a single text. Discussions of critical literacy frequently use the terms of literary theory, from "reader response" to "deconstruction," and the goals of literary theory instruction seem to match the goals of critical literacy instruction: the student should come to understand the role played by the perceiving subject in the creation of meaning for a given text and appreciate the potential for radically diverging readings of the same text. Thus, at the risk of oversimplification, critical literacy is defined in this essay as a form of instruction in literary theory—modified, of course, for application in the middle school, high school, and first-year college classroom.

Also recent is the publication of a number of resources that may be useful to teachers wishing to explore how to integrate theoretical perspectives and critical literacy into their teaching of Lee's novel. The year 2007, for example, saw the publication of both Marie K. Smith's *Teaching Harper Lee's "To Kill a*

Mockingbird" from Multiple Critical Perspectives, a resource complete with classroom activities and thus tailored specifically to the needs of the teacher, and *On Harper Lee: Essays and Reflections*, a collection of essays edited by Alice H. Petry tailored to a university-level audience or higher that is interested in reevaluations of the novel through a variety of approaches. The recent teachers' answers in the working sample and in the full collection of postings on *To Kill a Mockingbird* at eNotes.com give a sense of the extent to which such critical reevaluations of and teaching aides for Lee's novel have influenced how teachers at the middle school, high school, and first-year college level talk to students about the novel.

Looking for Critical Literacy

Many of the teachers' answers in the working sample demonstrate strong familiarity with a text-centered approach to literature that resembles New Criticism. Their answers frequently move back and forth among generalizations, brief quotations, and focused analyses of the quoted passages. For example, one teacher writes perceptively about the "strong dramatic irony" present in the scene in front of the jailhouse door:

> We [the readers] know that the group of men who confront Atticus at the jail is a lynch mob that has come for Tom Robinson. Scout, however, does not understand the danger of the situation as it unfolds. When she innocently places herself in the middle of it, she sees not a group of potential murderers but a neighbor she recognizes, Walter Cunningham.

At the same time, however, many of the teachers' answers also demonstrate a reliance on pre-critical terminology, such as "essential truth," and do not demonstrate a suspicion of "authorial intent," a concept that is antithetical to New Critical close readings of texts. As famously stated by the New Critics W. K. Wimsatt and Monroe C. Beardsley, "[T]he design or intention of the author is neither available nor desirable as a standard for judging the success of a work of literary art" Lee's biography is also not a common topic in the teachers' answers in the working sample or in the full set of answers, yet a series of text searches of the full collection show that many of the students' questions ask explicitly about the author's "intent," "choice," or "purpose." These questions often sound like homework assignments given by teachers to students, and the teachers' answers in the full collection never challenge the idea of speculating on authorial intent. When it comes to incorporating more recent (post–New Critical) theoretical perspectives on literature and modeling critical engagement with the text, the teachers' answers are often less successful.

MORAL CHARACTER

The answers contributing to the emerging theme of Moral Character demonstrate only a limited degree of critical literacy. The answer identifying "perhaps the only chink in [Atticus'] armor" is critically sophisticated in that it challenges the easy and widespread classification of characters into good and evil and even hints at the power of Lee's narrative in shaping the readers' opinion of the characters: "we [as readers] are supposed to like Atticus." Even the double turn in the short paragraph of this teacher's answer—with one "however" after another—shows an interest in ongoing exploration rather than premature judgment and closure. This answer thus demonstrates an approach aligned with reader response criticism and perhaps even with deconstruction, as the answer presents (in comparison to many of the other answers) a "reading against the grain." Two posted questions outside of the working sample also draw explicitly on reader response criticism; these questions come from tenth-grade students and ask how the reader "has . . . been positioned" to respond to specific characters in the novel. No other clear instances of reader response criticism are evident in the working sample or the full collection of postings. Instead, when talking about the characters in the novel, the answers tend to reduce the literary work to a moral lesson on how and how not to behave. Such answers pursue what is called a pre-critical approach; they seek to find a moral or general truth rather than to examine the particulars of the narrative being discussed. Critical literacy might be improved by exploring how the narrative is not impartial; the novel establishes for the reader a strong sense of familiarity with some characters (the Finches, in particular) and a lack of identification with others (such as the Ewell family and the hypocritical schoolteachers). The central symbol of the mockingbird—which is identified in numerous answers by teachers, all or nearly all of whom uncritically follow the novel's prompting, as a pure and innocent creature that does nothing but sing—can similarly be interrogated or deconstructed through a parallel reading of Ted Hughes' poem "Thrushes," which portrays the little song birds of the title as cold, calculating killers.

LIFE LESSONS

The bulk of the answers contributing to the emerging theme of Life Lessons similarly demonstrate only a limited degree of critical literacy, particularly in the area of gender criticism. The answers do not demonstrate the thoughts of resisting readers, readers who question both the promptings of the text and their own presuppositions as they make sense of the reading. The answer in the working sample that addresses Scout's education in gender identity or gender performance talks without irony about what "true Southern ladies" do and do not do. While a theoretical sampling of the full collection of answers shows that some teachers gently criticize what they see as Aunt Alexandra's "zeal to feminize Scout" by making her wear a dress and attend a formal tea party, for example, the teachers' posts in the full Question & Answer section tend toward a normalized reading of Scout's gender identity development. The transition from wearing overalls to wearing a dress is commonly described by teachers as desirable progress or maturation. Scout "moves through her tomboy stage," one teacher writes. Another teacher writes that she "has developed from a little rascal to a young lady who was just escorted from her home" (this teacher's reading or recollection contradicts the text, which repeatedly asserts that Scout, dressed in her overalls, does the escorting: "he allowed me to lead him," "I led him," "I would lead him" [*TKAM* 319]). A third teacher comments that "[p]art of the charm of the novel is watching Scout, the character, mature from a tomboy to the young lady who is narrating the story" and, in a separate answer, that "Scout has grown from a naive, tom boy to a sensitive and compassionate young lady." Only one answer outside the working sample, written by a doctoral student, identifies "gender ambiguity" and "gender slippage" in several characters in the novel. Critical literacy might be improved by encouraging readers to resist taking gender identities for granted, to focus on what the text says (e.g., Scout escorts Boo, she is not escorted by him), and to explore a wider range of possible meanings for the particular words, phrases, and scenes in the novel. For example, there are only two brief discussions in the full set of answers of the "morphodite snowman" in the novel and no consideration by teachers of the different meanings of the word "morphodite." In the American South, as demonstrated in various entries cited in the *Oxford English Dictionary*, "morphodite" has been used not only as a shortened form of "hermaphrodite" but also as a term for homosexual men or women, particularly those who engage in gender-transgressive behavior or dress. The term "morphodite" is used in this sense in the United States before 1941 and appears in Truman Capote's 1952 play *Grass Harp* as well as in later writings by other gay men, including Edmund White (see *The Beautiful Room Is Empty*, 1988) and Will Roscoe (see *Zuni Man-Woman*, 1991).

TEXT AND CONTEXT

The answers contributing to the emerging theme of Text and Context again demonstrate little critical literacy. The teachers' answers often pay close attention to the "world" within the novel but little attention to the world around it. Answers often include glancing historical references as well as implicit or explicit references to timeless "human behavior" or "human nature." One such answer includes the statement "[A]s so often happens, people turn their hatred upon the person who simply reminds them of what they are. So, Bob Ewell threatens Atticus." Critical literacy might be improved by encouraging students to view the narrative of Lee's novel as a retelling of or a response to one or more "real-world" developments in the civil rights struggles. The fate of Tom Robinson may be viewed in connection with rape trials or lynchings of black men, such as the Scottsboro boys' trial in the mid-1930s or the murder of Emmett Till in the mid-1950s. The small detail at the trial scene that "[f]our Negroes rose and gave [Jem, Scout, Dill, and Reverend Sykes] their front-row seats" (*TKAM* 164) may bring to mind the Montgomery bus boycott. The visit to Calpurnia's church, the relegation of blacks to the "far corner of the square" before the trial (*TKAM* 160, 162), and a number of other details in the novel may encourage students to reflect on the doctrine of "separate but equal" and the *Brown v. Board of Education* ruling. Finally, Mrs. Merriweather's condemnation of Northern hypocrites in chapter 24—"People up there set 'em free, but you don't see 'em settin' at the table with 'em" (*TKAM* 234)—may provide an opportunity to explore the sit-ins at lunch counters across the South that were just about to start as Lee's novel went to press.

A theoretical sampling of the entire Question & Answer section on *To Kill a Mockingbird* supports this characterization of the teachers' answers as lacking familiarity with different approaches in critical literacy and literary theory. In addition to other text searches, a search for the formal terms for different critical approaches yielded no instances of use of the following terms (and, where applicable, the adjectival forms of the terms): New Criticism, Marxism, New Historicism, and feminism.

Limitations

The strong presence of the three emerging themes and the weak presence of critical literacy perhaps cannot be generalized beyond the group of teachers who have recently contributed to the Question & Answer section on Lee's novel at eNotes. com. Such generalization is limited by the examination in this study of postings on only one Internet site. Reviewing a range of online discussion forums and using surveys and interviews to reach teachers who are not active in online discussion forums may reveal additional emerging themes and varying levels of critical literacy. Indeed, such a wider study may lead to a fuller understanding of how teachers at the middle school, high school, and first-year college level talk about Lee's novel. This limitation is true of all qualitative research; there is always more data to consider. Grounded theory and other methods of qualitative research seek to maximize the opportunities for gaining in-depth information and new insights, explains Michael Patton; these methods do not seek to produce a general "truth" that can be applied with absolute certainty across different settings and different populations.

Conclusion

Teachers in middle school, high school, and first-year college classrooms do have a lot to say about *To Kill a Mockingbird*, and what they say about the novel often reflects their strong attachment to the work and their equally strong interest in sharing that passion with students. Furthermore, what they say reflects a strong familiarity with text-based approaches to literature but a weak familiarity with critical literacy and literary theories and their possible applications to the novel for the purpose of moving past initial, often predetermined readings of the text. Perhaps surprisingly, the answers posted by teachers active at the senior high school and first-year college level do not show a higher level of theoretical sophistication than answers posted by teachers at the middle school and junior high school level.

Teachers should not be expected to engage their students solely in the abstract realm of critical literacy and literary theories, of course, and the absence of critical content in the answers posted by teachers in the *To Kill a Mockingbird* part of the Question & Answer section at eNotes.com should not be taken as an indication that the project of critical literacy has failed across the board. The project is worthwhile and, given more time and the creation of more resources tailored specifically to the needs of teachers of the novel at the secondary level, may very well produce more sophisticated students as well as new, insightful approaches to Lee's novel. When it comes to *To Kill a Mockingbird*—or pretty much any other complex work, for that matter—there is always much more to say.

Notes

1. This essay may be the first to apply a simplified grounded theory approach to the *To Kill a Mockingbird* part of the Question & Answer section at eNotes.com, but it does not represent the first time that Lee's novel has been mentioned in a study using grounded theory. At least two earlier studies have used grounded theory to explore the impact of different literary works on readers, including *To Kill a Mockingbird*. See the cited works by Els Andriga and by Caroline Clark and Carmen Medina.

2. I am not interested in taking part in the "persistent rhetorical wrestle" (Holton i) between the two cofounders of the grounded theory method, who now argue publicly

over its methodology, but my approach draws more from the model of Barney Glaser than from the more highly complex one of Anselm Strauss and Juliet Corbin.

Works Cited

Andringa, Els. "The Interface between Fiction and Life: Patterns of Identification in Reading Autobiographies." *Poetics Today* 25.2 (Summer 2004): 205–240.

Bogdan, Robert C., and Sari K. Biklen. *Qualitative Research for Education: An Introduction to Theory and Methods.* Boston: Allyn and Bacon, 1998.

Capote, Truman. *The Grass Harp, a Play.* New York: Random House, 1952.

Clark, Caroline, and Carmen Medina. "How Reading and Writing Literacy Narratives Affect Preservice Teachers' Understandings of Literacy, Pedagogy, and Multiculturalism." *Journal of Teacher Education* 51.1 (January–February 2000): 63–76.

Glaser, Barney G. *The Grounded Theory Perspective: Conceptualisation Contrasted with Description.* Mill Valley, CA: Sociology Press, 2001.

Glaser, Barney G., and Anselm L. Strauss. *The Discovery of Grounded Theory: Strategies for Qualitative Research.* Chicago: Aldine, 1967.

Hagood, Margaret C. "Critical Literacy for Whom?" *Reading Research and Instruction* 41 (2002): 247–264.

Holton, Judith A. "From the Editor." *The Grounded Theory Review* 6.3 (June 2007): i–iii.

Lee, Harper. *To Kill a Mockingbird.* 1960. New York: Harper Perennial Modern Classics, 2006.

McLaughlin, Maureen, and Glenn De Voogd. "Critical Literacy as Comprehension: Expanding Reader Response." *Journal of Adolescent & Adult Literacy* 48.1 (September 2004): 52–62.

Patton, Michael Q. *Qualitative Evaluation and Research Methods.* 2nd ed. Newbury Park, CA: Sage, 1990.

Petry, Alice H., ed. *On Harper Lee: Essays and Reflections.* Knoxville: U Tennessee P, 2007.

Roscoe, Will. *Zuni Man-Woman.* Albuquerque: U New Mexico, 1991.

Smith, Marie K. *Teaching Harper Lee's "To Kill a Mockingbird" from Multiple Critical Perspectives.* Clayton: Prestwick House, 2007.

Strauss, Anselm, and Juliet Corbin. *Basics of Qualitative Research: Grounded Theory Procedures and Techniques.* Newbury Park, CA: Sage, 1990.

White, Edmund. *The Beautiful Room Is Empty.* New York: Knopf, 1988.

Wimsatt, W. K., and Monroe C. Beardsley. "The Intentional Fallacy." In *The Verbal Icon: Studies in the Meaning of Poetry,* W. K. Wimsatt. Lexington: U Kentucky P, 1954. (3–18).

CHAPTER 2

Multimedia *Mockingbird:* Teaching Harper Lee's Novel Using Technology

Derek Blair and Cecilia Donohue

To Kill a Mockingbird (1960) has achieved the canonical staying power usually denied the "one hit wonder," the term used by Alice Hall Petry to describe author Harper Lee (144). Despite the novel's status as the lone full-length fiction Lee ever wrote and published, this Pulitzer Prize-winning work has been vigorously analyzed through the lenses of diverse critical schools while remaining a popular literary selection in the unit plans of secondary schools both across and outside North America. *To Kill a Mockingbird*'s designation as a favorite high school reading has led to a proliferation of Approaches to Teaching publications, both print and online, presenting anticipatory sets, writing prompts, and detailed lesson plans that provide instructors with a multiplicity of suggestions for teaching the texts of both the book and its film adaptation.

However, most of this material was compiled and published prior to today's technological revolution. This essay suggests that by harnessing the power of this technology, ELA (English Language Arts) educators can access an unprecedented array of learning tools that students will find engaging and, most importantly, that will prove remarkably effective in promoting higher-learning skills. Since we are in the midst of an era in which high school students are used to retrieving and receiving information quickly and visually, it has become, arguably, increasingly difficult to engage students with a 323-page novel and/or a 130-minute black-and-white motion picture. In light of these conditions, this essay will review the recent criticism relative to teaching the text; argue the rationale for *Mockingbird* lesson plans in which students learn with, rather than from, technology; and expand upon the existing pedagogical literature in its presentation of state-of-the-art, multi-genre approaches to teaching *Mockingbird.*

Critical Approaches Providing Teachable Moments

Recent scholarship on *To Kill a Mockingbird* runs the gamut from traditional to modern approaches that address issues evoking relevant talking points for classroom discussion. New Critical studies focusing on symbolism within the text are offered by Laurie Campion and John Carlos Rowe. Campion's 2003 *Explicator* entry suggests consistent representation of the concepts of "right" and "left" throughout the text, "'right' suggesting virtue and 'left' suggesting iniquity" (234). Rowe's 2007 essay, combining New Critical and Marxist approaches, explains the economic/symbolic significance of three material goods that figure prominently in the novel: the gifts Boo Radley deposits in the tree that are found by Scout, Jem, and Dill (of increased community value because they are shared); the chifforobe Mayella asks Tom to destroy (representing the class-based hopelessness of Mayella's situation); and Scout's ham costume (emblematic of the agrarian economy upon which Maycomb, Alabama, the novel's setting, is highly dependent). Hence, both writings provide a point of departure to launch a discussion of symbolism within the novel.

Most character analysis studies focus on Atticus Finch, primarily in his role as public defender of Tom Robinson. In a nod to deconstruction and reader response, Steven Lubet, in his 1999 article, asks us to consider the possibility that Mayella Ewell was telling the truth and that Tom Robinson was guilty of rape and how this scenario would impact reader impressions of Atticus Finch. Lubet inquires, "Whether Tom was innocent or guilty, Atticus no doubt fulfilled his obligations . . . but that only brings us directly to the hardest question of all: Is Atticus still a hero?" (1361). Tim Dare's 2007 study also challenges the oft-unassailed image of Atticus Finch. Dare cites a trio of points in the novel that he considers "of particular significance for lawyers and legal ethics" as they directly address the rule of law: "The first is Atticus' summation to the jury. . . . The second moment occurs after Tom's death [when the local newspaper publishes an editorial condemning the jury's guilty verdict]" (85). The third plot point, in which the rule of law is dismissed, provides ample fodder for discussion of ethics and equal treatment under the law. It revolves around the joint decision by Atticus and the sheriff not to prosecute Boo Radley for the death of Bob Ewell. As Dare expresses it, judgment of an individual in the "secret court of men's hearts" (*TKAM* 276), "a wicked thing in Tom's case is a good thing in Boo's case" (87).

The question of Atticus Finch's status as unblemished champion of civil rights has been recently challenged again in a *New Yorker* article by Malcolm Gladwell, who, in examining Finch's actions, sees him as a "good Jim Crow liberal [who] dare not challenge the foundations of [white Southern male] privilege" (32). Another approach is taken in Chris Crowe's article from 1999 and Kathryn Lee Seidel's 2007 essay, both of which focus on Atticus less as an attorney and more as a father. Seidel's article hails the powerful and positive influence Atticus exerts on Scout, his daughter and the first-person narrator of the novel. Seidel states that Atticus "counters [traditional] southern dicta for southern culture with a philosophy of calm courage and rational strength" (80). In Crowe's writing, Atticus is cited, alongside David Logan of Mildred D. Taylor's *Roll of Thunder, Hear My Cry* (1976) and Raymond Mendoza of Graham Salisbury's *Blue Skin of the Sea* (1992), as a highly desirable paternal exemplar in the burgeoning genre of young adult literature: "These father characters don't dominate the novels, but they do play key roles in the lives of their respective children" (Crowe 121). Crowe's declaration that "the involvement of a concerned and loving father is often crucial in a young person's development" (120) has obviously been heeded by authors of young adult novels published since this article. Kate DiCamillo's *Because of Winn-Dixie* (2000) and Gennifer Choldenko's *Al Capone Does My Shirts* (2004) are but two award-winning examples of young adult fiction featuring father figures who proactively participate in the maturation of a youthful protagonist/narrator. Most significantly, in 2007 Loretta Ellsworth published *In Search of Mockingbird*, in which the main character, Erin Garven, seeks closer connection with her late mother through reading her yellowed journals and her torn, much-read copy of *To Kill a Mockingbird*. Erin's quest, partnered with her apprehension about her father's impending remarriage, inspire the teenager to take a Greyhound bus trip to Alabama, intending to meet Harper Lee and ask if the writer ever answered the letter Erin's mother had sent to her. This novel is worthy of consideration as a tandem or supplemental text, and not only because of its strong referential connection with *To Kill a Mockingbird*. The character parallels between Scout and Erin also provide multiple teachable moments. In addition, Ellsworth's work treats the subject of father-child connections in the modulated yet positive way about which Crowe has written.

Feminist/gender, Marxist, and New Historical approaches to *To Kill a Mockingbird* have also served as interpretive lenses through which Lee's novel has been viewed and provide content for the literature classroom. Dean Shackelford's 1997 essay examines gender-based voicing both in the novel and in its film translation, along with his assessment of female characters in the novel ("few women characters . . . are very pleasant") (4). Shackelford attributes these characterizations to "Harper Lee's fundamental criticism of gender roles for women" (arguably accurate given Scout Finch's resistance to trading her tomboy togs for taffeta), and suggests that Lee's criticism of prescribed gender roles is manifested in the "novel's identification with outsider figures such as Tom Robinson, Mayella Ewell, and Boo Radley" (112). A gender-based/queer reading serves as the basis for Laura Fine's 2007 article on the character of narrator Scout Finch. Noting Scout's narrative laden with explicit "dissatisfaction with conventional [female] roles" (76), Fine sees Scout's potential as a "boundary breaking" young woman (66) and asserts that the novel's "narrative opens a path that will allow Scout to challenge her culture's prescribed sexual identities in the future (62).

Theodore and Grace-Ann Hovet's 2001 article addresses the nature of narrative in *To Kill a Mockingbird*, focusing on economic and regional (along with gendered) discourse as the means of painting an accurate and comprehensive societal portrait of the town of Maycomb to the reader: "Lee, following very closely the goals of the great female realists of the nineteenth century like Louisa May Alcott and Rebecca Harding Davis strives to present a 'realistic' portrayal of small town southern life which will make it known to readers outside the region" (69). Marxist theory also informs John Carlos Rowe's study of the "inherently racist" economy of Maycomb, "reliant on unquestioned hierarchies of gender, class and age that make southern racism . . . difficult to identify and overcome" (2). Patrick Chura's New Historicist approach to *To Kill a Mockingbird* details the similarities between the fate of Lee's Tom Robinson and the true story of Emmett Till, the African American teenager who was lynched in 1955 in Mississippi due to his alleged wolf-whistles at a white woman. Chura argues that Lee's novel presents "racial and social ideology that characterized not the Depression era [in which *To Kill a Mockingbird* is set] but the early civil rights era [concurrent with the novel's publication]" (2). Introducing the Robinson/Till case parallels in the secondary school classroom, as incorporated by Carol Ricker-Wilson in her teaching of *Mockingbird* in Toronto, Canada, fosters deeper student understanding of race-based attitudes in the mid-twentieth-century American South, while enhancing an interdisciplinary unit on literature and history (69).

"Approaches to Teaching" Articles and Volumes

A simple googling of "*To Kill a Mockingbird* lesson plans" will yield an extensive volume of information and advice for the instructor teaching this novel. Fully developed lesson plans featuring multidisciplinary and multimedia perspectives on the novel abound on such Internet sources as www.readwritethink.org/lessons, the lesson plan website of the NCTE (National Council of Teachers of English); www.pbs.org/teachers (the official website of public television); www.webenglishteacher.com; www.memory.loc.gov; and www.aresearchguide.com.

In addition, print articles have discussed both implemented and potential lesson plan foci. For example, Leslie Marx's 2007 essay chronicles assignments utilized in South Africa, where *To Kill a Mockingbird* was taught in diverse classroom settings "during the height of the [human rights] struggle years" (117). These assignments include discussing race relations, Scout's coming of age, and the heroism of Atticus; shifting the setting to South Africa and having students write excerpts based on the sociocultural differences; comparing and contrasting Maycomb with South African cities; and interpreting the content of photographs based on the messages conveyed in the novel. Susan Arpajian Jolley's 2002 article identifies numerous poems appropriate for study alongside *Mockingbird* in conjunction with the novel's themes of "courage . . . compassion, as well as what we can learn from history" (34).

Despite the wide variety of knowledge and guidelines shared on these websites, the teaching of *To Kill a Mockingbird* is not without its challenges. Ricker-Wilson discusses the "problematic reader response" to the novel from students who were uncomfortable with some of the characterizations. One example: "Somewhat troubling to my students was how . . . Lee invited her readers to have an informed and sympathetic understanding for . . . white characters who kept racism alive and well" (72). Other potentially controversial aspects of the novel, such as the frequent use of racial epithets, are discussed in Louel Gibbons' recently published NCTE volume, *"To Kill a Mockingbird" in the Classroom: Walking in Someone Else's Shoes* (2009).

Gibbons' volume packs a load of information within its 121 pages of text, including a generous selection of writing prompts to stimulate student/reader engagement; assignments connected to students' identification of the traditional elements of fiction; strategies to ensure close reading of the text as it informs punctuation and word choice; ideas for written responses to critical and evaluative essays on *Mockingbird*; and recommendations for teaching the film as a "text separate from the original novel" (103). Given the virtually up-to-the-minute copyright on this NCTE volume, references to teaching *To Kill a Mockingbird* with technology are likely to be expected by educators who read or consult this work. While Gibbons recommends "multimedia presentations" to illuminate character analysis (21) and reports her success using library "print and technological resources" to assemble a research project (37), she fails to make such approaches an integral focus. In this essay, we argue that multimedia/technology-related activities can and should be central to the lesson/unit plan and that it is no longer sufficient to implement technology as a supplementary or add-on classroom activity. Our conclusion is based on recent research, which suggests that student learning is directly related to the integration of technology into the curriculum, which is essential in developing media literacy and assuring overall student engagement in the twenty-first century. Since strategies related to teaching *To Kill a Mockingbird* can foster such connections, we offer some suggestions in the remainder of this essay.

Media Literacy and Twenty-first Century Skills

As author James Naisbitt wrote in his 1982 book *Megatrends,* "We are drowning in information but starved for knowledge" (24). This phenomenon of the information age has led many in the literary field to expand the concept of literacy to better prepare students for twenty-first-century realities. Consequently, formal media literacy curricula, as part of a complete ELA program, have been growing in scope and importance in school districts throughout North America and around the world. Various terms are used to describe this expanded definition of literacy that accounts for today's merging and converging media. "Media literacy," "media education," "twenty-first-century literacies," and others are used, but, for the purpose of this essay, we will utilize the term "media literacy."

Numerous organizations like CML (the Center for Media Literacy) and NAMLE (the National Association for Media in Education) have formed in recent years to promote the concept, but more interesting is the support for media literacy from groups like the near century-old NCTE and even the American Pediatrics Association.

The CML defines "media literacy" as follows:

> Media Literacy is a 21st century approach to education. It provides a framework to assess, analyze, evaluate and create messages in a variety of forms—from print to video to the Internet. Media Literacy builds an understanding of the role of media in society, as well as essential skills of inquiry and self-expression necessary for citizens of a democracy.

Similarly, a position statement adopted by the NCTE Executive Committee states, "As society and technology change, so does literacy. Because technology has increased the intensity and complexity of literate environments, the twenty-first century demands that a literate person possess a wide range of abilities and competencies, many literacies." In the same position statement, the NCTE lists key competencies for twenty-first century ELA students, all of which encourage a proactive rather than passive/receptive approach to technology:

To develop proficiency with the tools of technology
To build relationships with others to pose and solve problems collaboratively and cross-culturally

To design and share information for global communities to meet a variety of
   purposes
To manage, analyze and synthesize multiple streams of simultaneous information
To create, critique, analyze, and evaluate multi-media texts

In addition, a policy statement issued by the American Pediatrics Association in
August 1999 states that "given the volume of information transmitted through
mass media as opposed to the written word, it is as important to teach media
literacy as print literacy."

Why are pediatricians and ELA teachers, learned professionals who work
with children, supporting media literacy in the classroom? Simply put, com-
posing, implementing, and analyzing messages using the latest effective communication tools can greatly benefit today's students. The digital age has torn
down previously existing walls between media; the printed word, photography,
film, video, graphic art, animation, voice tracks, music, and the Internet now
constitute an emerging "mega-medium." As a result, everyone with access to a
computer can both consume and create massive amounts of information in various forms. Students must learn to master this flow of digital assets; one route to
this learning is through innovative teaching of literature.

Educators who first attempt to create and assemble a multimedia lesson/
unit plan will find that their students are exposed to and arguably bombarded
with a constant assault of information in various forms and of varying quality.
By introducing and embracing twenty-first-century technologies and curricula
in the classroom, teachers can train their students to be critical readers, view-
ers, and creators of all of this information. From digital photo essays, to character studies using Twitter, texts, and blogs, to electronic journalism reports—
the possibilities are seemingly endless. What have up to now been considered
by some as superficial social networking tools or multimedia software toys are
seen by "digital natives" like today's high school students as vital means of
communication. Best of all, when embedded in a well-developed lesson plan,
these tools can force students to use the higher-level thinking skills demanded
in our standards and benchmarks. To create an effective multimedia message,
students will, among other things, be required to analyze, appraise, select,
evaluate, assemble, write, design, and create remarkably effective communication projects.

Although "book culture" will continue to be valued and traditional literacy
media (i.e., the original printed publication) will remain an important component of ELA education, we encourage twenty-first-century teachers to throw
away the notion that *only* the printed word and classic means of information
transmission are worthy of critical analysis. For ELA students to be best prepared

for the information challenges of the twenty-first century, they need to become critical consumers and creators of nonprint information, communication, and entertainment. By embracing media literacy-based tools and lesson plans across the curriculum, including the traditional English classroom, we can help students to better navigate the sea of information while growing as well as feeding on a wealth of knowledge.

Learning with Technology, Not from Technology

Incorporating proactive multimedia and online research methodologies to teach *To Kill a Mockingbird* has great potential. However, technology alone is an ineffective teacher. For example, simply consulting one website for the definition of "Jim Crow laws" or downloading the film adaptation of *To Kill a Mockingbird* is not the most effective, efficient, or productive use of media in the classroom. These constitute passive learning *from* technology: that is, information is recorded through technological devices and the data is then delivered to the student, a passive recipient of technology's output. Unfortunately, this does not promote higher-level thinking skills, nor does it implement technology to the fullest potential.

Instead of students learning from the technology, they should be partnering with, or even "teaching," the computer as they learn. Technology must be perceived as more than hard- or software. David Jonassen, Jane Howland, Rose M. Marra, and David Crismond, in the book *Meaningful Learning with Technologies*, identify the underlying principles of learning with technology:

> Its designs, environments, and intellectual "tool kits" engage learners and build meaningful interpretations and representations of the world. It can be a reliable technique or method for engaging learning and encourage cognitive learning strategies and critical thinking skills. It encompasses any activity that engages learners in active, constructive, intentional, authentic and cooperative learning rather than passively conveying or communicating meaning. It fulfills a legitimate learning need. It is learner-initiated and learner-controlled. It fosters an intellectual partnership between learners and technologies. (8)

Technologies also foster learning by affording students the opportunity to convey ideas, understandings, and beliefs by creating and organizing their own multimedia messages. In this way, technology serves as a comprehensive information vehicle through which students assess information and compare/contrast perspectives, beliefs, and worldviews. Instead of consulting just one or two textbooks or library resources as in the past, students can now access and assess numerous information sources due to the power and speed of the Internet and other online tools. Students then can use this technology to create their own product or project. This supports students through learning by doing and by solving real-world problems.

Technology can also be used as a "social" medium, allowing learners to collaborate with others in the same classroom, or around the world. This can enable global discussion in which arguments, consensus, and synergistic discourse can be developed. Hence, technology can be an intellectual partner to students, helping them articulate and represent what they know, allowing them to reflect on what they have learned, and support mindful thinking (Jonassen et al. 5). It can also foster critical thinking, helping students learn from thinking about their actions, their beliefs, and the actions of others. According to Jonassen et al., a wide variety of thinking processes are fostered by learning with technologies, including causal or prediction; analogical (using analogies and comparing something to an idea that is already understood); expressive (where learners express what they know); experiential (personal experience that results in the most meaningful and resistant memories); and problem solving—what information to include, how to structure the information, and what form it should take (9). All of this can encourage students to build knowledge through open-ended, student-directed research projects where students are encouraged to "harvest" the Internet's vast information bank and learn as much as they can about a topic, determine what is important, and develop their own questions. It is essential that the students be in charge of the project, making key decisions about what topic to research and where to search for information as well as looking for primary as well as secondary information sources.

What should an open-ended, student-directed research project look like in the twenty-first century? One good example is the WebQuest. Like many new techniques and learning technologies, WebQuests have been misrepresented and misunderstood. The creator of the WebQuest, Bernie Dodge, did not intend for them to be simple electronic worksheets where students use the Internet to "fill in the blanks" in a set of questions. Instead, Dodge's intent is for students to incorporate cooperative learning, consider multiple perspectives (which the Internet makes remarkably easy), analyze and synthesize information, and create original products that demonstrate the acquired knowledge. An ideal WebQuest requires students to select and research the topics of their choice, provided that each meets the teacher's learning objectives. This is best done after a classroom brainstorming session. Effective WebQuests implement the GAP model (Caverly, qtd. in Jonassen et al. 25), which is comprised of the following steps:

- Gathering information
- Arranging information into meaningful formats
- Using technology tools to Present that new knowledge to others

All of this promotes higher-learning abilities and critical-thinking skills as students are forced to present and defend the information they found. Learners can use online tools, such as Inspiration software, to create concept maps of their projects and create Web files to compile and share information. As stated by Jonassen et al. in *Meaningful Learning with Technology*, "The cognitive and social skills required to construct WebQuests offer a motivating, deep learning experience. Students made interdisciplinary connections and were challenged intellectually. At the same time, they gained experience with technology presentation skills—and had fun!" (26).

Teaching *Mockingbird* with Technology

What makes *To Kill a Mockingbird* particularly appropriate for using multimedia learning tools is its potential for exploring the timeless issues and topics addressed in its plotline. The novel allows for the study of early twentieth-century American Southern history and culture as well as traditional, New Critical literary analysis. Although time constraints may limit the amount of time spent on the sociohistorical aspects, even limited attention can constitute an important step in the student's deeper understanding of its connection to the novel. Through extensive online research, partnered with proactive multimedia presentation methods, students can explore such historical topics as the civil rights movement of the 1960s, the Great Depression, racial inequality, the Scottsboro boys incident, and the Emmet Till trial—all of which have been identified as relevant to study in conjunction with the reading of *To Kill a Mockingbird.* Other aspects of the novel as analyzed in the critical literature, including characterization (particularly pertaining to Scout and Atticus), coming of age, and parent/child relationships, may also be explored through technology-driven teaching and learning. Some specific classroom activity ideas for teaching *To Kill a Mockingbird* using timely, interactive technology without sacrificing traditional literary and interdisciplinary content follow.

1. POWERPOINTS AND PHOTO ESSAYS TO TEACH *MOCKINGBIRD*-RELATED HISTORY

Students can demonstrate as well as actively convey their understanding of the historical contexts and events connected to *To Kill a Mockingbird* through the creation of PowerPoint/photo essays. An example of such an assignment is as follows: Students, working in groups, select one of the aforementioned historically related topics. They then research their topic by comparing and contrasting the content of at least four online resources, executing a critical analysis of the website material as they assess the reputation, organization, and accuracy of the website.

Armed with this information, the students select and assemble what they consider the most appropriate and important information on the topic. This information should be comprised of photographs and other graphic elements in addition to text. For example, photographs of key civil rights leaders and/or moments could provide the visual content. The final step requires the students to create, design, develop, and write a three- to five-minute, prerecorded PowerPoint and photo essay that effectively communicates their findings and interpretations to the class. After each presentation, students discuss the topics and the group's findings in a full class setting.

Simple and readily available software such as Microsoft PowerPoint or Apple Keynote can be used for a project such as this, making it an attractive assignment option even for the most technophobic instructor.

2. LITERARY THEMES EXPLORED THROUGH MULTIMEDIA

The study of the thematic elements of *To Kill a Mockingbird* also offers a plethora of creative opportunities for students to explore the novel's universal appeal and significance. In addition to the aforementioned historical perspectives, the issues of coming of age (or *To Kill a Mockingbird* as bildungsroman), justice, social castes, religious hypocrisy, heroism, childhood fears, and parent/child relationships have all been reported as key themes of the novel, worthy of additional research, discussion, and interpretation in the ELA classroom. One possible way of exploring these themes using technology in a proactive manner is through the use of published and/or original poetry or songs juxtaposed with visual elements to create videos. Here's how such an assignment might work: Students either write an original poem or song, or choose and interpret an existing selection that addresses a key theme of *To Kill a Mockingbird*. The aforementioned Jolley article provides a generous number of options if the instructor wishes to stick with already published works; among the selections she cites as thematically connected to the novel are Theodore Roethke's "My Papa's Waltz," Paul Lawrence Dunbar's "Sympathy," Jewel's "Hands," and Dudley Randall's "Ballad of Birmingham." Students who wish to select a song for this assignment and need help to jump-start their creativity could find some inspiration from the content of Christian Z. Goering's and Lauren Virshup's lesson plan posted on the www.littunes.com website, where the authors present specific ideas for songs that tie in with the themes of *Mockingbird.* Among the songs mentioned are "When Will I Get to Be Called a Man," a blues song by Big Bill Broonzy; "Walk a Mile in My Shoes" by Joe South; and "People Are People" by A Perfect Circle.

Students are then assigned to write a brief paragraph explaining why they chose the poem or song they selected, providing information on the poet's/artist-songwriter's background, and articulating their response to the poem, that is, the message and mood it conveys to them.

Students then view the acclaimed 1962 film version of *To Kill a Mockingbird.* While viewing, they look closely at each scene, choosing appropriate still images from the film that best complement the poem or song they have chosen; these will be assembled in a video montage. In executing this assignment, students utilize their creative, editorial, visual, and critical-thinking skills to decide on proper placement, pace, and mood within the poem or song.

For a lesson early in the unit studying the background information of the novel, students could alternatively use imagery from the African American civil rights movement, 1930s Alabama, or even modern-day civil rights struggles.

Students then design and create the final product utilizing simple slideshow software such as Microsoft Movie Maker, iMovie, or even PowerPoint synced to an audio track.

Students then produce a second short essay in which they reflect upon their multimedia work, stating whether or not they thought the video was effective and what they would do to improve it.

After students have determined and articulated what was successful and what needed improvement in each individual multimedia production, a final revised product can be created and presented in class along with a brief synopsis of their two paragraphs before and after their media presentation. Other students in the class then have the opportunity to appraise, compare, and evaluate the effectiveness of the work of their peers through constructive classroom discussion and examination.

3. CHARACTER STUDY THROUGH TWITTER, BLOGS, AND AVATARS

An effective way for students to engage with and delve into the heads of the characters of any book is through assuming the roles of characters in the novel. This can be done through technology using online social networking tools such as Twitter and Facebook. For educators and districts skittish about using these commercial websites, the more academically based blogging site www.wordpress.com is a viable alternative. To take this idea to the next level, students can be assigned to create digital portfolios or avatars of the characters through websites like www.secondlife.com. What makes social network–based assignments work so well is the fact that when creating their character "profile," students must be aware of intimate character details and make some intelligent critical decisions about their character in terms of their interests and outlook. Questions such as What would Scout do? How would Jem react? and How would Dill feel? should be informing student input in assignments like this. When creating the online discussion, students need to develop full knowledge of their respective characters so that he or she can be accurately brought to life via technology. Through this process, students will demonstrate a deeper understanding of the characters, examine important plot developments, question character motivation, and formulate original character dialogue.

Such an activity presents other advantages as well. Because students are comfortable and familiar with such interfaces, they are likely to "buy in" quickly to such assignments and unlikely to show resistance. In addition, such activities have the potential to transcend the classroom walls. With coordination and collaboration among teachers, students could be communicating about *To Kill a Mockingbird* with other students who might be anywhere—across the school corridor, across town, or perhaps across an ocean. Several innovative approaches to interactive assignments of this nature can be implemented. One potential class activity is to have the students divide into groups of three, with each student assuming the role of Scout, Jem, or Dill on the night before Tom Robinson is sentenced, and have the students craft dialogue for these characters at this particular point in time. If scheduling permits, another possibility is to have the students, again in assigned "character," create chapter-by-chapter blogs in which they expand on what is revealed in the text to show how they believe certain plot events have affected characters. In a classroom where *To Kill a Mockingbird* is being tandem-taught with Loretta Ellsworth's *In Search of Mockingbird*, students could be paired to assume the roles of Scout in *To Kill a Mockingbird* and Erin, the heroine of the Ellsworth book. "Scouts" and "Erins" could frame their conversations around one or more of their common bonds: their feelings about being raised by a single parent of the opposite sex; relationships with siblings; the events in their lives that are causing conflict; their budding relationships with young men; the reactions and responses to the older women they have encountered; and/or the societal pressures they are feeling as they grow up. Discussion of contextual literary symbolism could also be incorporated within this chat, as Scouts could discuss the material props that play a key role in the story (such as the items left by Boo Radley in the tree), and Erins could contribute reflections on her late mother's diary and dog-eared copy of a cherished book.

4. FINCH AND FANDOM

Yet another way for students to engage with *To Kill a Mockingbird* within the context of a participatory technological culture would be through the creation of online "fan fiction." On websites such as www.fanfiction.com, anyone can assume the role of author and create prequels, expanded chapters or sequels of existing literature. An effective assignment for teaching *To Kill a Mockingbird* using this modality is to ask students to write a chapter 32, provide an outline for a projected part 3 of the novel, or perhaps fast-forward the action ten or twenty years later and describe the principal characters as they would be then. Although hundreds of entries for *To Kill a Mockingbird* are already posted on this fan fiction website, the opportunities for students to create, collaborate, and publish in a broader community remain ample. The website www.google.com/talk (Google Talk) may also be utilized for such an assignment.

5. THE ROBINSON TRIAL AS "DEVELOPING STORY" ON CABLE NEWS

To Kill a Mockingbird can also be taught via interdisciplinary connections between literature and TV or radio broadcast journalism. Through the use of video equipment or simpler digital audio recorders and free audio editing software like Audacity (www.audacity.sourceforge.net), students are assigned to write and present newscasts on the proceedings of the trial. Students assigned the role of anchors in the "news studio" could ask questions of those students assuming the role of field reporter, as they emulate the correspondents who stand outside courtrooms on such networks as Tru TV (formerly Court TV). The correspondents respond to the anchorpersons' inquiries regarding the demeanor of witnesses, the mood of the crowd, reactions to testimony, speculation on which side is making the stronger case, and so on. An alternative assignment is for students to create video "mini-'mock'umentaries" on the city of Maycomb, Alabama, interviewing characters from the novel for inclusion in the radio or TV reports.

6. COMIC RELIEF

Other unconventional, yet effective plot and character studies lessons include the use of ComicLife software (www.comiclife.com), where students create comic book-style story boards, complete with scenes from the book and captions. Students must identify key elements to the story line, select appropriate images and text synthesizing the essence of a scene or chapter, and create and assemble an expressive and effective analysis of the plot.

7. BACKBEAT BIO

Students with an interest in music (and there are no shortage of those in any high school) may jump at the chance to create an original song that serves as a personal biography of any given character. Using music creation and editing software like GarageBand (www.apple.com), students write, record, mix, and create a song that clearly demonstrates the character's personality, traits, and role in the novel.

8. COMPLETE LESSON PLAN

The best part of these twenty-first-century tools and online resources is the collaborative nature of the technology and the fact that these educational resources will only continue to grow in the coming years as all of us continue to contribute and develop new ideas. Already, a number of organizations have multimedia lesson plans ready and waiting on a myriad of topics directly related to teaching *To Kill a Mockingbird* and necessary historical background information. On websites from PBS, NCTE, and others, educators can find lessons on everything from protest songs, to banned books, to breaking barriers—from specific plans for the novel that incorporate poetry and blues music, to lessons on Jim Crow laws and the civil rights movement. A quick look at some of these resources and the embedded links already included can give any educator an idea of the possibilities these powerful new tools offer. A few good sites to start with include www.readwritethink.org/lessons and www.pbs.org/teachers.

Conclusion

While some educators may remain skeptical about the quality of content delivery and the degree of learning effected by shifting away from traditional pedagogical methods, it is nonetheless possible to integrate multimedia technology into the teaching of a novel yet maintain the need for students to acquire authentic knowledge and skills relative to the work as they complete these tasks in these new modalities. In the aforementioned approaches, students may indeed be granted more leeway regarding the planning, organization, and execution of the suggested assignments, yet the need for instructors to assess such important rubric components as preparation, clarity, accuracy, completeness, insight, and ability to work collaboratively is still present and essential. In addition, these assignments, while providing showcases for demonstrating knowledge of the timeless issues addressed in *To Kill a Mockingbird*, also afford students the opportunity to acquire and sharpen their skill sets relative to the timely field of media literacy.

Works Cited

Campion, Laurie. "Lee's *To Kill a Mockingbird*." *The Explicator* 61.4 (2003): 234.

Caverly, D. C. "Technology and the 'Knowledge Age.'" In *Proceedings of the First Intentional Meeting on Future Directions in Developmental Education*. Ed. D. B. Lundell and J. L. Higbee. Minneapolis: U Minnesota, General College, and The Center for Research on Developmental Education and Urban Literacy, 2000. (34–36). http://www.education.umn.edu/CRDEUL/pdf/proceedings/1-proceedings.pdf

Choldenko, Gennifer. *Al Capone Does My Shirts*. New York: G.P. Putnam's Sons, 2004.

Chura, Patrick. "Prolepsis and Anachronism: Emmet Till and the Historicity of *To Kill a Mockingbird*." *Southern Literary Journal* 32.2 (2000): 1–26.

Crowe, Chris. "Atticus, David, and Raymond: Role Models for YA Males." *English Journal* 88.6 (1999): 119–121.

Dare, Tim. "Virtue Ethics: Lawyers and Harper Lee's *To Kill a Mockingbird*." *Journal of Interdisciplinary Studies* 19.1–2 (2007): 81–100.

DiCamillo, Kate. *Because of Winn-Dixie*. Cambridge, MA: Candlewick Press, 2000.

Ellsworth, Loretta. *In Search of Mockingbird*. New York: Henry Holt, 2007.

Fine, Laura. "Structuring the Narrator's Rebellion in *To Kill a Mockingbird*." In *On Harper Lee: Essays and Reflections*. Ed. Alice Hall Petry. Knoxville: U Tennessee P, 2007. (61–77)

Gibbons, Louel C. *"To Kill a Mockingbird" in the Classroom: Walking in Someone Else's Shoes*. Urbana: National Council of Teachers of English, 2009.

Gladwell, Malcolm. "The Courthouse Ring: Atticus Finch and the Limits of Southern Liberation." *The New Yorker* 10 August 2009: 26–32.

Goering, Christian Z., and Lauren Virshup. "Addressing Issues of Social Justice, Political Justice, Moral Character, and Coming of Age in *To Kill a Mockingbird*." Lesson plan. n.d. Web. 9 September 2009. http://www.corndancer.com/tunes/tunes_lp019/lp08_mckbrd.html

Hovet, Theodore R., and Grace-Ann Hovet. "'Fine Fancy Gentlemen' and 'Yappy Folk': Contending Voices in *To Kill a Mockingbird*." *Southern Quarterly* 40.1 (2001): 67–78.

Jolley, Susan Arpajian. "Integrating Poetry and *To Kill a Mockingbird*." *English Journal* 92.2 (2002): 34–40.

Jonassen, David, Jane Howland, Rose M. Marra, and David Crismond. *Meaningful Learning with Technology*. Upper Saddle River, NJ: Pearson Education, 2008.

Lee, Harper. *To Kill a Mockingbird.* 1960. New York: Harper Perennial Modern Classics, 2006.

"Literacy for the 21st Century: An Overview & Orientation Guide to Media Literacy Education." Center for Media Literacy. 2003, 2005. Web. 23 September 2009. http://www.medialit.org/pdf/mlk/01_MLKorientation.pdf

Lubet, Steven. "Reconstructing Atticus Finch." *Michigan Law Review* 97.6 (1999): 1339–1362.

Marx, Leslie. "Mockingbirds in the Land of Hadedahs: The South African Response to Harper Lee." In *On Harper Lee: Essays and Reflections.* Ed. Alice Hall Petry. Knoxville: U Tennessee P, 2007. (105–120)

Naisbitt, John. *Megatrends.* 1988. New York: Avon Books, 1990.

"The NCTE Definition of 21st Century Literacies." Position statement, the National Council of Teachers of English. 15 February 2008. Web. 9 September 2009. http://www.ncte.org/positions/statements/21stcentdefinition

"Media Education." Policy statement, Committee on Public Education, American Academy of Pediatrics. August 1999. Web. 9 September 2009. http://aappolicy.aap publications.org/cgi/content/full/pediatrics;104/2/341#B20

Petry, Alice Hall. "Harper Lee, the One-Hit Wonder." In *On Harper Lee: Essays and Reflections.* Ed. Alice Hall Petry. Knoxville: U Tennessee P, 2007. (143–164)

Ricker-Wilson, Carol. "When the Mockingbird Becomes an Albatross: Reading and Resistance in the Language Arts Classroom." *English Journal* 87.3 (1998): 67–72.

Rowe, John Carlos. "Racism, Fetishism, and the Gift Economy in *To Kill a Mockingbird.* In *On Harper Lee: Essays and Reflections.* Ed. Alice Hall Petry. Knoxville: U Tennessee Press, 2007. (1–17)

Salisbury, Graham. *Blue Skin of the Sea.* New York: Delacorte, 1992.

Seidel, Kathryn Lee. "Growing Up Southern: Resisting the Code for Southerners in *To Kill a Mockingbird.*" In *On Harper Lee: Essays and Reflections.* Ed. Alice Hall Petry. Knoxville: U Tennessee P, 2007. (79–92)

Shackelford, Dean. "The Female Voice in *To Kill a Mockingbird*: Narrative Strategy in Film and Novel." Web. 26 May 2009. http://vn.web.hwwilsonweb.com.madonnaezb.eiblime.com:2048/hww/results_single_ftPES.jhtml

Taylor, Mildred D. Taylor. *Roll of Thunder, Hear My Cry.* New York: Dial Books, 1976.

CHAPTER 3

A Soundtrack Approach to Teaching *To Kill a Mockingbird*

Christian Z. Goering and Cindy M. Williams

One of the most frequently taught pieces of book-length fiction in American secondary schools is Harper Lee's masterwork, *To Kill a Mockingbird.* And as many different approaches to teaching as there are out there, the varying pedagogical approaches to this novel are likely just as different as the people teaching it and the places where it is taught. We both taught the novel in our respective high school English classrooms, and it was received positively by our students, something not always the case when working with adolescents and books. Certainly one constant in the ever-changing adolescent landscape is music, and as secondary teachers, we tried to incorporate music whenever it was both educational and appropriate. One successful method we found to both incorporate music and simultaneously challenge our students was entitled The Soundtrack of the Novel (an example is provided in the box titled Student Handout after the conclusion). In this essay, we provide a foundational background for using music to teach canonical texts like *To Kill a Mockingbird*, offer and explain a widely adaptable pedagogical strategy, and then walk through the strategy ourselves, providing our musical interpretations of the novel while simultaneously giving practitioners a starting point in their own pursuit of strategies that both challenge and interest the twenty-first-century learner.

The soundtrack approach is a simple method of teaching a piece of fiction or nonfiction. It asks readers to make connections from a literary text to songs, describe and explain the connections made, and then collect the songs in the form of a letter entitled "Dear Listener." Good readers naturally connect with the characters, plot, themes, and settings of any given text. Sometimes those connections are to other works of fiction and nonfiction, various elements of popular culture, or past experiences from life. Sometimes those connections can cross into the realm of music. While simple to implement in any given literature classroom, this approach to teaching requires students to think creatively to make connections and then defend and explain the thinking behind such perceived parallels. Whether with music or without, this act of cerebral processing should be part and parcel of what students do in school. Everyone wins when students are engaged and challenged by a school assignment, and that is exactly what The Soundtrack of the Novel (TSOTN) approach sets out to accomplish.

In a classroom setting, each TSOTN assignment accompanies a piece of fiction or nonfiction that students are reading or preparing to read. In this discussion, we focus our attention around one novel being taught to a whole class, but teachers using independent and small-group approaches to literature can also employ this strategy. In our classrooms, we give students the first part of a TSOTN assignment as they prepare to read a novel for class. Then, after students read each chapter or section of the book, they perform this first step, which is to make and record a text-to-song connection. Either during the reading event or immediately following, students take their song connections, return to the text, and explicitly detail why they made each connection. Next, we ask students to collect the connections and explanations into a letter introducing and explaining the soundtrack as a whole as well as the individual tracks. Finally, the students create a visual interpretation—compact disc jewel case art, record album cover, concert poster, or web page—that represents their new soundtrack and eventually present this visual to the class. While our students in the past have found this assignment to be creative and fun, they have also often remarked about how difficult it is to make defendable connections, especially at some points in books.

Though it is not entirely clear where or when a soundtrack approach to teaching originated, the first publication of this approach came in the National Writing Project's *The Quarterly* in 2004 with "Music and the Personal Narrative: A Dual Track to Meaningful Writing." The Soundtrack of Your Life is a personal narrative writing assignment in which the students match memorable events, people, settings, or periods of their lives with the music of their choice. In much the same way, TSOTN hinges on students' abilities to make and explain connections to the classroom literature they are reading. These purposeful connections, referred to in a 2009 study as Musical Intertextuality (Goering; Goering, et al.), cause students to engage in a purposeful act of intertextuality, an educational theory tied directly to the seminal work of Louise Rosenblatt.

In her 1938 effort entitled *Literature as Exploration*, Rosenblatt contends the reader naturally "brings to the work personality traits, memories of past events, present needs and preoccupations, a particular mood of the moment, and particular physical condition . . . in a never-to-be-duplicated combination" (30–31). This reliance on prior knowledge and experience suggests readers bring with them not only past texts but also past forays into popular culture—movies, music, advertisements—as they approach each new text. In a 2001 study, Susan Lenski found that many competent readers make constant intertextual connections. She notes, "As readers experience a text, either by individual reading or through shared reading, they develop a provisional interpretation of that text" (314). In fact, these prior texts allow readers to construct meaning from the new, exacting a give and take "between the reader's evolving inner text, the new text, and the context of reading" (315). While some of our students possessed the literary background and ability to make vast intertextual connections between what they were assigned to read and what they had previously read, we must report most of them did not. Rather than lowering the curricular standards of time-honored texts like *To Kill a Mockingbird*, we preferred to find ways into such texts for our students. By practicing a skill competent readers do naturally and frequently with a less intimidating medium—music and lyrics—students not only gained the opportunity to catalogue a new piece of literature in their personal library but also experimented with a practice inherent to skilled readers.

TSOTN does rely, in part, on Rosenblatt's Reader Response Theory (1938), but the assignment goes beyond that initial connection, which can admittedly be superficial in nature. While that initial connection signals the beginning of an understanding, what student readers do with that initial connection may be far more important than the act of making it. By prompting students to explain their choices, TSOTN naturally requires higher levels of critical thinking and engagement, something very measureable in the writing they produce. This argumentative thinking model provides the basis for essay writing and a myriad of life skills requisite beyond the walls of school. At the core of any reading event are the reader and the text. The second aspect of TSOTN requires the reader to focus on two texts—song lyrics and the piece of literature—and to perform a close, analytical reading of each, ultimately deducing conclusions about their commonalities. New Criticism and Reader Response Theory can, in fact, work together toward common goals, something critics of Reader Response Theory claim is inconceivable (Carinicelli; Hirsch). That being said, we agree with Harris and McKenzie in their thinking that "readers have a crucial role to play in choosing and constructing meaning, drawing on their experiences with vast and evolving networks of texts" (35).

Some of these tensions take different sides in the national conversations of literary knowledge and literacy skills. Should high school students be learning how to read or reading in order to learn? The 2001 No Child Left Behind (NCLB) legislation put sinister pressures on the first of the two, a pressure that may cause some teachers to rethink using canonical texts like *To Kill a Mockingbird*. Since NCLB requires all students score at a relatively low level, that of "proficient," teachers are forced to focus on students that score in the bottom quartile on state reading assessments. This focus often neglects the teaching of literature in favor of stressing literacy skills, which are applied to lower level texts to meet the needs of the lower level learners. We wonder if both can be incorporated effectively and believe the TSOTN is but one of many approaches that meets both goals of literary reading and literacy skill improvement. In thinking about this assignment from a broader, educational context, it clearly serves different purposes of an English curriculum, addresses the needs of today's adolescents, and maintains significant texts in the classroom.

Soundtracks to *To Kill a Mockingbird*

As a method of experimenting with this approach ourselves, we created our own soundtracks of *To Kill a Mockingbird*. The boxes that follow reflect the connections we each made from the novel to our individual libraries of music. Each connection surely reflects our unique tastes in music and interpretations of the novel. In much the same way, soundtracks from current films often share both common themes and seemingly erratic choices in music. A cursory glance through our soundtrack lists will reveal music that works along with the novel but is often entirely different from each other's lists. Additionally, we each described a few connections we made to help illustrate the approach and the varying depths of connectivity.

EXPLANATIONS FROM CINDY

"I'm Still a Guy" by Brad Paisley has a similar message to that of chapter 13. The song talks about the many things that make the singer a "guy," and he insists that regardless of what current social standards entail, he is who he is, and he will not succumb to society's expectations of who he should be or how he should live. This is relevant to both the chapter and the novel in relation to Scout particularly. Her Aunt Alexandra insists that she become a part of the social class in an expected social manner appropriate to the Finch name. Clearly Scout is a tomboy, and although her character changes throughout the novel (she does begin to show more feminine tendencies), she does not succumb to social expectations and behaviors at the sacrifice of self. Rather, Scout and Jem both grow and change according to their understanding of their experiences and of their father's moral teaching and examples. The children are who they are,

Cindy's Soundtrack

Chapter	Song Title	Artist or Group
Chapter 1	The Way We Were	Barbra Streisand
Chapter 2	Playground in My Mind	Clint Holmes
Chapter 3	Hope for the Hopeless	Brett Dennen
Chapter 4	Summertime	Sam Cooke
Chapter 5	I Was Only Joking	Rod Stewart
Chapter 6	Little Lies	Fleetwood Mac
Chapter 7	Bad Blood	Neil Sedaka
Chapter 8	We Didn't Start the Fire	Billy Joel
Chapter 9	It Isn't Right	Platters
Chapter 10	Mockingbird	Carly Simon and James Taylor
Chapter 11	Devil Woman	Cliff Richard
Chapter 12	Go Your Own Way	Fleetwood Mac
Chapter 13	I'm Still a Guy	Brad Paisley*
Chapter 14	Runaway	Del Shannon
Chapter 15	Innocence	Kenny G
Chapter 16	Dressed To Kill a Mockingbird	Black Blondie
Chapter 17	Walk a Mile in My Shoes	Elvis Presley
Chapter 18	You've Got to Be Carefully Taught	Rodgers and Hammerstein*
Chapter 19	I Fall to Pieces	Patsy Cline
Chapter 20	Theme from Romeo and Juliet	Henry Mancini*
Chapter 21	The Night the Lights Went Out in Georgia	Vickie Lawrence
Chapter 22	Don't Stop Believing	Journey*
Chapter 23	High Cotton	Alabama
Chapter 24	The Great Pretender	Platters
Chapter 25	To Kill a Mockingbird	Dear Noel
Chapter 26	You Don't Mess Around with Jim	Jim Croce
Chapter 27	Against the Wind	Bob Seger
Chapter 28	Someone Saved My Life Tonight	Elton John
Chapter 29	I Can See Clearly Now	Johnny Nash*
Chapter 30	Braveheart	L 'Orchestra Cinematique
Chapter 31	I Believe	Brooks & Dunn

*Songs discussed at length.

similar to the song, and their change and growth is not brought about by social expectations.

In 1949, Rodgers and Hammerstein presented a controversial piece called "You've Got to be Carefully Taught" as part of their musical *South Pacific*. The song explains that in order for one to truly hate another because of race, he or

Chris's Soundtrack

Chapter	Song Title	Artist or Group
Chapter 1	Ghosts You Can See	Lost Immigrants
Chapter 2	A Blessing and a Curse	Drive-By Truckers
Chapter 3	Walk a Mile in My Shoes	Jimmy LaFave
Chapter 4	My Brother and Me	Bruce Robison
Chapter 5	Dead Flowers	The Rolling Stones
Chapter 6	God Bless this Town	Wade Bowen
Chapter 7	Mug Tree Lady	Still on the Hill
Chapter 8	California Snow	Tom Russell*
Chapter 9	Framed	Chris Knight
Chapter 10	Pugilist at 59	Tom Russell
Chapter 11	My Morphine	Gillian Welch
Chapter 12	Almost Grown	Jesse Malin
Chapter 13	The End of the Innocence	Don Henley
Chapter 14	What Do You Say in a Moment Like This	Reba McEntire
Chapter 15	If I Were You	Chris Knight*
Chapter 16	Time (the Revelator)	Gillian Welch
Chapter 17	Before You Accuse Me	Eric Clapton
Chapter 18	Reasons to Lie	Whiskeytown
Chapter 19	Southern Man	Neil Young
Chapter 20	Double Indemnity	Scott Miller
Chapter 21	If I Had Possession over Judgment Day	Robert Johnson
Chapter 22	Man in Black	Johnny Cash*
Chapter 23	Crooked Piece of Time	Todd Snider
Chapter 24	No Depression in Heaven	The Carter Family*
Chapter 25	Imagine	John Lennon
Chapter 26	Childish Things	James McMurtry
Chapter 27	Bad Moon Rising	John Fogerty
Chapter 28	Never Gonna Change	Drive-By Truckers
Chapter 29	In the Arms of the Angels	Sarah McLachlan
Chapter 30	Mockingbird	Ryan Adams
Chapter 31	Alright Guy	Todd Snider

Songs discussed at length.

she must be taught repeatedly, carefully, and early on. This song supports that hating and fearing what is different and what we do not understand are not innate behaviors; rather, these behaviors are learned at a very young age to the detriment of the learner. This particular song embodies the entire novel as well as offers a weak justification for Mayella's actions in chapter 18. Interestingly, her willingness to sacrifice her hatred for blacks to alleviate a moment of loneliness supports the fact that her hatred is not innate but learned. Nonetheless, when Mayella's father finds her in this situation, her fear of her father promotes another conflict between her learned hatred of blacks and her ability to tell the truth—something else she has not been taught. While Mayella's actions seem to be an exaggerated representation of Maycomb's prejudices, it is both Maycomb's and Mayella's willingness to embrace and practice their learned hatred of blacks that ultimately destroys an innocent man; thus, as the Rodgers and Hammerstein song iterates, teaching others to hate is a learned behavior that must be acted upon in order to keep it going.

"Theme from Romeo and Juliet" by Henry Mancini reminds the listener of an old, familiar Shakespearean tragedy that recognizes the tragic consequences of ingrained and imposed hatred and prejudice of a people against another people without explanation or cause. This attitude is reflected in chapter 20 both in Mr. Dolphus Raymond's need to justify his "unacceptable" preference for blacks by pretending to be an alcoholic, therefore giving the community members a way of writing off his peculiar behavior, and in Maycomb's view of all blacks as criminals, similar to Romeo and Juliet's families hating one another because of their names. In each case, an unjustifiable prejudice eventually contributes to the deaths of innocent people.

The song "Don't Stop Believing" by Journey connects to chapter 22 first through its title. It seemingly captures the essence of Miss Maudie's discreet encouragement to Jem when he is devastated over the outcome of Tom Robinson's guilty verdict. Jem has become disillusioned with his own idealistic view of justice and has gained a newfound understanding of the existence of hatred and prejudice in Maycomb. Miss Maudie reminds Jem of those who tried to do right, who were not cruel and heartless, and who tried to help Tom Robinson.

Through a similar theme, the Journey song opens with a reference to a lonely girl living in a small town and points out that people, strangers in their own cities, live for emotion and appear to be caught up in a world that seems like an ongoing movie out of control—victims of circumstance. While the essence of the chapter and the song both acknowledge the ugly side of the human condition, both also advocate looking past current circumstances to maintain hope and belief in that which is still good and has the potential to get better.

Chapter 29 reveals Scout's first clear view of Boo Radley—not just as the one who saved her and Jem, but as a human being. The song "I Can See Clearly Now" by Johnny Nash also reveals a similar story. The symbolism of the rain, dark clouds, and obstacles that prevent one from seeing clearly are gone; similarly, when Scout tells her story, she looks over at Boo and really sees him. Her judgment is no longer clouded by mysterious shadows or games nor is her judgment any longer impaired by fear of what she did not know—a theme common to the novel. The "rain and clouds" of hate and prejudice (born from fear) are lifted by the heroic actions of one of the innocent mockingbirds in the novel. Consequently, as Scout begins to see Boo differently and more clearly, her character's growth continues to be substantiated throughout the novel.

EXPLANATIONS FROM CHRIS

Expert songwriter Tom Russell addresses issues of immigration in "California Snow," a carefully woven tale of a border guard's experiences on the California-Mexico border. As illegal immigrants make the crossing into America, they find themselves unprepared for the cold, and the border guard in the song finds a husband and wife lying in a ditch. After the wife dies, the guard relates that the "next day we sent him back alone across the borderline" (Russell 26–27). The reader can immediately connect chapter 8 to this song as Scout and Jem were exploring the snow in their innocence. The two illegal immigrants must have had the same spirit as Scout and Jem, an innocent and pure vision of the world at that point. While the California snow crushes one vision, Scout and Jem's naïveté is first challenged by the fire at Miss Maudie's house and then by an even more sinister racism, one also spurred on by distinctions of race and class.

"If I Were You" by Chris Knight encapsulates one of the novel's central themes of empathy but does so in an unusual, unique way that relates well with chapter 15. In Knight's song, the narrator is a homeless person asking for spare change: "If I were you, I would gladly loan me a dollar or two" (line 1). As a reader, I connect this song both to the relegated social class of the angry mob attempting vigilante justice on Tom Robinson and to the desperate feeling that Scout and Jem experience seeing their father in apparent danger. Knight's character implores passersby for much more than spare change; he asks them for empathy, something Scout evokes from the members of the lynch mob through her actions when she diffuses the situation with the lynch mob.

In chapter 22 and throughout the book, Atticus Finch takes on the pain and anguish of others in a very selfless manner, a manner incredibly similar to the way Johnny Cash describes his own actions in "Man in Black." While the novel was written eight years before the song and no evidence of an explicit connection exists, it is nonetheless uncanny how similar Cash's portrayal is to that of Atticus Finch. The crooner explains, "I wear the black for the poor and the beaten down / Livin' in the hopeless, hungry side of town / I wear it for the prisoner who has long paid for his crime/ But is there because he's a victim of the times" (lines 5–8). Atticus wears black for the same unfortunate people in *To Kill a Mockingbird* by treating everyone as equals, representing Tom Robinson in a hopeless case, and even risking his family's well-being to do the right thing.

The Carter Family is widely considered the first family of country music, and A. P. Carter's legacy for the timeless songs such as "Wabash Cannonball," "Wildwood Flower," and "No Depression in Heaven" is eternal. Chapter 24 marks a point where few answers seem to quench the thirst of questions left by Tom's attempted escape from prison and death. In much the same way, the Great Depression left Americans with fewer answers than questions. Carter's words in "No Depression in Heaven" relate to both situations, "For fear the hearts of men are failing / For these are latter days we know" (lines 1–2) and are resolved by Carter's matriculation to heaven in the chorus. As both situations— the unfair racism in Maycomb and hopelessness during the Great Depression— cast a shadow over many, there is, in fact, relief in the future.

Discussion

While the example soundtracks provide two distinctly different perspectives on the novel, they also represent our thinking behind the connections we made. As students experience the process of making connections and being required to explain and defend them, they most certainly will have to perform close readings of each text—the novel and the lyrics—in order to make the connection clear to the audience. The unfortunate reality of students today, however, is that they see little relevance, if any, in what they are being asked to do and how the task will benefit them in the long term. Using the soundtrack lesson provides students the necessary relevance to utilizing and building schema and long-term comprehension. As students make connections between their understandings of music and what they may consider an archaic text, they are doing more than finding a song with a message that is similar to the chapter's. Like the different perspectives of our two example soundtracks, students' perspectives—via background knowledge—are also distinctly different from the teacher's and their peers. Oftentimes these differences contribute to what may be perceived as a lack of understanding, when in fact students are discovering, and thus learning, important facts of life. We must recognize that students see, read, and understand a simple theme differently than we do. The teacher, unfortunately, knowing the requirements and objectives of "understanding" a given theme, might interpret this difference as a failure to understand the text. However, this may not be true at all. For example, when a teacher explains (or lectures) to students the theme based on "loss of innocence," a student who may never have had the privilege of innocence may not understand the lectured concept; however, when students connect a message in a song—they have more than likely already made a self-to-lyric association—to the text, they are using the song's message as a bridge to broaden or clarify their understanding of the text. So, while a student may not seem to grasp the teacher's use of the expression "loss of innocence" as a thematic emphasis of *To Kill a Mockingbird*, her song choice may discuss poverty, parental neglect or aloneness (abandonment), abuse, or fear; in actuality, her connection to and identification with the parallels in the story are evidence she does "get it." As a result, by using this approach, the teacher is offering individualized instruction by relating students' understanding of the text to the required objectives. In so doing, the instructor works to bridge a gap in what may have originally appeared to be ineptitude but actually turns out to be a difference in the students' real-world concepts and their unfamiliarity/experience with educational jargon.

As teachers, we have come to understand that we teach students by way of content, but if we work toward understanding how students learn, we can be more creative by individualizing our teaching and providing students a choice in their learning style. Having such a chance is what makes TSOTN a more meaningful, purposeful, and engaging task. Using soundtracks as a connection to the text promotes a student-centered engagement where students explore, reason, infer, and problem-solve as they wrestle out their own understandings and misunderstandings in an attempt to discover what the text has to say. Eventually, they learn to read and write critically—another necessary long-term skill. Clearly, as students take an active role in their learning, such a hands-on method allows them to make connections with prior learning and personal experiences, and they consequently develop into successful learners following an instructional philosophy that is supported by such well-known educational theorists as Jean Piaget and Lev Vygotsky. Specifically, this philosophy asserts that when students construct their own understanding and knowledge of the world through their unique experiences and reflections on those experiences, learning becomes both more relevant and more ongoing. By using a soundtrack learning activity, educators can facilitate a long-term purpose—preparing students for life beyond school—and, at the same time, give them an opportunity to apply what they have learned in the classroom to various situations and tasks they will face in the future.

In addition, a central factor in creating relevance and maintaining an instructional purpose of the canonical text *To Kill a Mockingbird* is that educators ensure that their students have access to and learn from the content that has previously eluded them. TSOTN provides learning experiences and instruction that motivate students to learn in the ways that suit them best and simultaneously empowers them to take responsibility for their own learning. As students, with a cacophony of perspectives and musical backgrounds, connect ideas to the text, they learn not only to develop and defend their own points of view but also to subject their viewpoints to the analysis of others—a real-world consequence. Furthermore, instead of students being passive and powerless vessels, waiting to receive great shards of wisdom, the soundtrack activity teaches students to actively seek out answers about inevitable dilemmas, confusion, and contradictions found in the text. As they find answers and connect these issues to music, they "uncover" unique understandings as they attempt to make sense of their world. In such classrooms, students experience the stimulation of belonging to an intellectually challenging community—a group that formulates the necessary ingredient for transforming reading and writing connections into a lifelong skill.

Implications for Practice

Teachers planning to implement TSOTN in their classrooms should consider several characteristics of the assignment. We do not offer it as anything other than something that worked with our students. Certainly, adaptations and modifications can and should be made to fit a particular classroom or group of learners.

While the NCLB Act, formative and summative assessments, and state mandates and testing dictate a departure from "traditional" teaching, teachers and students are nonetheless held to measurable standards, and, therefore, teaching and learning must adhere to such requirements. In our implementation of the soundtrack-to-text lesson, we found that we had, in fact, redirected our teaching and thinking to look at what students are and should be learning—a necessary mandate. The need for the shift in thinking about traditional teaching practices is related to the shift from activity-driven curriculum to one driven by its desired end results for learners. For example, in the early 1900s, writing instruction focused on mechanics and grammatical preciseness. Students learned writing rules and rote memorization as a means for writing—an example of traditional activity-driven writing instruction. However, when writing instruction begins with desired end results—what the teachers want students to know and be able to do at the completion of a lesson—then writing instruction begins to shift from activity driven (with a focus on the teaching) to desired results driven (with a focus on the learning). For instance, in a traditional writing assignment, students might be asked to write a book report on *To Kill a Mockingbird* to check whether or not they read the text and could write about it in a grammatical fashion. A modernized version of that assignment might ask students to write a short summary that indicated their understanding of a specific theme or topic from the novel. Students might be asked to make connections in various writing modes to determine comprehension of content, thus the assignment becomes critical and/or analytical, more than a basic skills check (Bransford, Brown, and Cocking 24).

A major shift and departure from that traditional instruction focuses expectations on students' learning as they are acquiring an ability to analyze and interpret what is read with a critical eye and to respond in various genres and levels of writing. Such goals are exactly the premise of TSOTN. In responding to the reality that educational goals are very different for the twenty-first century, the use of soundtrack lessons serves to enhance instructional practices and to ensure understanding takes place on multifaceted levels. Teachers must realize though that such changes from traditional activity-driven instruction to more of an ends-results focus utilizing methods and lessons, however, require a deliberate and focused instructional design that will make an important shift in thinking about teaching. As advocates of such innovation we believe that when teachers implement TSOTN, they engage in a deep, broad study of the learning process they are charged to foster and encourage; as a result, they will hopefully become aware of the need for essential questions that should drive all instruction in this new era of educational accountability: What works? What doesn't? Where is student learning most successful, and why? How can we learn from that success? Where are students struggling to learn, and why? What can we do about it? We believe that utilizing the soundtrack-to-text lesson will allow the teacher to discover answers to these questions and in so doing, to address and respond to the individual educational needs of the learner.

Frameworks and testing standards require teachers to identify the desired results from what they find worthy and assessable in student understanding. But when teachers consider what the "big ideas" are that need to be uncovered, they ask if the targeted understandings are "framed by essential questions . . . provoking, arguable, and likely to generate inquiry around the central idea?" (Wiggins and McTighe 28). And, are the goals—content standards and objectives—appropriate? Teachers and curriculum designers then begin to move away from content coverage (implying a march through vast amounts of material)—as the traditional tendency in response to state curriculum guides and frameworks and more toward an uncoverage, in-depth teaching that focuses on the learning instead of the material (Wiggins and McTighe 28).

Furthermore, because content standards and text do not explicitly highlight the key concepts behind the content of reading or writing instruction, we must "unpack" the standards and, consequently, uncover the key, or big ideas within the content and then develop essential questions that explore these ideas (Wiggins and McTighe 35). Numerous researchers have demonstrated the fact that when students understand the key ideas embedded in the content standards, they learn specific facts, concepts, and skills that help them to be better readers, writers, and learners. As we reflected on our soundtracks for the novel and as we made our text-to-song connections, we were reminded as literacy teachers of the importance of teaching for understanding and of remembering ourselves that instruction works best, and students learn best, when it concentrates on thinking and understanding rather than on rote memorization. As we sought out methods to achieve this end, we began to see a greater coherence among teaching and learning experiences, desired results, and key performances, which resulted in better student performance—the stated goal for NCLB and for education in general.

By placing student learning at the helm of our teaching, our long-term goals create a stronger, more meaningful curriculum for students. In short, "covering" frameworks and/or teaching skills out of context or by presenting a canonical text such as *To Kill a Mockingbird* using the traditional approach in planning and teaching is not enough. These tired methods of teaching start at the beginning of a text, cover the information for a test in isolation, and, unfortunately, omit opportunities for students to wrestle with genuine problems and ideas that would allow them to make meaning of their learning. When teachers use thought-provoking, engaging, and interactive educational strategies, students walk away with powerful, meaningful interpretations of the understandings they gain from such approaches. Not only that, but students who have been taught using these strategies are not "covering" information from a text; they are "uncovering" essential questions and demonstrating how to apply their knowledge in various situations. As noted previously, the results from research support the uncoverage approach to improve student achievement (Wiggins and McTighe 35; Emberger). Specifically, it demonstrates unequivocally that teaching for meaning and understanding leads to more lasting and significant student learning and simultaneously meets appropriate educational outcomes without having to "teach to the test."

When students understand, they can proceed to explain, interpret, and apply skills to make sense of their world through assessments that demand transfer of learning. And as students gain such perspective on their own learning, their success at transfer depends on a realization of how to connect otherwise isolated or inert facts, skills, and experiences to the real. By using TSOTN on *To Kill a Mockingbird*, our students were able to connect an otherwise isolated text to real-life experiences and understandings discovered in their world of music. Thus, TSOTN is more process than product since genuine learning is never finished. The primary goal of our literacy classrooms should be to help students learn how to learn. They are not tabulae rasae upon which knowledge is etched nor are they empty vessels for teachers to fill with knowledge.

Instead, we as educators must realize that our students come to learning situations with their own knowledge, ideas, and understandings. Through activities such as making text-to-song connections, students can discover their ideas and recognize that they are sometimes invalid, incorrect, or insufficient to explain current experiences and understandings. When students learn new pieces of information, they compare the information to the knowledge and understanding they already have, and when the new information matches up with previous knowledge, students add it to their comprehension—though this sometimes takes some work (Smith 13).

TSOTN includes, reinforces, and sustains the development of students' thinking skills. These skills then enable students to transfer their learning to real-world applications. They learn to solve problems, and, thereby, they learn to consider multiple and flexible perspectives of understanding and thinking (in themselves and about others). By varying opportunities for learning, we can provide students an opportunity to engage in assessment that more specifically meets their individual learning needs/styles. Clearly, accepting the premise that students' learning should drive instruction and committing to ongoing professional knowledge and skill development serves to create lifelong learners and to empower students to explore, reason, infer, problem-solve, and grapple with their understandings and misunderstandings to discover meaningful, purposeful, and engaging learning.

Conclusion

In a welcome address to the parents of incoming students at the Boston Conservatory, Dr. Karl Paulnack, pianist and director of the music division, explained that "music is one of the ways we make sense of our lives, one of the ways in which we express feelings when we have no words, a way for us to understand things with our hearts when we can't with our minds." When we ask students to connect music to the text, we are, in essence, asking them to filter their understanding of an obscure text through the lenses of sensibility in their music—the place where many of today's teens go to discover meaning in and to make sense of their lives. As a consequence, students will find opportunities to express their understanding of a text through their understanding of self. As Paulnack asserts, music allows us to "move around those big invisible pieces of ourselves and rearrange our insides so we can express what we feel even when we can't talk about it." When students create a soundtrack of the novel, they are connecting, learning, and demonstrating newfound skills. Their writing reveals not a product but a process of growth and maturation, one similar to that which Scout and Jem experience in *To Kill a Mockingbird.*

Student Handout

IMAGINARY SOUNDTRACK OF THE NOVEL

Music has become an integral part of human existence. It motivates us, calms us, inspires us, at times irritates us, and basically becomes the backdrop against which we live our lives. Songs can bring vivid memories of persons, places, and events from our own past and serve to document our thoughts, feelings, and emotions at a given time or place. One especially rich time for these songs to enter our consciousness is when we read other people's words.

Part I Assignment

Imagine you were asked to compile a soundtrack for *To Kill a Mockingbird*. What songs would you include? Collect the titles of at least eight songs that are meaningful to the group and that the group feels document what is actually happening in the chosen chapters (the minimum is eight songs regardless of number of chapters—you may do more than eight). Your songs should be listed in the chronological order of the chapters/events they document. Put some thought into the order of your songs and the complete package you are presenting to the class. School appropriateness is based on group conferencing.

	Song Title	*Artist or Group*
Track 1		
Track 2		
Track 3		
Track 4		
Track 5		
Track 6		
Track 7		
Track 8		
(extra)		
(extra)		

Part II Assignment

Now that you have created the imaginary soundtrack to this novel, write a reflective letter (addressed to "Dear Listener,") that explains why you chose the particular songs that you did. For each song you will need to reflect on the events, characters, settings, and so on that inspired this selection. Again, for the purposes of this assignment, be sure that this letter is school appropriate. Use the outline here to help you construct this letter. You need to cover each topic listed in the appropriate number of paragraphs; however, the questions listed are only there to help you begin thinking about the topic. You do not need to answer each and every question or any of the questions as long as you have sufficiently explained the topic of each section. Be sure to include specific details of the connections made so we, your readers, will understand your thinking behind each. Finally, please use proper MLA parenthetical citations.

Topic 1—Explanation of This Soundtrack (one paragraph)

This paragraph outlines your rationale or purpose in creating this soundtrack:

> What is this album you have created?
> Why are you completing it? (because it is an assignment is NOT an answer!)
> What do you hope to get out of this project?
> What goals did you have for creating it?

Topic 2—Explanation of Each Song on the Soundtrack (one paragraph per song)

This section is made up of many smaller paragraphs. Be sure to explain your choices song by song and address the following questions:

> What is the name of the song and the artist?
> Why is each song important to this particular chapter?
> How does each song connect to the novel?
> What does each song reveal about the chapter and why do you think it is representative of the chapter?

Topic 3—Final Remarks and Reflection on the Soundtrack as a Whole (one paragraph)

This paragraph is your group's conclusion in which you should thank your reader for taking the time to listen to your soundtrack and offer any final reflections upon this project as a whole.

Songs from Goering and Virshup's lesson plan "Addressing Issues of Social Justice, Political Justice, Moral Character, and Coming of Age in *To Kill a Mockingbird* on LitTunes.com http://www.corndancer.com/tunes/tunes_lp019/lp08_mckbrd.html.

THEME 1: SOCIAL INEQUALITY

"Baloney Again" by Mark Knopfler
"Law Is for the Protection of the People" by Kris Kristofferson
"People Are People" by A Perfect Circle
"Shine" by Ry Cooder
"Simon" by Lifehouse

THEME 2: POLITICAL INEQUALITY

"Alabama Blues" by J. B. Lenoir
"When Will I Get to be Called a Man" by Big Bill Broonzy
"The Lonesome Death of Hattie Carrol" by Bob Dylan
"Strange Fruit" by Billie Holiday
"Jena" by John Mellencamp

THEME 3: MORAL CHARACTER

"There but for Fortune" by Phil Ochs
"I Choose" by India.Arie
"Hands" by Jewel
"What Say You" by Travis Tritt
"He Was My Brother" by Simon and Garfunkel
"Lie on Lie" by Chalk Farm
"Atticus Taught Me" by Cary Cooper

THEME 4: LOSS OF CHILD INNOCENCE

"Don't Laugh at Me" by Mark Wills
"Walk a Mile in My Shoes" by Joe South
"Everyday People" by Sly and The Family Stone
"Walk Tall" by John Mellencamp
"All Kinda People" by Robert Palmer

Works Cited

Bransford, John D., Ann L. Brown, and Rodney R. Cocking, eds. "The Design of Learning Environments." In *How People Learn: Brain, Mind, Experience and School.* Washington, DC: National Academy Press, 2000. (131–154)

Carnicelli, Thomas. "The English Language Arts in American Schools: Problems and Proposals." In *What's at Stake in the K-12 Standards Wars: A Primer for Educational Policy Makers.* Ed. Sandra N. Stotsky. New York: Peter Lang, 2000. (211–231)

Emberger, Marcella. "Assessing the Assessments: Helping Teachers Think Like Asses-sors." *Principal,* March 2006: 39–40. Retrieved December 2009 from www.naesp .org/Principal2006M-A.aspx.

Goering, Christian Z. "Music and the Personal Narrative: The Dual Track to Meaning-ful Writing." *The Quarterly* 26.4 (December 2004): 11–17.

———. "Open Books, Open Ears, and Open Minds: *The Grapes of Wrath,* the 'Broken Plow,' and the LitTunes Approach." In *Dialogue 7: "The Grapes of Wrath": A Recon-sideration.* Ed. Michael J. Meyer. Amsterdam: Rodopi, 2009. (801–817)

Goering, Christian Z., Katherine Collier, Scott Koenig, John O. O'Berski, Stephanie Pierce, and Kelly Riley. "Musical Intertextuality in Action: A Directed Reading of *Of Mice and Men.*" In *The Essential Criticism of Of Mice and Men.* Ed. Michael J. Meyer. Lanham, MD: Scarecrow, 2009. (307–330)

Harris, Pauline and Barbra McKenzie. "Networking around the Waterhole and Other Tales: The Importance of Relationships among Texts for Reading and Related Instruc-tion." *Literacy,* 2005: 31–37.

Hirsch, E. Donald. *The Knowledge Deficit.* Boston: Houghton Mifflin, 2007.

Lenski, Susan D. "Intertextual Connections during Discussions about Literature." *Read-ing Psychology* 22.4 (October 2001): 313–335.

Paulnack, Karl. "Karl Paulnack to the Boston Conservatory Freshman." The Boston Conservatory. March 2009. http://www.bostonconservatory.edu/s/940/Bio.aspx?sid =940&gid=1&pgid=1241.

Rosenblatt, Louise. *Literature as Exploration.* New York: Appleton-Century Crofts, 1938.

Smith, Mark K. "Jerome Bruner and the Process of Education." The Encyclopedia of Informal Education. http://www.infed.org/thinkers/bruner.htm.

Wiggins, Grant, and Jay McTighe. *Understanding by Design.* Expanded 2nd ed. Upper Saddle River NJ: Pearson Education, 2005.

Part 2

TO KILL A MOCKINGBIRD
AND THE JUSTICE SYSTEM

CHAPTER 4

The Courthouse Ring: Atticus Finch and the Limits of Southern Liberalism[1]

Malcolm Gladwell

In 1954, when James (Big Jim) Folsom was running for a second term as governor of Alabama, he drove to Clayton, in Barbour County, to meet a powerful local probate judge. This was in the heart of the Deep South, at a time when Jim Crow was in full effect. In Barbour County, the races did not mix, and white men were expected to uphold the privileges of their gender and color. But when his car pulled up to the curb, where the judge was waiting, Folsom spotted two black men on the sidewalk. He jumped out, shook their hands heartily, and only then turned to the stunned judge. "All men are just alike," Folsom liked to say.

Big Jim Folsom was six feet eight inches tall, and had the looks of a movie star. He was a prodigious drinker, and a brilliant campaigner, who travelled around the state with a hillbilly string band called the Strawberry Pickers. The press referred to him (not always affectionately) as Kissin' Jim, for his habit of grabbing the prettiest woman at hand. Folsom was far and away the dominant figure in postwar Alabama politics—and he was a prime example of that now rare species of progressive Southern populist.

Folsom would end his speeches by brandishing a corn-shuck mop and promising a spring cleaning of the state capitol. He was against the Big Mules, as the entrenched corporate interests were known. He worked to extend the vote to disenfranchised blacks. He wanted to equalize salaries between white and black schoolteachers. He routinely commuted the death sentences of blacks convicted in what he believed were less than fair trials. He made no attempt to segregate the crowd at his inaugural address. "Ya'll come," he would say to one and all, making a proud and lonely stand for racial justice.

Big Jim Folsom left office in 1959. The next year, a young Southern woman published a novel set in mid-century Alabama about one man's proud and lonely stand for racial justice. The woman was Harper Lee and the novel was *To Kill a Mockingbird*, and one way to make sense of Lee's classic—and of a controversy that is swirling around the book on the eve of its fiftieth anniversary—is to start with Big Jim Folsom.

The Alabama of Folsom—and Lee—was marked by a profound localism. Political scientists call it the "friends and neighbors" effect. "Alabama voters rarely identified with candidates on the basis of issues," George Sims writes in his biography of Folsom, "The Little Man's Best Friend." "Instead, they tended to give greatest support to the candidate whose home was nearest their own." Alabama was made up of "island communities," each dominated by a small clique of power brokers, known as a "courthouse ring." There were no Republicans to speak of in the Alabama of that era, only Democrats. Politics was not ideological. It was personal. What it meant to be a racial moderate, in that context, was to push for an informal accommodation between black and white.

"Big Jim did not seek a fundamental shift of political power or a revolution in social mores," Sims says. Folsom operated out of a sense of noblesse oblige: privileged whites, he believed, ought to "adopt a more humanitarian attitude" toward blacks. When the black Harlem congressman Adam Clayton Powell, Jr., came to Montgomery, on a voter-registration drive, Folsom invited him to the governor's mansion for a Scotch-and-soda. That was simply good manners. Whenever he was accused of being too friendly to black people, Folsom shrugged. His assumption was that Negroes were citizens, just like anyone else. "I just never did get all excited about our colored brothers," he once said. "We have had them here for three hundred years, and we will have them for another three hundred years."

Folsom was not a civil-rights activist. Activists were interested in using the full, impersonal force of the law to compel equality. In fact, the Supreme Court's landmark desegregation ruling in *Brown v. Board of Education* ended Folsom's career, because the racial backlash that it created drove moderates off the political stage. The historian Michael Klarman writes, "Virtually no southern politician could survive in this political environment without toeing the massive resistance line, and in most states politicians competed to occupy the most extreme position on the racial spectrum." Folsom lost his job to the segregationist John Patterson, who then gave way to the radical George Wallace. In Birmingham, which was quietly liberalizing through the early 1950s, Bull Connor (who notoriously set police dogs on civil-rights marchers in the 1960s) had been in political exile. It was the Brown decision that brought him back. Old-style Southern liberalism—gradual and paternalistic—crumbled in the face of liberalism in the form of an urgent demand for formal equality. Activism proved incompatible with Folsomism.

On what side was Harper Lee's Atticus Finch? Finch defended Tom Robinson, the black man falsely accused of what in 1930s Alabama was the gravest of sins, the rape of a white woman. In the years since, he has become a role model for the legal profession. But he's much closer to Folsom's side of the race question than he is to the civil-rights activists who were arriving in the South as Lee wrote her novel.

Think about the scene that serves as the book's centerpiece. Finch is at the front of the courtroom with Robinson. The jury files in. In the balcony, the book's narrator—Finch's daughter, Jean Louise, or Scout, as she's known—shuts her eyes. "Guilty," the first of the jurors says. "Guilty," the second says, and down the line: "guilty, guilty, guilty." Finch gathers his papers into his briefcase. He says a quiet word to his client, gathers his coat off the back of his chair, and walks, head bowed, out of the courtroom. "Someone was punching me, but I was reluctant to take my eyes from the people below us, and from the image of Atticus's lonely walk down the aisle," Scout relates, in one of American literature's most moving passages:

> "Miss Jean Louise?"
> I looked around. They were standing. All around us and in the balcony on the opposite wall, the Negroes were getting to their feet. Reverend Sykes's voice was as distant as Judge Taylor's:
> "Miss Jean Louise, stand up. Your father's passin'."

If Finch were a civil-rights hero, he would be brimming with rage at the unjust verdict. But he isn't. He's not Thurgood Marshall looking for racial salvation through the law. He's Jim Folsom, looking for racial salvation through hearts and minds.

"If you can learn a simple trick, Scout, you'll get along a lot better with all kinds of folks," Finch tells his daughter. "You never really understand a person until you consider things from his point of view . . . until you climb into his skin and walk around in it." He is never anything but gracious to his neighbor Mrs. Dubose, even though she considers him a "nigger-lover." He forgives the townsfolk of Maycomb for the same reason.

They are suffering from a "sickness," he tells Scout—the inability to see a black man as a real person. All men, he believes, are just alike.

Here is where the criticism of Finch begins, because the hearts-and-minds approach is about accommodation, not reform. At one point, Scout asks him if it is O.K. to hate Hitler. Finch answers, firmly, that it is not O.K. to hate anyone. Really? Not even Hitler? When his children bring up the subject of the Ku Klux Klan's presence in Maycomb, he shrugs: "Way back about nineteen-twenty there was a Klan, but it was a political organization more than anything. Besides, they couldn't find anyone to scare. They paraded by Mr. Sam Levy's house one night, but Sam just stood on his porch and told 'em things had come to a pretty pass. . . . Sam made 'em so ashamed of themselves they went away." Someone in Finch's historical position would surely have been aware of the lynching of Leo Frank in Marietta, Georgia, in 1915. Frank was convicted, on dubious evidence, of murdering a thirteen-year-old girl, Mary Phagan. The prosecutor in the case compared Frank to Judas Iscariot, and the crowd outside the courthouse shouted, "Hang the Jew!" Anti-Semitism of the most virulent kind was embedded in the social fabric of the Old South. But Finch does not want to deal with the existence of anti-Semitism. He wants to believe in the fantasy of Sam Levy, down the street, giving the Klan a good scolding.

In the middle of the novel, after Tom Robinson's arrest, Finch spends the night in front of the Maycomb jail, concerned that a mob might come down and try to take matters into its own hands. Sure enough, one does, led by a poor white farmer, Walter Cunningham. The mob eventually scatters, and the next morning Finch tries to explain the night's events to Scout. Here again is a test for Finch's high-minded equanimity. He likes Walter Cunningham. Cunningham is, to his mind, the right sort of poor white farmer: a man who refuses a W.P.A. handout and who scrupulously repays Finch for legal work with a load of stove wood, a sack of hickory nuts, and a crate of smilax and holly. Against this, Finch must weigh the fact that Cunningham also leads lynch mobs against black people. So what does he do? Once again, he puts personal ties first. Cunningham, Finch tells his daughter, is "basically a good man," who "just has his blind spots along with the rest of us." Blind spots? As the legal scholar Monroe Freedman has written, "It just happens that Cunningham's blind spot (along with the rest of us?) is a homicidal hatred of black people."

Finch will stand up to racists. He'll use his moral authority to shame them into silence. He will leave the judge standing on the sidewalk while he shakes hands with Negroes. What he will not do is look at the problem of racism outside the immediate context of Mr. Cunningham, Mr. Levy, and the island community of Maycomb, Alabama.

Folsom was the same way. He knew the frailties of his fellow-Alabamians when it came to race. But he could not grasp that those frailties were more than personal—that racism had a structural dimension. After he was elected governor a second time, in 1955, Folsom organized the first inaugural ball for blacks in Alabama's history. That's a very nice gesture. Yet it doesn't undermine segregation to give Negroes their own party. It makes it more palatable. Folsom's focus on the personal was also the reason that he was blindsided by Brown. He simply didn't have an answer to the Court's blunt and principled conclusion that separate was not equal. For a long time, Folsom simply ducked questions about integration. When he could no longer duck, he wriggled. And the wriggling wasn't attractive. Sims writes:

> In the spring of 1955, he repeated portions of his campaign program that touched the issue of desegregation tangentially and claimed that he had already made his position "plain, simple, and clear." He frequently repeated his pledge that he would not force black children to go to school with white children. It was an ambiguous promise that sounded like the words of a segregationist without specifically opposing segregation. Speaking to the Alabama Education Association in 1955, the governor recommended a school construction bond issue and implied that the money would help prolong segregation by improving the physical facilities of Negro schools.

One of Atticus Finch's strongest critics has been the legal scholar Steven Lubet, and Lubet's arguments are a good example of how badly the brand of Southern populism Finch represents has aged over the past fifty years. Lubet's focus is the main event of *To Kill a Mockingbird*—Finch's defense of Tom Robinson. In "Reconstructing Atticus Finch," in the *Michigan Law Review*, Lubet points out that Finch does not have a strong case. The putative rape victim, Mayella Ewell, has bruises on her face, and the supporting testimony of her father, Robert E. Lee Ewell. Robinson concedes that he was inside the Ewell house, and that some kind of sexual activity took place. The only potentially exculpatory evidence Finch can come up with is that Mayella's bruises are on the right side of her face while Robinson's left arm, owing to a childhood injury, is useless. Finch presents this fact with great fanfare. But, as Lubet argues, it's not exactly clear why a strong right-handed man can't hit a much smaller woman on the right side of her face. Couldn't she have turned her head? Couldn't he have hit her with a backhanded motion? Given the situation, Finch designs his defense, Lubet says, "to exploit a virtual catalog of misconceptions and fallacies about rape, each one calculated to heighten mistrust of the female complainant."

Here is the crucial moment of Robinson's testimony. Under Finch's patient prodding, he has described how he was walking by the Ewell property when Mayella asked him to come inside, to help her dismantle a piece of furniture. The house, usually crowded with Mayella's numerous sisters and brothers, was empty. "I say where the chillun?" Robinson testifies, "an' she says—she was laughin', sort of—she says they all gone to town to get ice creams. She says,

'Took me a slap year to save seb'm nickels, but I done it. They all gone to town.'" She then asked him to stand on a chair and get a box down from the chifforobe. She "hugged him" around the waist. Robinson goes on:

> "She reached up an' kissed me 'side of th' face. She says she never kissed a grown man before an' she might as well kiss a nigger. She says what her papa do to her don't count. She says, 'Kiss me back nigger.' I say Miss Mayella lemme outa here an' tried to run but she got her back to the door an' I'da had to push her. I didn't wanta harm her, Mr. Finch, an' I say lemme pass, but just when I say it Mr. Ewell yonder hollered through th' window."
>
> "What did he say?"
>
> . . . Tom Robinson shut his eyes tight. "He says you goddam whore, I'll kill ya."

Mayella plotted for a year, saving her pennies so she could clear the house of her siblings. Then she lay in wait for Robinson, in the fervent hope that he would come by that morning. "She knew full well the enormity of her offense," Finch tells the jury, in his summation, "but because her desires were stronger than the code she was breaking, she persisted in breaking it." For a woman to be portrayed as a sexual aggressor in the Jim Crow South was a devastating charge. Lubet writes:

> The "she wanted it" defense in this case was particularly harsh. Here is what it said about Mayella: She was so starved for sex that she spent an entire year scheming for a way to make it happen. She was desperate for a man, any man. She repeatedly grabbed at Tom and wouldn't let him go, barring the door when he respectfully tried to disentangle himself. And in case Mayella had any dignity left after all that, it had to be insinuated that she had sex with her father.

It is useful, once again, to consider Finch's conduct in the light of the historical South of his time. The scholar Lisa Lindquist Dorr has examined two hundred and eighty-eight cases of black-on-white rape that occurred in Virginia between 1900 and 1960. Seventeen of the accused were killed through "extra legal violence"—that is to say, lynched. Fifty were executed. Forty-eight were given the maximum sentence. Fifty-two were sentenced to prison terms of five years or less, on charges ranging from rape and murder to robbery, assault and battery, or "annoying a white woman." Thirty-five either were acquitted or had their charges dismissed. A not inconsiderable number had their sentences commuted by the governor.

Justice was administered unequally in the South: Dorr points out that of the dozens of rapists in Virginia who were sentenced to death between 1908 and 1963 (Virginia being one of the few states where both rape and attempted rape were capital crimes) *none* were white. Nonetheless, those statistics suggest that race was not always the overriding consideration in rape trials. "White men did not always automatically leap to the defense of white women," Dorr writes. "Some white men reluctantly sided with black men against white women whose class or sexual history they found suspect. Sometimes whites trusted the word of black men whose families they had known for generations over the sworn testimony of white women whose backgrounds were unknown or (even worse) known and despised. White women retained their status as innocent victim only as long as they followed the dictates of middle-class morality."

One of Dorr's examples is John Mays, Jr., a black juvenile sentenced in 1923 to an eighteen-year prison term for the attempted rape of a white girl. His employer, A. A. Sizer, petitioned the Virginia governor for clemency, arguing that Mays, who was religious and educated, "comes of our best negro stock." His victim, meanwhile, "comes from our lowest breed of poor whites. . . . Her mother is utterly immoral and without principle; and this child has been accustomed from her very babyhood to behold scenes of the grossest immorality. None of our welfare work affects her, she is brazenly immoral."

The reference to the mother was important. "Though Sizer did not directly impugn the victim herself, direct evidence was unnecessary during the heyday of eugenic family studies," Dorr writes. "The victim, coming from the same inferior 'stock,' would likely share her mother's moral character." The argument worked: Mays was released from prison in 1930.

This is essentially the defense that Atticus Finch fashions for his client. Robinson is the churchgoer, the "good Negro." Mayella, by contrast, comes from the town's lowest breed of poor whites. "Every town the size of Maycomb had families like the Ewells," Scout tells us. "No truant officers could keep their numerous offspring in school; no public health officer could free them from congenital defects, various worms, and the diseases indigenous to filthy surroundings." They live in a shack behind the town dump, with windows that "were merely open spaces in the walls, which in the summertime were covered with greasy strips of cheesecloth to keep out the varmints that feasted on Maycomb's refuse." Bob Ewell is described as a "little bantam cock of a man" with a face as red as his neck, so unaccustomed to polite society that cleaning up for the trial leaves him with a "scalded look; as if an overnight soaking had deprived him of protective layers of dirt." His daughter, the complainant, is a "thick-bodied girl accustomed to strenuous labor." The Ewells are trash. When the defense insinuates that Mayella is the victim of incest at the hands of her father, it is not to make her a sympathetic figure. It is, in the eugenicist spirit of the times, to impugn her credibility—to do what A. A. Sizer did in the John Mays case: *The victim, coming from the same inferior stock, would likely share her father's moral character.* "I won't try to scare you for a while," Finch says, when he begins his cross-examination of Mayella. Then he adds, with polite menace, "Not yet." We are back in the embrace of Folsomism. Finch wants his white, male jurors to do the right thing. But as a good Jim Crow liberal he dare not challenge the foundations of their privilege. Instead, Finch does what lawyers for black men did in those days. He encourages them to swap one of their prejudices for another.

One of George Orwell's finest essays takes Charles Dickens to task for his lack of "constructive suggestions." Dickens was a powerful critic of Victorian England, a proud and lonely voice in the campaign for social reform. But, as Orwell points out, there was little substance to Dickens's complaints. "He attacks the law, parliamentary government, the educational system and so forth, without ever clearly suggesting what he would put in their places," Orwell writes. "There is no clear sign that he wants the existing order to be overthrown, or that he believes it would make very much difference if it were overthrown. For in reality his target is not so much society as 'human nature.'" Dickens sought "a change of spirit rather than a change in structure."

Orwell didn't think that Dickens should have written different novels; he loved Dickens. But he understood that Dickens bore the ideological marks of his time and place. His class did not see the English social order as tyrannical, worthy of being overthrown. Dickens thought that large contradictions could be tamed through small moments of justice. He believed in the power of changing hearts, and that's what you believe in, Orwell says, if you "do not wish to endanger the status quo."

But in cases where the status quo involves systemic injustice this is no more than a temporary strategy. Eventually, such injustice requires more than a change of heart. "What in the world am I ever going to do with the Niggers?" Jim Folsom once muttered, when the backlash against Brown began to engulf his political career. The argument over race had risen to such a pitch that it could no longer be alleviated by gesture and symbolism—by separate but equal inaugural balls and hearty handshakes—and he was lost.

Finch's moral test comes at the end of *To Kill a Mockingbird.* Bob Ewell has been humiliated by the Robinson trial. In revenge, he attacks Scout and her brother on Halloween night. Boo Radley, the reclusive neighbor of the Finches, comes to the children's defense, and in the scuffle Radley kills Ewell. Sheriff Tate brings the news to Finch, and persuades him to lie about what actually happened; the story will be that Ewell inadvertently stabbed himself in the scuffle. As the Sheriff explains:

Maybe you'll say it's my duty to tell the town all about it and not hush it up. Know what'd happen then? All the ladies in Maycomb includin' my wife'd be knocking on his door bringing angel food cakes. To my way of thinkin', Mr. Finch, taking the one man who's done you and this town a great service an' draggin' him with his shy ways into the limelight—to me, that's a sin. It's a sin and I'm not about to have it on my head. If it was any other man it'd be different. But not this man, Mr. Finch.

The courthouse ring had spoken. Maycomb would go back to the way it had always been.

"Scout," Finch says to his daughter, after he and Sheriff Tate have cut their little side deal. "Mr. Ewell fell on his knife. Can you possibly understand?"

Understand what? That her father and the Sheriff have decided to obstruct justice in the name of saving their beloved neighbor the burden of angel food cake? Atticus Finch is faced with jurors who have one set of standards for white people like the Ewells and another set for black folk like Tom Robinson. His response is to adopt one set of standards for respectable whites like Boo Radley and another for white trash like Bob Ewell. A book that we thought instructed us about the world tells us, instead, about the limitations of Jim Crow liberalism in Maycomb, Alabama.

Note

1. Reprinted from *The New Yorker*, Politics and Prose, 10 August 2009: 26–32.

CHAPTER 5

To Kill a Mockingbird: Fifty Years of Influence on the Legal Profession

Ann Engar

Voted best legal film of all time by the American Film Institute, cited by numerous lawyers as the book and film that most inspired their decisions to pursue a career in law, claimed to be the impetus for constructive changes in Southern justice during the civil rights movement, *To Kill a Mockingbird* in its novel, film, and play versions has deeply influenced the legal profession in the past fifty years. In this essay, I will examine carefully the impact the story has had on the legal profession, an important component of the book's story particularly since it has inspired much more legal scholarship than literary criticism ("Note" 1685). How has the book been used by the legal profession, and what does the story—and, in particular, its character Atticus Finch—represent to lawyers? I will argue that Atticus Finch speaks to the deepest of attorneys' longings and insecurities: their desire for public respect and influence and for private balance and wholeness.

For at least the past two generations, the book and film have attracted numerous individuals to the legal profession through their depiction of a gallant, eloquent, and courageous attorney defending an innocent man. Voted the number one movie hero of the past one hundred years by the American Film Institute, Atticus Finch bestows respectability and honor upon the legal profession. Attorney Richard Brust, assistant managing editor of the *ABA Journal*, has described Atticus Finch as the "epitome of both moral certainty and unyielding trust in the rule of law . . . the self-assured lawyer and upright human being we all hope to be." Steven Lubet, professor of law at Northwestern University, with a note of criticism, contends that Finch "saves" the legal profession "by providing a moral archetype, by reflecting nobility upon us, and by having the courage to meet the standards we set for ourselves but can seldom attain. . . . His potential justifies all of our failings and imperfections. . . . All of his choices are brave and noble, which is why the community of Maycomb ultimately put its faith in him" (Lubet, "Reconstructing Atticus Finch" 1340). Rob Atkinson uses similar religious and mythic language to describe how attorneys view Atticus Finch: "[Harper] Lee has given us the Gospel According to Atticus in the words of his chief disciple Scout. . . . But we [attorneys] are the ones who continue to work and worship Atticus' golden image" (1371). Atkinson deems Lee to be the maker and marketer of an icon. Though Atkinson's comments are somewhat sensationalistic, Lee does invite reverential respect for her character, especially in a scene oft quoted by lawyers—the scene in which Atticus exits the courtroom and Reverend Sykes tells Scout, "Miss Jean Louise, stand up. Your father's passin'" (*TKAM* 241) as the black audience in the balcony all get to their feet.

Scenes from the book and film are frequently played and discussed at bar association conventions. At the 2006 Minnesota Bar Convention, for example, the film was used in continuing education courses by the Criminal Law Section. Panelists critiqued the legal performance of Atticus Finch as portrayed by Gregory Peck. Advice given by the panel included avoiding clutter (Atticus' defense table is bare), keeping it simple (Atticus' point that no doctor was called although the right side of Mayella's face was injured), and picturing the witness' home life (Mayella's lack of friends and alcoholic father) ("Legal Education Seminar"). The succeeding year at the convention, the History Theater presented "Atticus Finch: The Search for Humanity," followed by Minnesota Supreme Court Chief Justice Russell A. Anderson moderating a panel on professionalism and ethics ("Minnesota Bar Buzz").

As a public figure, Atticus is praised for his skill at advocacy, his concern for social justice, and his morality. In his analysis of the films *A Few Good Men*, *Body Heat*, and *To Kill a Mockingbird*, attorney Aaron Peron Ogletree points to Atticus Finch as a lawyer willing to do almost anything to protect his client, including risking his life. Ogletree asserts that these films present the image of lawyers as counselors who develop relationships with the family members of clients, who keep the family informed of case developments, and whose relationships never create an issue of conflict of interest (334). Atticus and the lawyers in the other films exhibit courtroom demeanors of preparedness, ability to think quickly when necessary, relentlessness in cross-examination, and flexibility in fitting changing circumstances. Atticus remains calm no matter what the trying circumstances are, including being spat upon and experiencing threats against his children's lives. Hofstra University law professor Monroe H. Freedman praises Finch for being a superb advocate, wise counselor, and conscientious legislator (76), one who Scout tells us is reelected year after year with no opposition (37). Similarly, Steven Lubet, while he criticizes much of the adulation of Atticus, does praise his skill in compelling a "bigoted Alabama jury to hesitate before convicting an innocent black man" ("Reconstructing Atticus Finch" 1361). Finally, Gary B. Pillersdorf discusses how in films and media, great lawyers give summations that are the most dramatic and dynamic part of the case, with Atticus being no exception. Pillersdorf does comment, though, that it is a myth that a great orator can salvage a far-fetched case (70).

Also, Atticus is concerned about justice not only for the rich but also for those like the Cunninghams, who can pay him only with a bag of nuts or whatever other items of produce they might have. As a white attorney defending a black man accusing of raping a white woman in Alabama in 1935, Atticus is viewed by some lawyers as a symbol of a fighter for civil rights and social justice. Freedman writes that, for some lawyers, Atticus' hero of justice is a "mythological paragon of social activism" (67). Atticus' fight for justice for the oppressed has even in recent years been transferred from the oppression of the poor and of African Americans to the oppression of political dissidents. The *St. Louis Daily Record* reported in 2005 that Joshua Dratel, the defense attorney for David Hicks, a man captured by the Northern Alliance in Afghanistan and transported to the U.S. naval station in Guantanamo Bay, sent his client a copy of *To Kill a Mockingbird*. Dratel recounts, "The whole Guantanamo experience was encapsulated for me when I sent him [the book]—and they [military officials] rejected it. A classic piece of American fiction that I don't think has caused a revolution yet. But maybe the story of someone wrongly charged with a crime hits too close to home!" ("A Guantanamo Test Case").

One of Atticus' most moral moments comes as he explains to Jem and Scout why he will defend Tom Robinson:

> All I can say is, when you and Jem are grown, maybe you'll look back on this with some compassion and some feeling that I didn't let you down. This case, Tom Robinson's case, is something that goes to the essence of a man's conscience—Scout, I couldn't go to church and worship God if I didn't try to help that man. . . . [People are] entitled to full respect for their opinions, but before I can live with other folks I've got to live with myself. The one thing that doesn't abide by majority rule is a person's conscience. (*TKAM* 120)

Atticus certainly tries to live up to the demands of his conscience, his God, and his personal ethics as others concerned with social justice have.

It is this kind of reflective passage in the book that has led lawyers to invoke Atticus as a moral exemplar. Thomas L. Shaffer, emeritus law professor at the University of Notre Dame and the nation's most prolific legal scholar, wrote in

1991 that Atticus appears in all of his (Shaffer's) books and asserted that people the ages of his law students from 1963 to 1991 knew the novel better than they knew the Bible (Shaffer, *American Lawyers* 223–224). Shaffer says Atticus has been cited as a paragon, role model, and professional exemplar; and he himself uses Atticus as an example of a good person (14), the embodiment of the American gentleman-lawyer (28). Shaffer also claims that it is significant that Atticus does not disassociate from his background but works conscientiously without losing his sense of self (35). Shaffer admiringly describes Atticus as he defines "discrimination humbly when he [tells] his children that before one acts with (or acts upon) the other fellow, he has to get inside his skin, a particularly poignant metaphor when one theme in the story is racism" (45). Moreover, Atticus is depicted as "heroic in telling the truth" (85) and as a protector of the weak (93).

It is evident that present-day attorneys play upon this image of Atticus in pleas for their colleagues to become involved in pro bono and low-cost legal work. Nevett Steele, Jr., director of a Baltimore organization that helps solo and small-firm attorneys provide low-cost legal help to the traditionally underserved, identifies Atticus as a great legal hero and says, "I know this is an idealized sort of thing, but you seek to have [lawyers] make a living and also to provide some tremendous service to individuals and the community and really set an example" (*The Daily Record*). One of the most extreme uses of Atticus as a moral exemplar and pro bono savior appears in the writing of Ted D. Lee in the *Texas Intellectual Property Law Journal*. Lee calls Atticus his "all time favorite hero" because he "stood up for what was right even though he knew it was unpopular and he would never be paid for his services." Invoking the earlier-mentioned reverential worship of Atticus, Lee gives the same advice about moral decision making and Atticus that preachers give about Jesus: "Each of us, when considering whether to undertake a representation or how best to represent our client, should ask ourselves, 'What would Atticus Finch do?' Do the right thing. You may not receive monetary rewards here on this earth, but you will receive respect from those who matter" (593–595). Having worked his readers into moral fervor in Southern preacher–style rhetoric, Lee then invites attorneys to work for the Pro Bono Task Force.

Why does the character of Atticus speak so strongly to attorneys? In popular culture lawyers are one of the few groups about whom it is politically correct to joke. They often appear as "parasitic, devious, greedy and cynical" immoralists (Economides and O'Leary 16). Associating with criminals, they at times are depicted as not far from criminals themselves. The generation that, as juveniles, read *To Kill a Mockingbird* as it was first published and were inspired by the movie version, watched as young professionals the corruption of Watergate fueled by the actions of attorneys Richard Nixon, John Dean, John Ehrlichman, G. Gordon Liddy, John Mitchell, and others. Far from being Supermen who defend "truth, justice, and the American way," today's lawyers often seem to have a reputation in the public eye for twisting truth or for being unconcerned with it and for flouting justice in favor of winning for their wealthy clients. A *New York Times* review, for instance, stated that "the greatest of all oxymorons" is the term "legal ethics" (quoted in Dershowitz 151). Dershowitz goes on to label law an "ethically treacherous profession" (151) and has created a litany of charges against lawyers: they "overprepare witnesses, oversell their relationships with prosecutors and judges, and overbill or charge for hours when they are doing over things" (182).

Yet many attorneys originally choose law precisely because they see themselves as champions of the oppressed and because they care deeply about justice, equity, and rules. In a survey taken by Mike Papantonio of over two hundred attorneys in the southeastern United States in the 1990s, some 48 percent of respondents said, "I have or will have made meaningful impact to better society as a whole by the time I leave my practice as a trial lawyer" (27). Besides Watergate, another lesson about law in the twentieth century came from the civil rights movement, which was championed by lawyers such as Thurgood Marshall, who used the courtroom rather than relying on recalcitrant legislatures to abolish the inequities of segregation, inequities that take so prominent a place in *To Kill a Mockingbird.*

Added to the controversial public image of attorneys is the very complexity of the legal system itself. Lay people are often incensed that defense attorneys argue effectively for clients who they know are guilty. They are appalled when they hear professors like Abbe Smith of Georgetown state things like "Proof, not truth, is the currency in our courtroom." They do not realize that attorneys and judges are often lifetime associates, while many clients are "one-shotters" who can easily misunderstand or be run over by the system. Alan Dershowitz has his "Thirteen Rules of the Criminal Justice Game," which most participants in the criminal justice system understand but many lay people do not:

Rule I. Most criminal defendants are, in fact, guilty.
Rule II. All criminal defense lawyers, prosecutors, and judges understand and believe Rule I.
Rule III. It is easier to convict guilty defendants by violating the Constitution than by complying with it, and in some cases it is impossible to convict guilty defendants without violating the Constitution.
Rule IV. Many police lie about whether they violated the Constitution in order to convict guilty defendants.
Rule V. All prosecutors, judges and defense attorneys are aware of Rule IV.
Rule VI. Many prosecutors implicitly encourage police to lie about whether they violated the Constitution in order to convict guilty defendants.

Rule VII. All judges are aware of Rule VI.

Rule VIII. Most trial judges pretend to believe police officers who they know are lying.

Rule IX. All appellate judges are aware of Rule VIII, yet many pretend to believe the lying police officers.

Rule X. Most judges disbelieve defendants about whether their constitutional rights have been violated, even if they are telling the truth.

Rule XI. Most judges and prosecutors would not knowingly convict a defendant who they believe to be innocent of the crime charged (or a closely related crime).

Rule XII. Rule XI does not apply to members of organized crime, drug dealers, career criminals or potential informers.

Rule XIII. Nobody really wants justice. (80–81)

Dershowitz labels these rule-bending, end-justifies-the-means proceedings as "benign corruption" (80). But complicity in such a system cannot help but make those outside the law cynical and those inside the law feel compromised and conflicted. As Calvin Woodard, Woodard Professor Emeritus of Law at University of Virginia, says, "Scout has questions and doubts about the law that even Atticus—the consummate man of law—cannot adequately explain" (153).

Given these images and the amorphous ethics of the law, it is no wonder that attorneys turn Atticus Finch into an icon. Who would not wish to be aligned with a man who instructs the jury,

> I'm no idealist to believe firmly in the integrity of our courts and in the jury system—that is no ideal to me, it is a living, working reality. Gentlemen, a court is no better than each man of you sitting before me on this jury. A court is only as sound as its jury, and a jury is only as sound as the men who make it up. I am confident that you gentlemen will review without passion the evidence you have heard, come to a decision, and restore this defendant to his family. In the name of God, do your duty. (*TKAM* 233)

But Dershowitz also claims that although lawyers tend to be hero-worshippers, they need to avoid hero-worshipping, even of attorneys like Clarence Darrow, Oliver Wendell Holmes, Hugo Black, and William O. Douglas (3). Instead, lawyers should emulate admirable traits of individual attorneys but recognize that "even singular characteristics will rarely be without flaws" (9). He summarizes, "There is no perfect justice, just as there are no absolutes in ethics. But there is perfect injustice, and we know it when we see it" (9).

The adulation of Atticus Finch has blinded some readers to the complexity of his character. Some of that adulation undoubtedly stems from the point of view of the novel, a young child telling the story of her father, a story written by a daughter—Harper Lee—who adored her own attorney father. Atticus himself confronts the lack of perfect justice: in a perfect world, an innocent client would be freed. Atticus also confronts the problem of no absolutes: in a world of absolutes, he would not have to impugn the character of a young woman whose father abuses her. Perfect injustice would have been for Tom Robinson not to have had his point of view heard, not to have had the ability to appeal, not to have had good representation. Calpurnia recognizes the law's complexity and unpredictability when she tells a friend, "First thing you learn when you're in a lawin' family is that there ain't any definite answers to anything" (*TKAM* 237).

Dershowitz further suggests that obsession over the conflict between legal ethics, which require legal advocacy on behalf of both innocent and guilty clients, and personal morality, which requires decency and honesty in all dealings, is actually a mark of a good lawyer. In fact, he says,

> there are no perfect resolutions to these and other conflicts. An effective lawyer must do everything on behalf of his client that is not forbidden by the law or the rules of the legal profession. But a good person should always be uncomfortable about doing anything that does not meet his or her personal standards of morality. . . . If you are a decent and thinking person, you will never grow entirely comfortable with some of the tactics you will be required to employ as an effective and ethical lawyer (158).

It is this more human lawyer, the uncomfortable lawyer, whom Harper Lee reveals under the adulation of her narrator Scout and who attracts real-life lawyers to the book.

It is also the Atticus Finch that emerges from legal critics who complain that Atticus is not the paragon portrayed by his worshippers. Atticus does not volunteer to defend Tom Robinson but instead is appointed. Atticus tells his brother, Jack, "I'd hoped to get through life without a case of this kind, but John Taylor pointed at me and said, 'You're It'" (*TKAM* 93). Far from a Savior figure, Atticus is more the kind of person Jack describes in his response—"Let this cup pass from you, eh?" But Atticus takes on the case in order to "face" his children (93). He admits to a profound distaste for criminal law and does not take on pro bono cases in order to overcome evil. Miss Maudie says that his specialty is more along the lines of drawing up wills: "he can make somebody's will so airtight can't anybody meddle with it" (95). Malcolm Gladwell, a columnist for the *New Yorker*, even asserts that Atticus is no moral activist because he is not brimming with rage because of Robinson's unjust verdict and because he does not take the problem of racism outside of the immediate context of Maycomb (26–32).

Steven Lubet similarly deconstructs Atticus by labeling him "not a fire-brand or a reformer" or "civil rights defender" ("Reconstructing Atticus Finch" 1360). According to Lubet, Atticus does not care about the relative truth of the charges and the defense. Lubet questions whether Finch's virtue depends on Robinson's innocence or on Atticus' use of his skills, even if it is in aid of the guilty. To Lubet, there are two alternatives: Atticus is either a "paragon of honor" or a "slick hired gun" (1362). More probably the latter, Atticus, Lubet claims, uses the standard technique of mid-1930s rape cases—the "she wanted it" defense—to humiliate Mayella Ewell with his politeness, relying upon cruel stereotypes and "playing the 'gender card'" (1345–1348, 1362). Lubet argues that there are crucial gaps in Robinson's story, yet Atticus does not insist the Robinson explain them (1347). Lubet closes his argument with statements close to Dershowitz's—"real lawyers must struggle with unending moral complexity"—but adds that "public support for the adversary system . . . [is] weakened by the unconditional insistence that all advocacy is for the better" ("Reply to Comments" 1383–1384).

Lubet's provocative article, most recently quoted by Malcolm Gladwell in his August 2009 *New Yorker* article, originally appeared in the *Michigan Law Review* in May 1999. It was followed by five responses by law school professors and deans from prestigious law schools, including Stanford and University of Chicago. Lubet, in turn, commented on their responses. What is amazing is that a book, often read by junior high school students and put in the juvenile sections of libraries, almost forty years after its initial publication, would draw such attention and strong passions from such distinguished readers and that those passions would still be inflamed ten years later.

Each of the attorneys who responded to Lubet, though not agreeing with Lubet's depiction of Atticus as a hired gun, debunks the mythologizing of Atticus Finch in favor of more realistic view of the legal profession. Each also clearly admires Lee's skill in creating such a character and finds Atticus a hero.

Ann Althouse, a professor at University of Wisconsin Law School, baldly states that *To Kill a Mockingbird* does not depict Atticus "as a brave and idealistic man who took unpopular cases and stood up to the evils of his society" (1364). Instead, he is shown as a man who accepts assignments and is willing "to continue to work within the system really living in the world he is born into," a "model of toleration of an imperfect world and acceptance of the limited effect of one's proper performance of one's own assigned role" (1364). While Lubet faults Atticus for not having the persistence to discover the truth about Mayella's life, Althouse suggests he appropriately focused on his own client (1368). Rather than insisting on absolutes, especially in judgments and revelations of truth, Atticus, according to Althouse, exemplifies someone who "has found a way to live and work as a good person in a deeply flawed society" (1369). The dialectic between Lubet and Althouse illustrates the tension between those who long for clear-cut truths in law (like Lubet, who criticizes Atticus for not living up to an ideal) and those who maintain that law is limited both by those who participate in it and by its inherent structure (Althouse's position).

Burnele V. Powell, dean at University of South Carolina School of Law, continues Althouse's line of argumentation. He pictures lawyers as actors in a "theatrical social production called a criminal trial" (1373). For him Atticus is a hero because he provides Robinson with the kind of defense that our society has defined as desirable. Atticus demands the freedom "to make arguments within the bounds of the law that are necessary for the full ventilation of issues in a criminal case" (1375). William H. Simon, Stanford University Law School professor, similarly questions whether Finch is an "icon of virtue" but also suggests treating the novel as a "professional responsibility hypothetical" through which one can judge Atticus' conduct to be "ethically plausible" both in terms of bar norms and more ambitious conceptions of justice (1376). Yet Simon asks whether Atticus entirely fulfills the strictures of the law since, at the end of the novel, he collaborates in covering up the murder of Bob Ewell, a collaboration that could be called an "obstruction of justice," but which he accedes to in order not to expose Boo Radley to the curiosity of townspeople in a public trial (1377).[1] Simon, like Dershowitz, underlines the difference between personal morality and the law.

Randolph N. Stone, law professor at University of Chicago, combats Lubet's claims with his own advocacy of vigorous and zealous defense, which he feels Atticus rendered to Robinson. To Stone, too, the question of guilt is irrelevant, especially when so much in law is stacked against the defendant, including racial profiling, prosecutorial overcharging, discriminatory jury selections, disproportionate sentencing and confinement policies, and wrongful convictions (1381).

Thus, the public character of Atticus Finch appeals to legal readers on the surface level because of his skills in presenting a defense, cross-examining, and carrying out a summation; because of his defense of the poor and oppressed; and because of his desire to live according to the dictates of his conscience. His own community of Maycomb admires and trusts him as a man of decency and principle. Beneath the surface, Atticus is more complex but no less attractive: no civil rights activist, he does his duty, which includes an energetic defense involving exposure of the victim, airing of his client's point of view, working within a limited system, and eventually subverting the system in order to avoid exposing a troubled and suffering young man.

Lawyers at times confront the difficulty of bridging between professional and personal behavior. Dershowitz, as previously mentioned, writes that criminal defendants have the constitutional right to zealous representation that includes going right up to the line of legally and ethically permissible conduct.

Yet, Dershowitz comments, lawyers can become entangled in their inability to distinguish that this kind of license extends only to the defense of others and not to their own personal and professional decisions about life (148). In *To Kill a Mockingbird*, Miss Maudie posits that Atticus has no such problem: he is the same in the house as he is in public (*TKAM* 50). A *Harvard Law Review* note, "Being Atticus Finch: The Professional Role of Empathy," employs Atticus Finch to demonstrate that ritual can be used to channel empathetic feelings successfully to bridge the divide between professional and personal self, between nonjudgmental detachment and moral activism.

Empathy in *To Kill a Mockingbird*, according to the *Harvard Law Review* note, can be disempowering (as it is with Scout's new teacher), can lead to "paternalistic pity" (as it allows Bob Ewell to break laws with impunity), can encourage self-deception (Atticus' belief that he can "stand in Bob Ewell's shoes" but talk derisively of "his kind"), or can produce inability to face ugliness (Dill's crying at the cross-examination of Robinson) ("Note" 1686–1688). But it can also be positive: it is manifest in Atticus' teaching his children to remain courteous to Mrs. Dubose despite her taunts and threats and to allow them to retain enough empathy so that they can ultimately learn about her courage. Ritual again is manifest as Atticus is friendly and "polite to a fault" in his cross-examination of Mayella Ewell. But Atticus also breaks from ritual at specific times, such as at the trial when he takes off his coat and unbuttons his vest, in order to appeal to the emotions of the jury (1687–1688).

The note closes by adjuring lawyers to adopt some form of personal ritual in order to keep empathy within the bounds of professionalism and also to employ it in its service. It recommends adopting Atticus' "brand of (semi)detached civility; subjecting every professional decision to a specific, searching series of questions, or mandating a certain amount of pro bono work for oneself" (1701). Aside from its advice on maintaining professionalism and benevolence and its plea for pro bono work, the note demonstrates the major appeal of Atticus Finch to attorneys: his ability to bridge the public and private worlds and to be a success in each, thus presenting Atticus as "the classic model of how to pursue a career and raise a family with grace and integrity" (1688).

With lawyers working sixty to eighty hours per week on average at big law firms, there is often little time or energy for a successful home life. Atticus' home with its curious and lively children who respect and emulate their father is thus very appealing. Scout says that she and Jem "found our father satisfactory: he played with us, read to us, and treated us with courteous detachment" (*TKAM* 6). In addition, the children mirror their father by playing at law with Scout as probate judge, Jem as sheriff, and Dill as the criminal (43–44), and Jem even admits to wanting to become a lawyer (55). Clearly, Atticus is intent on surrounding his children in a world of law: he tells his daughter, "Law remains rigid, Miss Scout Finch. . . . You must obey the law" (34) and calls Jem's snowman "near libel" (76). When he uses "last-will-and-testament diction," the children feel free at all times to interrupt him for a translation when it is beyond their understanding (35). And when Uncle Jack berates Scout, she yells at him because Atticus would have listened to both of the children's sides before judging (97). The *Massachusetts Lawyers' Weekly*, in reviewing a performance of the theatrical version of the story at the Wheelock Family Theater in 2007, recommended that lawyers take their children to the play because it could help parents explain to their children what they do as advocates, since their professional choices can be a challenge, especially if they are representing unpopular clients ("*Mockingbird* Still Soars"). The book thus shapes a view of an attorney who, despite having a not-easily-presented profession, plays an integral role in parenting and creating a happy private life.

Mike Papantonio, in his book *In Search of Atticus Finch: A Motivational Book for Lawyers*, well expresses the longing for a balanced life, a good public and private life, that Atticus Finch represents. His aforementioned survey found 76.2 percent of all respondents said, "I need to take more time from my day-to-day practice to improve my quality of life" (27). Papantonio looks nostalgically at the slow-moving, small community–based world of Maycomb where, Papantonio asserts in an obvious oversimplification, "things mean what they mean, people are what they are and seldom change" (32). For him, the book represents an effective counter to the frenzied world of the 1990s with "contentious, combative" trial lawyers, lawyers focused on monetary rewards, and lawyers consumed by stress and burnout (35–36).

Papantonio sees Atticus as the solution to these problems. In his opinion, Atticus is a "tremendously complex yet simply drawn character who possesses almost every attribute a human being and a trial lawyer might wish to have" (11). Papantonio, like the *Harvard Law Review*, speaks of Atticus' ability to link public and private worlds through the "quality" he epitomizes in his functions (11). Atticus represents a person who knows himself, who is defined by his beliefs, values, and lifestyle. In short, he lives a full and meaningful life. One of the biggest issues to Papantonio is the respect in which Atticus is held. "I saw great contrast between the way Atticus is regarded in his community and the way lawyers are regarded today" (25). Today's lawyers, he bemoans, are seen as self-serving rather than serving their communities. Though Papantonio describes Atticus as almost god-like in ennobling "all who come in contact with him" (25), his study of *Mockingbird* is correct in saying that, although many of Atticus' neighbors believe he is wrong and while his friends believe he is naïve and blind and his detractors viciously convey their disapproval of his defending a black man, none excoriates him for being dishonorable (26). On the whole, Atticus has the respect of his community, yet he does not depend upon it. He "does not define his successor value as a person by his level of acceptance or by his material worth" (43). What Atticus stands for is clear and definable. Papantonio, like Ted D. Lee, even goes so far as to encourage lawyers to "develop a habit of asking themselves, 'What would Atticus Finch do and how would he do it?'" (45), in order to live a balanced and fulfilling life.

The difficulty, again, is that Atticus and his life are much more complex than Papantonio presents. Although Lee herself characterized her tale as "a love story pure and simple" (quoted in Lubet, "Reconstructing Atticus Finch" 1341), Atticus' private life has its weaknesses. Scout herself admits, "Atticus ain't got time to teach me anything. . . . Why he's so tired at night he just sits in the livingroom and reads" (*TKAM* 19). Atticus is so deeply involved in his book that he does not even hear his children as they peek in the shutters of Boo Radley's house. In fact, the person who does fulfill the parental role teaching the children, especially about morality, is Calpurnia, the housekeeper. Although Atticus does exemplify and confirm what she teaches (Shaffer, "Learning" 142), Calpurnia remains the teacher, the one who is watching over Scout and Jem during most of their waking hours. In truth, Atticus and his children are fortunate to be surrounded by a number of women who enable him to be a respected attorney with a happy family. Besides Calpurnia (as previously stated), Miss Maudie and Aunt Alexandra also fulfill these maternal roles for Jem and Scout since Atticus has no wife with whom to maintain a relationship and seems not to be seeking one. Also, although the novel occurs in the depths of the Depression and Atticus does assist those who can pay little, he seems to have no material worries: he lives in a comfortable, two-story house and has the money to pay a servant.

So, for all Atticus means to attorneys as both an honorable public servant and a loving father, should he be a hero to lawyers? Examination of his actions fits into the law and literature movement in which narrative literature is used as a mean of improving the moral character of the law and the lives of lawyers. Yet to what extent is it valid and even healthy to use a fictional character to represent a complicated, evolving, and sometimes morally ambiguous profession such as law? Fictional characters face fictional difficulties and challenges and are shaped by their authors to perform actions that might have happened, that, as Aristotle said, are probable and not actual, more universal and singular (353). Ann Althouse takes this tack as she notes that *To Kill a Mockingbird* says much about rape in its own fictional world but little about rape cases in the real world (1367). When honoring Frank Armani, a New York attorney who did not reveal that his client had confessed to him four murders and the place he dumped the bodies, law professor Lisa G. Lerman likened Armani to Atticus but underlined that "the difference is that, unlike Atticus Finch, Frank Armani is a real person" (Hansen 30). A comment by Dershowitz mentioned earlier in this essay is applicable here: one should choose heroic characteristics rather than a heroic person. And, it might be added, choose a real person rather than a fictional character, no matter how multilayered a creation he might be. William H. Simon, too, has questioned whether icons of virtue are what attorneys should look for in novels (1377) or whether they should seek real-life role models.

Nonetheless, *To Kill a Mockingbird* has attracted two generations of lawyers to the profession and, in its depiction of a dedicated, empathetic, and skilled attorney, has inspired hero-worship and impassioned debates, especially over legal ethics and the limitations of the legal system. Lawyers' reactions to the novel reveal their deep need to be seen as respected public servants, individuals with strong moral cores who can effectively navigate their professional and family lives while simultaneously coping with their discomfort with the ethically ambiguous waters that swirl around them.

As fifty years have passed since the novel's publication and nearly fifty years since the film's release—years filled with racial, gender, and technological revolutions—the question remains: Will the novel and film still hold their appeal and power? How dated are they? The film, as a classic of American cinema, will certainly continue to be watched by lovers of movies, even black-and-white, non-digitized ones. But, if the small poll of my freshman university pre-law class is any indication, it is the book itself that will endure and continue to draw young people to the law. On the first day of this fall's semester, I asked the thirty students in the class, "Who has read *To Kill a Mockingbird?*" An amazing seventeen out of thirty had. I then asked how many had seen the movie. Hands went down until only two remained. Finally, I asked the seventeen how many had decided to explore becoming a lawyer because of the book: three answered affirmatively. Thus, either the book inspired them to want to become lawyers or they were motivated to read the book because of their interest in law. Either way, the legal profession will continue to benefit from a novel written about three children and the summer when they first had the idea of making Boo Radley come out.

Note

1. Thomas Shaffer earlier commented on Atticus' lie to protect Boo Radley as an example of a gentleman-lawyer story where the lawyer strives to protect the weak who are not weak. The gentleman-lawyer cannot prevent pain so he "hides from what he cannot

do in the delusions of his optimism. These delusions corrupt his ethic by turning it from an ethic of the virtues to an ethic of honor and shame" (*American Lawyer* 93).

Works Cited

Althouse, Ann. "Reconstructing Atticus Finch? A Response to Professor Lubet," *Michigan Law Review* 97.6 (May 1999): 1363–1369. LexisNexis *Academic*. Web. 2 November 2009.

American Film Institute. "AFI's 100 Years: 100 Heroes & Villains." 2003. Web. 9 October 2009. http://www.afi.com/tvevents/100years/handv.aspx

Aristotle. *The Pocket Aristotle.* Ed. Justin Kaplan. New York: Simon and Schuster, 1991.

Atkinson, Rob. "Comment on Steven Lubet, 'Reconstructing Atticus Finch.'" *Michigan Law Review* 97.6 (May 1999): 1370–1372. LexisNexis *Academic*. Web. 2 November 2009.

Brust, Richard. "The 25 Greatest Legal Movies," *ABA Journal* 94.8 (August 2008). LexisNexis *Academic*. Web. 26 September 2009.

The Daily Record (Baltimore, MD), 27 January 2006. LexisNexis *Academic*. Web. 16 October 2009.

Dershowitz, Alan. *Letters to a Young Lawyer.* New York: Basic Books, 2001.

Economides, Kim, and Majella O'Leary. "The Moral of the Story: Toward an Understanding of Ethics in Organizations and Legal Practice." *Legal Ethics* 10.1 (Summer 2007): 5–21. LegalTrac. Web. 10 November 2009.

Freedman, Monroe H. "Atticus Finch—Right and Wrong." In *Racism in Harper Lee's "To Kill a Mockingbird": Social Issues in Literature.* Ed. Candice Mancini. Detroit: Greenhaven, 2008. (67–76)

Gladwell, Malcolm. "The Courthouse Ring: Atticus Finch and the Limits of Southern Liberalism." *The New Yorker,* 10 August 2009: 26–32. Web. 10/17 August 2009.

"A Guantanamo Test Case." *St. Louis Daily Record,* 27 November 2005. LexisNexis *Academic*. Web. 16 October 2009.

Hansen, Mark. "The Toughest Call: Lawyer's Life Changed When He Decided to Keep Client's Confession." *ABA Journal* 93 (August 2007): 28–30. LegalTrac. Web. 10 November 2009.

Lee, Harper. *To Kill a Mockingbird.* New York: Harper Perennial Modern Classics, 2006.

Lee, Ted D. "Letter from the Chair." *Texas Intellectual Property Law Journal* 16.3 (Spring 2008): 593–595. LexisNexis *Academic*. Web. 6 October 2009.

"Legal Education Seminar in Minneapolis Compares Criminal Law to Sales, Acting." *St. Louis Daily Record,* 19 April 2006. LexisNexis *Academic*. Web. 10 October 2009.

Lubet, Steven. "Reconstructing Atticus Finch," *Michigan Law Review* 97.6 (May 1999): 1339–1362. LexisNexis *Academic*. Web. 2 November 2009.

————. "Reply to Comments on "Reconstructing Atticus Finch," *Michigan Law Review* 97.6 (May 1999): 1382–1384. LexisNexis *Academic.* Web. 2 November 2009.

"Minnesota Bar Buzz," *Minnesota Lawyer,* 18 June 2007. LexisNexis *Academic.* Web. 9 October 2009.

"*Mockingbird* Still Soars with Stirring Message on Race." *Massachusetts Lawyers Weekly,* 5 November 2007. LexisNexis *Academic.* Web. 7 October 2009.

"Note: Being Atticus Finch: The Professional Role of Empathy in *To Kill a Mockingbird," Harvard Law Review* 117.5 (March 2004): 1682–1702. LexisNexis *Academic.* Web. 29 October 2009.

Ogletree, Aaron Peron. "Film Reviews: *A Few Good Men, Body Heat, To Kill a Mockingbird." Contemporary Justice Review* 9.3 (September 2006): 333–335. LexisNexis *Academic.* Web. 6 October 2009.

Papantonio, Mike. *In Search of Atticus Finch: A Motivational Book for Lawyers.* Pensacola, FL: Seville Publishing, 1995.

Pillersdorf, Gary A. "Great Endings." *Trial* 40.12 (November 2004): 70–74. LegalTrac. Web. 10 November 2009.

Powell, Burnele V. "A Reaction: (Stand Up, Your Father [a Lawyer] Is Passing." *Michigan Law Review* 97.6 (May 1999): 1373–1375. LexisNexis *Academic.* Web. 2 November 2009.

Shaffer, Thomas L. "Learning Good Judgment in the Segregated South." In *Racism in Harper Lee's "To Kill a Mockingbird": Social Issues in Literature.* Ed. Candice Mancini. Detroit: Greenhaven, 2008. (137–146)

Shaffer, Thomas L. with Mary M. Shaffer. *American Lawyers and Their Communities.* South Bend, IN: U Notre Dame P, 1991.

Simon, William H. "Moral Icons: A Comment on Steven Lubet's 'Reconstructing Atticus Finch.'" *Michigan Law Review* 97.6 (May 1999): 1376–1377. LexisNexis *Academic.* Web. 2 November 2009.

Smith, Abbe. "Case of a Lifetime." *Rhode Island Lawyers Weekly,* 17 November 2008. LexisNexis *Academic.* Web. 11 September 2009.

Stone, Randolph N. "Atticus Finch in Context." *Michigan Law Review* 97.6 (May 1999): 1378–1381. LexisNexis *Academic.* Web. 2 November 2009.

Woodard, Calvin. "Listening to the Mockingbird." In *Racism in Harper Lee's "To Kill a Mockingbird": Social Issues in Literature.* Ed. Candice Mancini. Detroit: Greenhaven, 2008. (147–158)

CHAPTER 6

Bending the Law: The Search for Justice and Moral Purpose

Jeffrey B. Wood

Scout, Jem, and Atticus Finch may be endearing and memorable characters in a work of classic fiction, but I would contend the main character of Harper Lee's *To Kill a Mockingbird* is the law. The law is the protagonist essentially because the novel describes in detail the ways that law governs social conduct and how society shapes its laws, and because Lee leads the reader to question the law's higher purpose and how to bend and change the law in order to meet its ideals. The story of the arrest and conviction of Tom Robinson personalizes and starkly exemplifies the way the law had so completely failed African Americans in the South before the civil rights movement of the 1960s (an era in which the novel became a celebrated and influential narrative of injustice). Indeed, fifty years after its publication, the novel remains a clarion call for racial justice and legal reform. Lee piercingly dissects the failure of Southern jurisprudence and explores its myriad contributing factors and devastating human consequences, through stories, characters, and—above all—the deep thoughts of Scout and Atticus Finch. Lee also uses Tom's story in a broader sense to explore themes critical to a reformed jurisprudence: equality before law, mutual understanding and respect, dignity, wise judgment, mercy, and humility. Thus Lee writes about a great injustice and at the same time teaches us about justice.

What should be done about injustice? A growing number of critics, including some in this volume, assert that Atticus Finch does not go far enough to adequately combat the unjust, prejudicial, and evil legal system of the Jim Crow South. This criticism is anachronistic and misses the point. Atticus may be a product of his time and society—"Maycomb County born and bred"—and he may appear at times to excuse the excesses of his neighbors. Notwithstanding these potential weaknesses, on every moral issue in the book, Atticus chooses the side that most nearly preserves human dignity, the common good, love of neighbor, equality, fairness, and the progress of humanity toward these values. Atticus is in many ways a barometer and expositor of Lee's ideas about the purpose of the law, especially in his insistence on the evil nature of institutionalizing such negative personality traits as prejudice, hatred, and narrow-mindedness.

Moreover, Atticus seems to understand that lasting legal change will not succeed unless people's hearts and minds also change, unless the law embodies the highest and best values of collective society, and unless the law is flexible enough to accommodate special circumstances. Lee suggests repeatedly throughout the novel that bending the law a little bit is appropriate and is preferred over strict adherence to rigid rules. At the same time, Lee suggests that the best way to achieve long-lasting legal reform is also a process of bending the law, a process that must be undertaken with care and understanding, particularly the understanding that flows from standing in others' shoes. The resulting changes in the law will of necessity be incremental and will occur over time, as society itself adapts and recognizes the need for such changes. Thus, the law will bend and will ultimately be reshaped by revisions and reforms that will preserve the highest and best aspects of jurisprudence, community, and culture, while correcting and attempting to eliminate its evil and its unjust failures. Lee's hope seems to be that the law will ultimately redeem itself, and therefore *To Kill a Mockingbird* is full of hope and expectation for this redemption.

Examining the way that the law bends in the novel as a result of facing particular challenges, therefore, is like studying the growth and development of a novel's protagonist. The protagonist usually always meets challenges and makes critical decisions about facing those challenges in the context of the events and stories in the narrative, interactions with other characters, and his or her own thoughts or ideas about life. If the law is the protagonist of *To Kill a Mockingbird*, therefore, exploring the dual meanings of "bending the law" in the context of the novel's stories and characters, as seen through the perceptive eyes of Scout and with the clarified wisdom of Atticus, is essential if readers want to understand the novel's enduring lessons about justice, legal reform, and social change.

The novel begins with Scout recalling the way Atticus resolves a dispute between Scout and Jem over what started it all (*TKAM* 3). Atticus contends that both Scout and Jem are both right, signaling his ability to weigh opposing principles and find the good aspects of each. By balancing such competing values, as Atticus continually does throughout the novel, he demonstrates his tendency to always look for the higher good, particularly for the higher good that the law can serve. He appears to realize that competing truths are not always inconsistent. Instead, apparently contradictory ideas can coexist, and the crucible of competing values can help forge stronger and more long-lasting resolutions to the problems we face. Results reached by consensus over time are ultimately more successful because more people have an interest in seeing them succeed.

Lee's initial biographical sketch of Atticus Finch describes a stark and tragic example of the law's power when it bends, while also foregrounding the ignorance and fruitlessness of persisting in efforts to maintain a rigid, obstinate legal position. Lee recounts that early in his legal career, Atticus represented two men of the Haverford clan who killed the town's leading blacksmith in the presence of three witnesses and who then refused to accept the state's plea bargain in order to escape the death penalty (*TKAM* 5). Lee describes the plea bargain as "generous" and likens the Haverford name and the family's local reputation to the pejorative term "jackass." As Lee revisits the resulting conviction and hangings, she records that the event left Atticus with a "profound distaste" of the practice of criminal law.

This story shows that the law can be most powerful and useful to society when it is flexible. When the prosecution offers a plea bargain rather than insisting on the rigid prosecution of defendants to the full letter of the law, the prosecutor not only exhibits mercy and caring but also conserves resources, while still ensuring a certain level of punishment for the crime (because every prosecutor knows there is a risk of the jury overly sympathizing with the defendant, no matter how good the evidence). In the case of the Haverfords, a plea bargain could have mercifully allowed the defendants to live and would have preserved the possibility of their redemption and eventual contribution to society, their families, and posterity. Conversely, the rigid insistence on their innocence foreclosed these benefits and ultimately cost the Haverfords their lives. Lee underscores the point by linking the Haverford name with "jackass." In addition, she emphasizes the profound dissatisfaction Atticus has with the experience, precisely because it fails to meet his ideals of flexibility within the legal process. The Haverfords' execution could easily have been avoided, if only the Haverfords could have bent a little bit from their obstinate legal position.

Lee's retelling of Arthur Radley's teenage difficulties just a few pages later also exemplifies the law's ability to bend to meet special circumstances. The younger Radley boy hung around with a rowdy gang and soon came before a judge on charges of disorderly conduct (*TKAM* 11). Ironically, Radley's father rejects the judge's decision to send his son to the state industrial school (itself a humane approach to juvenile delinquency, as Lee wryly notes that the "punishment" rendered to the other boys in the gang actually gave them access to the best secondary education available in the state), and instead convinces the judge to release Arthur on the promise that he would ensure that the boy would cause no further trouble. In Lee's estimation, the judge "was glad to do so," realizing that Mr. Radley's promise was his "bond."

In this case, it may be said that the judge exercised extreme judicial flexibility by setting young Radley free on the basis of his father's word alone, with no financial obligation, no collateral, no probation, and no court supervision or any other involvement whatsoever. This example also shows the societal and legal importance of extrajudicial covenants; the judge valued Radley's promise as a bond even though it had no legal standing. Subsequently, young Radley— "Boo" as he became known—spent fifteen years confined at home under his family's tyrannical presence. Still later he spends some time being locked in the courthouse basement after reportedly stabbing the elder Radley in the leg with scissors. Boo ultimately returns to the family house, where he stayed, like a ghost.

In Boo's case, the law adjusted the punishment to the circumstances, recognizing the potential of parental supervision to produce reform and change. It is very clear that on several occasions, the judge, the sheriff, and the town council search for unique ways to give Boo Radley a second chance. The Radley narrative, however, also points out the unfortunate result of Mr. Radley's overbearing and vindictive nature. This lack of flexibility—in fact, the rigidity of his disciplinary actions—causes Boo to become a ghostly recluse because his father is unwilling to give him the freedom to make any more mistakes. Here, the law bends, but the elder Radley does not, an action that has several detrimental effects on his adolescent son.

Lee pointedly describes Mr. Radley as having colorless eyes, a thin upper lip, and ramrod-like posture, features that signal his rigidity and lack of empathy. Emphasizing that Mr. Radley's eyes did not reflect light and that God's law was his only law, Lee suggests that his inflexibility is a flaw of character dictated by a moral and religious intransigence and that his demeanor is unlikely to change. Colorless eyes also signify apathy, show indifference to Arthur's real needs, and imply dullness in the extreme. Indeed Calpurnia describes Radley as "the meanest man ever God blew breath into" (*TKAM* 13). It is clear that Lee rejects the older Radley's tyrannical approach to punishment precisely because it lacks any sense of effectiveness or appropriateness in the specific circumstances.

Interestingly, during the first ten pages of the novel, Lee has already led the reader to draw several key observations about the law. First of all, she implies that the law must weigh differing values, ideals, and interests that may sometimes compete but may also be reconciled with care and wisdom. Second, the law can achieve the most goodness when people recognize that its power comes from gentleness and mercy. Moreover, she has indicated that the law's mercy is not universally recognized, and it is frequently refused rather than cultivated. Finally, the law is what people say it is; in the novel, not only judges, sheriffs, and council members, but also fathers, cooks, teachers, and peers establish complex regimes and rules that govern social conduct. For example, a baseball hit into the Radley yard was a lost ball with no questions asked—a rule that didn't bend (*TKAM* 10). In addition, Scout's battles with Calpurnia, the family household helper and cook, were "epic and one-sided"—Calpurnia always won (*TKAM* 6). As we have seen, old Radley dictates the stark existence of the Radley household, and his authority is upheld by a shaky covenant with the town authorities. Prosecutors attempt to find good results by offering plea bargains. Judges sometimes accept nontraditional penalties. Rules are sometimes rigid, sometimes bent.

In the second chapter of the novel, Lee further explores the complex folkways of Maycomb County through the example of the Cunningham clan, independent and self-reliant country people who refuse charity no matter how bleak their existence. Scout encounters young Walter Cunningham on the first day of school, recollecting her fascination with the senior Cunningham's payment to Atticus for legal services: stove wood, hickory nuts, smilax, holly, and turnip greens (*TKAM* 23). She attempts to explain the Cunningham clan's trait of self-sufficiency to her schoolteacher, Miss Caroline Fisher, who is new to Maycomb, to help her understand why young Walter wouldn't accept money from the teacher to pay for a lunch (having none and not having forgotten one)—only to receive the teacher's confused scorn at her attempted explanation and an unexpected punishment as well. Although Lee implies the importance and vitality of all of these interrelated unwritten norms, she also notes the unbridled discretion of teachers (and others in authority) to decide for themselves whether to honor a departure from absolute rules and expectations.

The Cunningham clan plays a crucial role in the novel and seems to represent Everyman, individuals struggling to maintain their independence and common decency in the midst of the Great Depression. They pay their bills in kind—in fact, at times providing more than they owe. They send their children to school. They seemingly accept with general acclamation the common assumptions of social life—barter, self-reliance, honesty, frugality, attending school and church—and they passively tolerate the racism, segregation, and prejudice of the time as well. While Atticus Finch stands apart from the racism of Maycomb society, the Cunninghams are caught up in it, like most Southerners of the era. Yet their racism is not totally intransigent.

At the attempted lynching of Tom Robinson, for example, it is Walter Cunningham, Sr.'s, self-realization and awareness of other viewpoints that ultimately thwarts the lynching (*TKAM* 175). Likewise, during the jury deliberations, a juror who is connected to the Cunninghams holds out for hours. Although the juror's actions are insufficient to actually render justice in Tom's case, they give Atticus (and the reader) hope for a "shadow of a beginning" of change (*TKAM* 253). The Cunningham clan's willingness to bend a little and to consider a different viewpoint, both at the attempted lynching and during jury deliberations, constitutes one of the great revelations of the novel. In one sense, the Cunningham clan is a microcosm of a society bending to achieve long-lasting legal change, incrementally, slowly, perhaps uneasily, and not as fast as one might desire. Their bravery in resisting Maycomb's long-tolerated racist viewpoints, while not strong enough to save Tom's life in this one case, is clearly what Lee hopes will ultimately transform society.

After her experiences on the first day of school learning more about the Cunninghams and various other peculiarities in the Maycomb community, Scout engages Atticus in an extended discussion about another Maycomb clan, the Ewells, and their avoidance of truancy laws and hunting restrictions (*TKAM* 33–35). "Sometimes it's better to bend the law a little in special cases," highlights Atticus as he explains the unorthodox arrangements that Maycomb authorities have uneasily and tacitly worked out with the Ewells. Unlike the Cunningham clan, the Ewells have not accepted community standards. Destitute and reliant on community handouts, the Ewells represent the Downcast, not Everyman. Perhaps out of pity for their lower-class status and their negative reputations in the community, the truancy officer has agreed to look the other way, as long as the Ewell children attend school one day a year. As Atticus explains it, the town leaders have agreed the Ewell children are not likely to gain any benefit from school whatsoever, so it would be "silly" to force them to attend school.

Although this explanation may seem flippant, Atticus goes on to explain his analysis for determining whether or not to rigorously enforce the truancy law in the case of the Ewells. While his statement that it would be "silly" to insist on school attendance suggests a gut feeling and may appear somewhat arbitrary or ad hoc, his rationale is in fact logical and thorough. Atticus considers the children involved—their way of living, their nature, their lack of interest in education, and their alcoholic father. Therefore, Atticus condones bending the law in this case based on an intimate and deep knowledge of the Ewells and the Maycomb community as a whole. He tries to envision what it would be like to force the Ewells to attend school. He weighs the public and governmental effort that would be required to get the Ewells to conform to regular school attendance, considering not only the likely response of the Ewells but also the disruption it would cause in the classroom. Lee's depiction of Burris Ewell on the first day of school makes it clear that schooling would be wasted on him, and that enforced rules in this case would be perhaps pointless—even worthless.

Likewise, the town authorities, recognizing that the Ewell children would probably starve otherwise, permit Bob Ewell to hunt and trap out of season. While Atticus concedes that hunting and trapping out of season is against the law and morally wrong, he also understands that denying food to hungry children would be a greater evil. Once again Atticus employs his deep knowledge of the community in reasoning that bending the law in this instance is correct.

In his estimation, Maycomb landowners, who essentially have had their game stolen by Ewell, would not begrudge the Ewell children an occasional meal. Atticus balances these opposing principles—property rights, law, community order, and majority rule on the one hand, and child welfare, grace, and compassion on the other—and supports bending the law rather than enforcing rigid legal rules. To Atticus, bending the law is more than simply not enforcing the strict letter of the law; it means looking to the spirit of the laws and upholding the moral purpose they serve. It is this higher purpose that makes the pursuit worthwhile, that vindicates the somewhat gritty and uneasy process that bending the law might involve.

A few pages later, Atticus draws a distinction between bending the law and making a compromise. When Atticus agrees to continue reading with Scout, he makes a compromise with her—an "agreement reached by mutual concessions" (*TKAM* 34). In Scout's case, the rigid legal rules apply—she must go to school, unlike the Ewells. But Atticus agrees to continue to teach reading to Scout despite her teacher's request that he desist. In return, Scout agrees to continue to attend classes regardless of her feeling that they are not only unnecessary but restrictive and demeaning as well.

In this episode, Lee again suggests that bending the law is a higher task than mere arrangements among disputing parties. Bending the law is primarily a moral task. It involves searching for the "higher law" or the higher purpose that is involved. It considers the greater good for society and the individual before deciding what is "right." In a sense, bending the law is relativistic—it considers the relative values of competing propositions and rejects an automatic and rigid application of firm rules in every case. It is clear that Atticus always chooses to uphold a higher purpose. Yet while demonstrating that bending the law involves making moral choices, Lee also asserts that those choices depend on far more than the personal preferences of an individual. Thus by his choice to do good for society and individuals, Atticus offers an indication that he wants the law to do the same.

Application of the higher law, therefore, involves more than choosing one set of moral values over another set of moral values. It requires individuals to search for the highest and best purpose in each decision. At the same time, one must acknowledge that bending the law may not create the perfect solution for every case. The motive for bending the law must never be arbitrary, self-centered, biased, or discretionary. Instead, it should be painstaking, humble, and full of effort. It is primarily a craft, like building a fine musical instrument or conducting careful surgery of the brain. In short, Lee suggests that bending the law requires the use of a scalpel, not an old, blunt kitchen knife. Lee's text acknowledges that both have great power: a kitchen knife can kill racists like Bob Ewell, but by wielding a scalpel to attempt to excise the tumor of racism,

Atticus proves more successful in achieving a long-lasting resolution of a severe societal problem.

As the novel progresses, Lee continues her explication of the higher moral purpose. Another example occurs when Atticus is called to shoot a rabid dog (*TKAM* 109); normally one doesn't shoot other people's dogs, any more than one hunts out of season, but Atticus is called upon to shoot Harry Johnson's dog Tim (the "pet of Maycomb") in order to protect the community from danger. Here is a case where it is not only permissible but essential to bend the law to protect the common good and ensure safety. Lee's emphasis on the popularity of Tim Johnson and the dramatic necessity of shooting him in order to save the community from a greater danger also serves as a metaphor that illustrates the community's prevailing prejudice and the necessity of removing the danger posed by institutionalized racism. The episode parallels the larger problem that Maycomb and Atticus must face head-on later in the novel.

In addition, this episode highlights the eagle eyes of Atticus Finch (eyes that earn him the nickname of "One-Shot Finch"), in contrast to the dull, colorless eyes of the elder Radley (which, as noted earlier, suggest his rigidity and tyranny). Atticus shoots Tim Johnson dead in the forehead, slightly to the right (*TKAM* 110), even after his glasses fall to the ground. He then grinds the broken lens to a powder, emphasizing they are not necessary to him. By submitting to the local sheriff's insistence that he be the one to shoot when the first shot would be the only shot, Atticus demonstrates a deadly aim that instantly eradicates the danger posed by the rabid dog. In a similar manner, he submits to Judge Taylor's insistence that he be the one to defend Tom Robinson, and he demonstrates his clear vision of the necessity of eradicating the evil stain that threatens to harm the community. Although Atticus does not succeed in convincing the jury to acquit Robinson, he helps some in the community to see, albeit with blurred vision, the evil caused by rampant racism. Moreover, Atticus can evision with hope a future of racial justice.

Following the shooting, Atticus makes it clear in another encounter that the quality of courage needed to fight for the higher moral purpose involves more than the skilled use of a weapon. The story of Mrs. Dubose's battle with morphine addiction culminates in the message from Atticus that courage is not a man with a gun in his hand but "when you know you're licked before you begin but you begin anyway and you see it through no matter what" (*TKAM* 128). Mrs. Dubose dies of cancer, but she wins her battle with morphine and dies "beholden to nothing and nobody" (*TKAM* 128). Her higher purpose is freedom from the customary but addictive medical treatment the doctor provided to ease her pain. Wanting to end her dependence on the narcotics he provides, Mrs. Dubose chooses to reject the assumption that the medication is required and asserts her freedom. Indeed, the customary medical treatment she had received is parallel to the customary treatment of African Americans in Maycomb by the white majority: it may be routine, taken for granted, and ingrained, but such "required behavior" is addictive and damaging all the same. In another metaphorical interpretation, Mrs. Dubose's determination to end her addiction serves as a symbolic inspiration to Atticus and others to end the addiction to racism that plagues Maycomb society. The freedom Mrs. Dubose seeks, and the courage it takes for her to achieve that status, exemplifies another facet of the moral quest for the higher purpose that the novel espouses.

In addition to Mrs. Dubose, Lee uses still other characters to highlight the search for a higher moral purpose and to illuminate how bending the law serves to promote a better society. For example, Calpurnia seems to represent the stern taskmaster with a wide, hard hand and a tyrannical presence (*TKAM* 6). But while the tyrannical Mr. Radley's eyes are dull and colorless, Calpurnia's eyes suffer from nearsightedness, and she squints constantly. Calpurnia's squinting may be her way to ascertain what is actually going on in the Finch household among her charges, but it may also be symbolic of a larger quest. Calpurnia is a seeker; she squints to learn things, narrowing the scope of her vision to see more clearly. Described as one of four literate members of the First Purchase African M.E. Church, Calpurnia uses her squinting vision to foster close reading and to create unusual discoveries. Significantly, Calpurnia's reading ability is acquired from reading Blackstone's *Commentaries on the Laws of England*, an influential eighteenth-century treatise on the development of the common law in England and in the American colonies.

"Common law" is distinguished from statutory law passed by elected legislatures; the common law is the collective decisions of judges over the centuries, which are often referred to as "precedent," used to resolve subsequent cases involving similar disputes. Lee attended law school at the University of Alabama in the 1940s, when Blackstone was still revered as a source of wise legal rules, and she studied literature in England, the source of the common law. Thus, it is clearly possible that Lee's references to Blackstone and the common law, particularly in connection with Calpurnia, who is seemingly always squinting and searching with nearsighted eyes, may suggest and even accentuate the novel's approach to legal reform. Lee knew that common law was developed through a painstaking application of precedent with care and wisdom. In such situations, the law develops slowly and incrementally, always pushing and thrusting toward a more perfect whole, always working toward discovery of the most consistent, righteous, and socially beneficent purpose, purposes that are deemed consistent with past principles. In much the same way, the optimism Atticus demonstrates after Tom Robinson's trial is based on making progress over time, realizing that perfection in the law may not be accomplished immediately. Atticus is not discouraged or deflated by the unfair verdict. This is precisely because he realizes how slowly real change is attained. Bending the law a little bit, striving to be flexible, considering other people's viewpoints, and offering mercy and accepting it are all necessary steps before any real, long-lasting legal change can occur.

In addition to her unusual connection with the searching and slowly developing common law, Calpurnia, like Atticus, has an uncommon fortitude and humility. The altercation that occurs between Calpurnia and Lula in front of First Purchase, when Calpurnia brings Scout and Jem to church on Sunday, dramatically reveals the contrast between her searching, steady, wise, compassionate, and open-minded approach and Lula's bitter, separatist, and closed-minded outlook. While Lula argues that whites and African Americans should worship at separate churches and tries to capitalize on Calpurnia's status as a mere servant at the Finch household in order to denigrate Calpurnia's vision of hosting the Finch children at her church as her "company," Calpurnia (although flustered by Lula's abrasive manner) clearly wins the argument about different churches with her short defense: "It's the same God" (*TKAM* 136). It's clear that Lee uses this scene to emphasize that color barriers will only be broken down by steady and persistent effort to seek a remedy for wrongdoing even in the face of strident, separatist opposition from both races—whites as well as African Americans— who want to remain separate out of anger, fear of change, and self-importance. Lee shows that society and whole communities are required to bend in order for changes in the law to succeed.

Moreover, Calpurnia, like Atticus, exemplifies wise thinking and well-developed analyses of her opinions. One instance of this occurs when Calpurnia helps Scout understand why she speaks differently at the Finch household when talking with the children than the way she speaks at First Purchase when talking with fellow African Americans. Calpurnia makes several points regarding her speech choice: (1) different conversation fits different settings; (2) certain ways of speaking might be taken as condescending; (3) restraint in conversation is ladylike and modest; (4) it's not necessary to show all your knowledge; (5) it's difficult to force change on others; and (6) people need to want to change themselves (*TKAM* 143). Indeed, Lee seems to suggest here that changing the law, particularly in connection with race relations, depends on people wanting to change their opinions and expectations. Thus, throughout the novel, Lee emphasizes the need for individuals to change first in order to make larger social change possible. Furthermore, in order for people to change, they must first *want* to change. The novel emphasizes that embracing change must begin with the recognition of a *need* to change.

Aunt Alexandra is another crucial character who illustrates that the way to change the law and society is gradual and subtle. Significantly, Aunt Alexandra bends. Lee compares Alexandra to Mount Everest ("cold and there") and describes her bearing as "formidable" from any angle (*TKAM* 145). Lee also highlights Alexandra's boarding-school manners, her inclination toward noblesse oblige, her penchant for upholding absolute morality in any setting, and her utter lack of self-doubt. Aunt Alexandra's great passions include maintaining the Finch family reputation and presiding at missionary teas where the society ladies of Maycomb fret over the native Mruna tribe and other unfortunates (*TKAM* 260). Perhaps most important, Aunt Alexandra's name itself hearkens to classical Greece and seems to denote a repository of civilization that resembles the famous library that was located in Alexandria. Lee's depiction of Alexandra makes her the last person in the book that one would expect to bend.

For Alexandra, however, an awakening moment of realization—an understanding of the necessity for change and flexibility—occurs during the ladies' tea. In Lee's account, Alexandra is "pierced" and even gratified when Miss Maudie Atkinson subtly but sharply defends Atticus from Mrs. Merriweather's racial criticism (*TKAM* 266). Shortly thereafter, in the Finch kitchen, Alexandra talks with Maudie and Scout after Atticus and Calpurnia leave to tell Helen Robinson that her husband, Tom, was killed trying to escape Enfield Prison Farm (*TKAM* 269). In her reactions, Alexandra first grieves for the effect of racism and prejudice on Atticus, and then she continues by acknowledging the fear behind racism, expressing her despair that people in society rely on Atticus rather than working to eradicate racism themselves ("what they're afraid to do themselves," she cries). Eventually Miss Maudie underscores this realization of Alexandra's when she describes the handful of people in Maycomb who "say that fair play is not marked White Only" as people with "background," a categorization that can only appeal to Alexandra's sense of gentility and class. Notably, Alexandra's treatment of Scout after this realization is no longer chiding or overbearing; instead, she smiles at Scout and invites her to pass a tray of cookies to the ladies (*TKAM* 271); later, after Scout's rescue, Alexandra hands Scout overalls to wear and calls her "darling" (*TKAM* 303). Now governed by compassion and understanding, rather than by rules and social expectations, Alexandra bends.

Alexandra's transformation, however slight it may seem in the powder-puffed context of the ladies' missionary society, demonstrates that legal and social change starts in individual hearts. Lee also uses Aunt Alexandra to show that fighting racism and prejudice is civil, moral, and just. A bastion of civility like Aunt Alexandra—representing classical Greece—would naturally support compassion, fairness, and equality. Indeed, the development of such personal traits demands that fighting racism become one of the highest and best purposes of society. In addition, Lee shows us that there is more than one way to be a civil rights advocate; while civil disobedience, marches, sit-ins, and federal declaratory judgment actions certainly have their place, fostering changes in the individual heart are just as significant, if not even more important. Readers here sense that common civility and fairness on the street corner, when multiplied by thousands, will lead the way to widespread racial justice.

Lee also uses several other characters to highlight different ways of bending the law in order to achieve legal reform. One powerful example of this is the case of Mr. Link Deas. Sensing powerlessness and the need to help Tom Robinson during the trial, Deas takes matters into his own hands and interrupts the decorum of the courtroom, bursting out, "I just want the whole lot of you to know one thing right now. That boy's worked for me eight years an' I ain't had a speck o'trouble outa him. Not a speck" (*TKAM* 222). This outburst prompts Judge Taylor to evict Deas from the courtroom, perhaps overreacting to Deas' improper but honest affirmation of Tom's fine character. Interestingly, both Link Deas and Judge Taylor bend the law, in different ways, in their attempts to give Tom Robinson every possible advantage. Deas interrupts the trial, risking contempt of court sanctions, to tell the community and the jury that Tom Robinson has good character and is not a troublemaker. Similarly, while Taylor always strives to maintain a fair trial, in his case management techniques he (true to his name) tailors the case in order to help Tom. For example, Taylor appoints Atticus rather than another attorney to shape Robinson's defense, knowing that such an upright man would not provide a customary or lackadaisical defense for an African American accused of raping a white woman. Additionally, Taylor seems to shade the evidence in order to provide the jury a sense of the real story. As Atticus notes after the trial, Taylor looks at Ewell during the trial as if he were a "three-legged chicken" or a "square egg" (*TKAM* 287). "Don't tell me judges don't try to prejudice juries," Atticus concludes. Thus Deas and Judge Taylor both represent different attempts at influencing the jury to help Tom—influencing or bending the law themselves by trying to persuade the jury itself to bend. Deas bends the decorum of the trial and Judge Taylor bends the rules of impartiality required of a jurist. Each man's endeavor goes about as far as possible without giving cause for declaring a mistrial.

The trial of Tom Robinson, of course, constitutes the main narrative of the novel. Despite expectations to the contrary, all sorts of bending goes on in any trial. The adversarial system in jurisprudence encourages this, by ethically charging each attorney to represent the client—either the "people" or the defendant, as the case may be—to the best of his or her ability. Consequently, each attorney tries to bend the jury to see the facts of the case a certain way and uses every tool at hand to do so. Scout repeatedly acknowledges this duty by her matter-of-fact assessment of the prosecutor's sharp cross-examination of Robinson, while the same actions drive Dill to tears. Uniquely, Lee describes the prosecutor, Mr. Gilmer, as having a slight cast in one of his eyes, which he uses to his advantage; he seems to be looking at someone when he is not, causing juries and witnesses to pay closer attention, thinking themselves to be under Gilmer's scrutiny (*TKAM* 189). In contrast to Atticus' piercing, eagle eyes or to Calpurnia's squinting, searching eyes, Gilmer apparently has trick eyes that he uses to deceive and intimidate people—albeit completely within ethical, moral, and legal guidelines. By investing Gilmer with such a supernatural gift, Lee seems to highlight similar traits in Atticus, while drawing a distinction between Atticus' keen sight, employed to save the community from a rabid dog, and Gilmer's deceptive vision, employed to persuade the susceptible jury to convict an innocent man.

Could Tom Robinson possibly have been guilty? Significantly, Lee allows the reader to decide this important question, never absolutely revealing his innocence in so many words, while giving signs throughout the novel that make Tom's innocence appear to be an inescapable conclusion. Even so, Lee's decision to imply rather than inform the reader on this important point has sadly given provocative law professors an opening to question and castigate the trial techniques of Atticus Finch on the basis of an almost—but not totally—impossible presupposition that Tom is somehow guilty and that Atticus knows it. The resulting debate completely loses sight of the main focus of the novel on the evil effects of racism in society and the need for people and society to bend in order to change it. On the contrary, Lee leaves the question of Tom's innocence to the reader in order to heighten the dramatic tension of the novel, particularly in the trial narrative, and to allow the reader to discover the truth on his or her own. This method seems to highlight the ways that the law is bent and shaped by factors other than the innocence or guilt of one person. Indeed, the reader discovers the truth of Tom's innocence and must come to terms with the reality of institutional racism. Scout bluntly confirms what the reader is led to expect: "Tom was a dead man the minute Mayella opened her mouth and screamed" (*TKAM* 276). After Tom's death, editor B. B. Underwood of the local Maycomb newspaper makes the point suggested by the title of the novel: Tom's death is like the senseless slaughter of songbirds by hunters and children (*TKAM* 275).

Atticus stands against the prejudice, hate, and senseless killing that are clearly understood by both Scout and Underwood: "Shoot all the bluejays you want, if you can hit 'em, but remember it's a sin to kill a mockingbird" (*TKAM* 103). Miss Maudie Atkinson explicates this comment of Atticus by noting the innocence of mockingbirds and their beautiful, freely given songs. Because Atticus is relentless in his pursuit of moral improvement, he quite rightly considers Hitler a maniac—"the only time I ever saw Atticus scowl," notes Scout—but he still is able to instruct Scout: "It's not okay to hate anybody" (*TKAM* 282). In the moral worldview of Atticus Finch, Hitler is a despicable psychopathic dictator who should be deposed, but Atticus simultaneously acknowledges that hatred is evil and harmful for all of society. Hatred harms the beholder as much as, if not more than, the object of hatred.

Despite critics' protests to the contrary, Atticus is completely consistent in his search for the higher moral purpose in every aspect of life. He tells Scout that Tom's case "goes to the essence of a man's conscience" and confesses that he could not attend church and worship God if he didn't try to help Tom (*TKAM* 120). But when Scout responds that most of Maycomb thinks he's wrong in his espousal of Tom's cause, Atticus grants his opponents "full respect" for their opinion but continues to stress the fact that he must be at peace with his own conscience in order to live with other folks (*TKAM* 120).

For Atticus, defending an innocent man, preventing hatred of others from infecting society, and protecting innocent songbirds are all ways of living out his conscience, his God-given purpose, his moral obligation. So in order to meet his calling, Atticus consistently believes that bending the law is appropriate. He goes further and does everything he can to make the law more flexible and to change the shape of things for the future. "In the name of God, do your duty," he implores the jury. "In the name of God, believe him" (*TKAM* 234).

In his every act, Atticus consistently opposes hatred, racism, and common prejudice, and therefore serves as an example to his children as well as to Maycomb as a whole. Scout and Jem also search for the higher moral purpose throughout the narrative. Jem's search is almost tortured at times, as he frequently goes off and ponders in silence, much like Atticus reflects by himself (so much so that he worships at church by himself, leaving Jem and Scout to sit separately). One scene in the novel troubles some commentators who see in it an inconsistency in Atticus and his search for truth throughout the narrative. This event occurs when Nathan Radley upsets Jem by plugging the knothole in the tree along the children's path to school, a knothole where Boo Radley (unbeknownst to Scout and Jem) left them two soap dolls, a broken watch and chain, a pair of good-luck Indian-head pennies, and other presents (*TKAM* 67–71). Radley tells Jem he plugged the hole because the tree was dying, a lie later confirmed by Atticus who notes the tree's green and full leaves and the lack of brown spots. But when Jem tells Atticus that Radley said the tree was dying, Atticus responds: "Well maybe it is. I'm sure Mr. Radley knows more about his tree than we do" (*TKAM* 71).

The way Atticus reverses his opinion on the question of the tree's health is not an example of a vacillating stance as some commentators contend, but rather the action serves to pinpoint his flexibility and his consistent search for the higher moral purpose. His reply is seemingly more concerned with helping to preserve his neighbor's standing and autonomy than verifying the truth or falsity of his claim. It appears that to Atticus, neighborly generosity and benevolence prevails over maintaining a truth that may be relatively insignificant. At the same time, it's clear that Jem is emotionally disturbed by this scene, although it's not clear what brings him to tears—Atticus' puzzling response, Radley's concealment, or just the plug in the knothole. Atticus notably does not either agree with Radley or lie to Jem; he merely says that Radley's explanation might be the case, and then he accepts Radley's right to ascertain the status of his own trees. Atticus refuses to call Radley a liar, just as he refuses to denigrate or retaliate against Bob Ewell and just as he refuses to openly castigate his neighbors for their racism. Indeed, Atticus goes further than that. He generously grants his neighbors' opinions the same status as his opinions: "They're entitled to full respect for their opinions," he tells Scout (*TKAM* 120). His quiet and solitary search for the higher purpose in all things explains the potentially confusing juxtaposition of moral values that Atticus espouses throughout the novel. He somberly weighs competing values and tries to discover the good points in all.

In this way, Atticus is Christlike, a description many commentators agree upon (see, for example, Shaffer), noting several Christlike parallels: taking Ewell's spit in his face without retaliation (*TKAM* 248); protecting the community from the rabid dog (*TKAM* 110); doing what society cannot do itself (*TKAM* 269); and helping the innocent both by defending Tom and by protecting him from an attempted lynching (*TKAM* 169–176). His quiet search for the higher purpose also appears Christlike: he withdraws in church and ponders; he reads alone and reflects on truth and values; he contemplates basic philosophical principles and explains them succinctly to Scout. All the while, Atticus exhibits a generous spirit toward his neighbors, even those who are enmeshed in the racism of the time, following the Christlike example demonstrated when Jesus dined with prostitutes, tax collectors, and sinners, and called all people his "brother" and "sister" while accepting and forgiving their failings. Jesus, too, bent the law, for example, by healing people on the Sabbath day; in doing so, Jesus looked for the higher good (the cure of disease and brokenness) rather than upholding the narrow, rigid Sabbath restrictions of the Jewish authorities.

The moral searching of Atticus Finch reaches a climax in the final pages of the novel as he struggles to understand Heck Tate's insistence that Bob Ewell fell on his knife—another lie, though not as obvious as Nathan Radley's attempted deception about his tree. At first, Atticus stubbornly insists that he won't hush up Ewell's death—thinking that Jem somehow had stabbed Ewell—because he could never look Jem in the eye after being compliant in such a cover-up. Atticus asserts that he can not live one way in public and another way at home (*TKAM* 314). But when he is eventually persuaded that Boo Radley, not Jem, has stabbed Bob Ewell, Atticus finally accedes to Heck Tate's fictional construct in order to protect Boo Radley's shy, sheltered, and innocent reclusivity.

Atticus relents because Boo Radley has acted to prevent a crime from being committed. As Tom Robinson is the wrong man in the wrong place at the wrong time and so is unfairly convicted of a rape he does not commit, Boo Radley is the right person in the right place at the right time and is mercifully freed from public attention for a killing he does commit. Boo saves Jem and Scout in much the same way that Atticus saves the community from the rabid dog. When Atticus asks Scout if she could possibly understand, she responds: "Mr. Tate was right. . . . It'd be sort of like shootin' a mockingbird, wouldn't it?" (*TKAM* 317).

Lee leaves it to Scout to weigh the ultimate moral quandary of the novel. Boo Radley's childlike gifts of carved soap and shiny pennies are like the song of the mockingbird, his innocence like Tom's, his peaceful nature like the songbird's. Boo's eyes, colorless like his father's, are so gray and empty that Scout thinks he might be blind—but nonetheless Boo actually sees Ewell's threat to Jem and Scout and saves "his" children. These qualities of blindness and innocence, and the visible need to protect Boo Radley's privacy (which Atticus has advocated since the very beginning of the novel whenever Jem, Scout, and Dill attempted to make Boo "come out" from his chosen seclusion) clearly prevail over any desire Atticus might have to reveal or publicize the mere factual events of the stabbing. Despite the argument some make that Tate is asking Atticus to lie, Atticus indeed does uphold the truth, because he chooses to grant precedence to the higher moral truth that it's a sin to kill a mockingbird.

Bending the law a little bit in order to achieve a higher moral purpose is the lasting legacy of Atticus Finch, along with the understanding that establishing long-lasting legal change—albeit a slowly won achievement—is often attained by bending the law and striving for flexibility. By bending the hearts and minds of individuals in society like the Cunninghams, the law can be reshaped and reformed, so that more perfect justice can be achieved. Harper Lee's narrative and characters, along with the deep and sensitive thoughts of Atticus and Scout, lead to hope and anticipation for this change, and no doubt will continue to inspire generations of readers to join in efforts to redeem the law from its failure and to bend it toward a future of equality, compassion, and justice.

Works Consulted

Johnson, Claudia Durst. *"To Kill a Mockingbird": Threatening Boundaries.* New York: Twayne, 1994.

Lee, Harper. *To Kill a Mockingbird.* 1960. New York: Harper Perennial Modern Classics, 2006.

Lubet, Stephen. "Reconstructing Atticus Finch." *Michigan Law Review* (May 1999): 1339–1362.

Osborn, John Jay. "Atticus Finch—The End of Honor." *University of San Francisco Law Review* (Summer 1996): 1139–1142.

Phelps, Teresa Godwin. "The Margins of Maycomb: A Rereading of *To Kill a Mockingbird.*" *Alabama Law Review* (Winter 1994): 511–530.

Roark, Marc L. "Loneliness and the Law: Solitude, Action, and Power in Law and Literature." *Loyola Law Review* (Spring 2009): 45–77.

Shaffer, Thomas L. "Growing Up Good in Maycomb." *Alabama Law Review* (Winter 1994): 531–561.

———. "The Moral Theology of Atticus Finch." *University of Pittsburgh Law Review* (Winter 1981): 181–224.

Shields, Charles J. *Mockingbird: A Portrait of Harper Lee.* New York: Henry Holt, 2006.

Woodard, Calvin. "Listening to the Mockingbird." *Alabama Law Review* (Winter 1994): 563–584.

Part 3

THEMES, IMAGERY, AND STRUCTURAL CHOICES

CHAPTER 7

Unlikely Duos: Paired Characters in *To Kill a Mockingbird*

Robert C. Evans

> I think I see what it really is—a child's book. When I
> was fifteen I would have loved it. Take out the rape and
> I think you've got something like Miss Minerva and Wil-
> liam Green Hill. I think for a child's book it does all right.
> It's interesting that all the folks that are buying it don't
> know they're reading a child's book. Somebody ought to
> say what it is.
>
> —Flannery O'Connor on *To Kill a Mockingbird* (411)

Although Harper Lee's *To Kill a Mockingbird* is one of the most widely read
and widely taught novels of all time, surprisingly little academic criticism has
been devoted to it (Johnson, *Threatening* 20). This neglect seems to have resulted, in part, from several assumptions: first, that the book is intended mainly
for adolescents and is not a piece of serious, "mature" literature; second, that
the book is mostly valuable for the social and moral lessons it teaches, so that
its artistry and craft are relatively unimportant; and, finally, that *Mockingbird*
in fact contains little real artistry and craft but is instead relatively simple and
unsubtle. The novel has been criticized, for instance, for allegedly failing to
integrate its two main plots—a criticism that has been effectively refuted by
Claudia Johnson[1]—and in general it has been assumed to lack any very complex
aesthetic design. In this essay, I hope to address some of these criticisms, especially by focusing on the ways Lee compares and contrasts two key characters:
Boo Radley and Bob Ewell. I hope to show how these characters act as foils to

one another throughout the text, so that their final confrontation at the conclusion of the novel is not a merely convenient contrivance (with Boo as a kind of small-town Southern deus ex machina) but the culmination of a pattern that has run throughout the text.[2]

I

Before focusing on the contrasts between Boo and Bob, however, it may be worthwhile to suggest the ways in which numerous similar sets of paired characters help to structure this allegedly unsophisticated novel. By setting a whole series of characters in relevant relations to one another, Lee produces something more than a simple narrative for children; instead, she produces a work of art that is carefully designed to achieve significant thematic and aesthetic coherence. Some paired characters are obviously compared; others are clearly contrasted. In either case, however, Lee seems to have used pairing as a way of structuring her novel and reinforcing its major themes. Even the overall structure of the book—which is broken into two major parts—suggests that pairing is crucial to the fundamental design of *To Kill a Mockingbird*. Likewise, the fact that the narrative revolves around the experiences of two young siblings (rather than just a single child), and that the two children consist of a boy and a girl, helps illustrate the many ways in which pairings are essential to the general design of Lee's novel.

Boo Radley and Tom Robinson, for instance, are obviously similar characters. Both are quiet and reserved; both are the victims of obvious prejudice; and both have run-ins with the local legal system. Yet Boo—because of his race, his family connections, and, ultimately, his mental handicap—is treated far more leniently by the law than is Tom. This is the case even though Boo is actually guilty of various kinds of misconduct (including, eventually, a killing), while Tom is completely innocent of a major crime. Both men, of course, are "innocent" in the most fundamental sense, but the important similarities between them also help to highlight significant contrasts and thus help reinforce a major theme of the novel: Boo, because he is white and therefore automatically privileged, repeatedly benefits legally, whereas Tom is sent to prison (and ultimately dies) on the basis of one false accusation.

Ironically, another significant pairing in the book involves the modest Tom Robinson and Bob Ewell, Tom's arrogant accuser. Both men and their families live in poverty on the edge of town, and in fact it is because of this physical proximity that Tom actually does have some real and undeniable contact with Ewell's daughter. Both men are, to some degree, outsiders in genteel Maycomb—Tom simply because of his race and Ewell because of his lower-class economic standing as well as his low-class character. Both men are fathers to a significant number of children, but Tom is clearly a loving and beloved paternal figure, while Ewell is negligent and even abusive. Tom is loved both by his children and by his wife, whereas Ewell's wife is long since dead, and an incestuous relationship with his daughter is implied in courtroom testimony. Thus, Tom is at the center of a healthy (if impoverished) family, while Ewell presides over a family of children who are unfortunate in practically every way, especially in the character of their father. Both the similarities and the contrasts between Tom and Ewell, then, help reinforce many of the novel's major themes, especially the theme of race. If it were not for Tom's race, his sterling character might make him a respected member of the community; likewise, if it were not for Ewell's race, Ewell would have almost no social standing at all.

A similar kind of pairing can be seen by comparing and contrasting Bob Ewell and Atticus Finch. Both men are fathers (and fatherhood is indeed one of the most significant themes of this novel), but it would be hard to imagine two fathers more strikingly different. Atticus is a constant, loving, gentle, and inspiring presence in the lives of his children, whereas Ewell is negligent, self-centered, unloving, and hard-tempered. Both men are widowers, but whereas Atticus obviously adores his son and daughter and provides a stable and affectionate home life for them (including a kind of surrogate mother in Calpurnia), even the mere number of Ewell's children is unknown ("Some people said six; others said nine" [*TKAM* 194]), and Ewell obviously could not care less about his children's education, their health, or even their cleanliness (193–194). Atticus's gentle nature makes him reluctant to hurt anyone or anything, including animals, although he is able and brave enough to kill a rabid dog when circumstances make the killing necessary. Ewell, in contrast, is by nature a vicious man—willing to lodge a false and potentially deadly accusation, and willing (eventually) to attack two innocent children, though only in the dead of night. Atticus and Ewell could hardly be more different, and their courtroom confrontation is simply the highpoint of many episodes in which their contrasts are either highlighted or implied.

Another such pairing involves Scout, the young narrator of the novel, and Mayella Ewell, the nearly adult woman who accuses Tom (at her father's insistence) of sexually assaulting her. Both girls are motherless, and in each case the girl's father is the major influence on her life. Scout, though, is obviously an embodiment of youthful innocence, whereas Mayella (who in various ways seems a victim of her father) comes to seem a rather corrupt figure by the end of the book. Her corruption is rooted not in her sexual desire for Tom but rather in her willingness (however coerced she may feel by Bob Ewell) to connive in sending an innocent man to potential death. Scout, obviously, has some flaws of her own (especially in her initial mockery of Boo Radley and also in her somewhat callous treatment of Walter Cunningham when he visits her home), but whatever faults Scout exhibits are quickly corrected by her father or by Calpurnia, both of whom provide strong moral guidance both for Scout and for her brother Jem. Mayella, however, lacks such guidance from her own father, and one of the tragedies of the book is that Bob Ewell manages to pervert Mayella so thoroughly by the end of the trial that he almost turns her in some ways into a carbon copy of himself. Ewell may or may not sexually assault his daughter (although this possibility is strongly implied [*TKAM* 221]), but he clearly helps to corrupt her ethics. In contrast, the relationship between Scout and Atticus is everything one could hope for in the bond between a parent and a child. Atticus definitely has physical contact with Scout, but it is always of the most tender and innocent kind. Most important, however, is the moral guidance Atticus provides. Scout can always respect her father in ways that Mayella can never really respect Bob Ewell.

Finally, one more instance of paired characters—this time a rather comic one—deserves examination. In the opening chapters of the book, Lee goes out of her way to contrast Atticus Finch as an influence on children with Miss Caroline Fisher, the young new teacher at Scout's school. Miss Caroline, whose inadequacies as an instructor result not only from practical inexperience but also from exposure to "pernicious" modern educational theories, displays little skill as a teacher and little talent in relating to other human beings. She insults the intelligence of all her students by reading them ridiculously infantile stories, and she particularly insults the intelligence of Scout, who is already a highly skilled reader thanks to the example and encouragement of her father, whom Miss Caroline then proceeds to denigrate as a negative influence on Scout's learning (*TKAM* 18–20). Before long, the teacher is so frustrated with Scout that she actually raps the girl's hand with a ruler (*TKAM* 24), punishing the girl physically in a way that Atticus never would (because Atticus would never need to). Atticus, instead, shows his children intellectual and moral respect, treating them as young persons who are developing quickly into adults and who are capable of understanding reason. He doesn't hesitate to criticize them when they are wrong (as when he rebukes them for acting out episodes from the life of Boo Radley in the public streets), but he never once hits his children, nor does he act condescendingly to children in general, as Miss Caroline does. In fact, Atticus treats children with the dignity and respect he shows everyone, including Scout's teacher herself, whom he easily forgives for her mistakes. By contrasting Miss Caroline and Atticus, Lee once more uses paired characters to underscore important ideas and to strengthen the structure of her novel.

Many more examples of these kinds of pairings of characters might easily be cited. The firm but loving Calpurnia, for instance, is clearly contrasted with bossy, fault-finding Aunt Alexandra as a female influence on Atticus's children, just as Atticus himself is obviously contrasted with the intolerant Alexandra (his own sister) as a parental figure. Likewise, the generous-spirited Calpurnia, who takes the Finch children to an all-black church with her, is sharply contrasted with a black woman named Lula, who censures Calpurnia's behavior (*TKAM* 135–136). The gossipy Stephanie Crawford is contrasted, as a neighbor, with the far more appealing Miss Maudie Atkinson. Atticus is clearly a far different kind of parent than Mr. Radley, Boo's father, and he provokes a far different kind of response from his children than does Mr. Radley, whom Boo attacks with a pair of scissors.

To Kill a Mockingbird is clearly built around an ever-lengthening series of paired characters—characters whose similarities and differences are both often illuminating. By structuring the book in this way, Lee gives it a kind of artistic coherence that makes it far superior to the mere rambling reminiscence it might easily have been. Scout may be recalling events and personalities she first encountered when she was a very young girl, but those events and personalities are presented with a good deal of deliberate design—design that helps make the novel more than simply a book for (or about) children. The more one examines *To Kill a Mockingbird*, the more one finds it deserves the stature it has obviously won as one of the most widely taught and widely appreciated of all American novels. It is not simply a book that is valuable for its ethical "message"; rather, it is a well-structured work of art in which the pairing of various characters is central to an impressive artistic coherence.

II

Of all the pairings of characters in *To Kill a Mockingbird*, perhaps none is more intriguing than the unlikely combination of Boo Radley and Bob Ewell. The similarity of their first names, differing only by a single letter, is the first potential indicator of such a pairing.[3] Boo Radley seems, at first, to reflect a highly romantic, gothic, and childish view of evil. Yet "evil" is not only nonexistent in Boo but in fact turns out to be a source of positive good. Bob Ewell, on the other hand, embodies a kind of evil that is unfortunately all too real, malevolent, and undeniable. In shifting her narrative focus from Boo to Bob, Lee also alters the tone and atmosphere of the novel, turning what begins as mainly a nostalgic, amusing children's book into a highly disturbing exploration of personal and social immorality. As the novel develops, readers come to realize that Boo, far from being the source of fear that his very nickname suggests, is in fact a source of genuine kindness and altruistic benevolence. By the middle of the novel, it is entirely obvious that Boo is far more sinned against than sinning; he is a victim rather than a victimizer; and although he has good reason to be bitter and angry, for the most part he responds to his misfortunes with simple stoic withdrawal. He does, it is true, unexpectedly lash out at his chief tormentor—his father—with a pair of scissors, but that random act of spontaneous violence seems to be simply a one-time, impulsive outburst until he later (much later) stabs and kills Bob Ewell to protect the Finch children from Ewell's vicious nighttime attack. Ironically, even this act of extreme and literally fatal violence only enhances our sense of Boo's basic benevolence. He uses his knife not in his own interests but rather in the interests of others. In this respect as in so many others, he is the exact opposite of Bob Ewell.

Ewell is an obviously malevolent figure right from the start, but by the end of the novel he has gone from bad to worse. His narrative trajectory, in fact, is precisely the opposite of Boo Radley's, for whereas Boo goes from seeming a mysteriously gothic villain to being a kind of actual if inadvertent hero, Bob develops from an obviously bad man (willing to abuse his own adolescent daughter and then put an innocent man's life at risk) to something even worse: a lurking, potentially murderous assailant who threatens and stalks utterly defenseless children. Ewell is loud, crude, self-centered, and vicious, whereas Boo is quiet, thoughtful, modest, and compassionate. Boo only *seems* a villain, whereas Ewell's villainy is instantly apparent and only grows more and more clearly malignant as the book develops. Ewell is a corrupt and cruel father to his own children, whereas Boo acts as an increasingly compassionate and even protective parental figure to the Finch children as the novel progresses. At the beginning of the book, Boo merely leaves small trinkets for them in the hollow of a tree; at the end of the novel, he has saved their very lives. Ewell, in contrast, goes from seeming an almost comically malign figure (a man who quickly makes a fool of himself in the courtroom) to being a deeply vicious and increasingly dangerous villain who cannot refrain from revenge, even when he has technically won his case. Boo is thought to be mentally disturbed, but it is actually Bob who seems murderously unbalanced. In all these ways and in many others, then, Boo Radley and Bob Ewell are clear narrative foils, and by comparing and contrasting these two figures, Lee adds an element of structural sophistication to her text—an element that has often been overlooked.

Lee's use of Boo and Bob as ironic counterparts becomes especially apparent when the novel is re-read, although the contrasts are obvious enough even during an initial perusal of the text. The novel is constructed in ways that highlight the significant parallels and differences between the lives and living conditions of the two characters. The run-down, dilapidated condition of the Radley home, for instance, foreshadows the later, even more decrepit appearance of the Ewell shack. Thus, Lee writes that the Radley Place

> was once white with a deep front porch and green shutters, but had
> long ago darkened to the color of the slate-gray yard around it. Rain-
> rotted shingles drooped over the eaves of the veranda; oak trees kept
> the sun away. The remains of a picket drunkenly guarded the front

yard—a "swept" yard that was never swept—where Johnson grass and rabbit-tobacco grew in abundance. (*TKAM* 9)

The Radley home thus symbolizes the decay and deterioration of the Radley family itself, including its isolation from the rest of the community. The Ewell home, however, is even more clearly a reflection of the family who lives within it:

> Maycomb's Ewells lived behind the town garbage dump in what was once a Negro cabin. The cabin's plank walls were supplemented with sheets of corrugated iron, its roof shingled with tin cans hammered flat, so only its general shape suggested its original design: square, with four tiny rooms opening onto a shotgun hall, the cabin rested uneasily upon four irregular lumps of limestone. Its windows were merely open spaces in the walls, which in the summertime were covered with greasy strips of cheesecloth to keep out the varmints that feasted on Maycomb's refuse. (*TKAM* 193–194)

The fact that Bob Ewell raises his family in what "was once a Negro cabin" seems not only significant but intensely ironic: it helps explain his need, later in the novel, to assert his superiority over blacks and to identify himself with the novel's other white characters, even though many of the white citizens of Maycomb regard him as the epitome of white trash (a fact symbolized by the location of his shack). The Ewells, despite being white, are a far less healthy and productive family than most of the black families depicted in the book, including the family of Tom Robinson. Although Ewell cannot stand to think of himself as being inferior to the novel's blacks, it is clear that his accusations against Tom Robinson are rooted, in part, in his realization that he is, in fact, a figure of contempt and disdain among the novel's other whites. The only way in which Ewell enjoys any social distinction is because of his skin color; otherwise he is as isolated—and as much a figure of derisive ridicule—as Boo Radley himself.

However, whereas Boo Radley would once have been welcome in middle-class Maycomb society if he had not been isolated by his father, Bob Ewell has deliberately chosen to isolate himself and his family from any kind of healthy contact with, or respect from, the rest of the community. Here as elsewhere in the novel, then, Boo is merely a victim, whereas Bob is a victimizer. Boo and Bob both live in run-down, ramshackle houses, but Boo bears no responsibility for his unattractive living conditions, whereas Bob Ewell bears full responsibility for his. No other houses in the novel are described in such unappealing terms as the homes of Boo Radley and Bob Ewell, but in this case as in so many other instances, the similarities between Boo and Bob also help highlight the significant differences between them.

The novel's first references to Boo actually help foreshadow the later appearance and activities of Bob Ewell. Thus, early in the novel, Scout reports that inside the Radley house "lived a malevolent phantom. People said he existed, but Jem and I had never seen him. People said he went out at night when the moon was down, and peeped in windows" (*TKAM* 9). Scout then notes the widespread belief among the town's citizens that any "stealthy small crimes committed in Maycomb were his [Boo's] work," and she reports that once "the town was terrorized by a series of morbid nocturnal events" that were quickly (if falsely) attributed to Boo (*TKAM* 9).

All of this frightening and fantastic phrasing, of course, foreshadows the later—and quite real—malevolence of Bob Ewell in the aftermath of the trial. Thus, Ewell pays a strange nocturnal visit to the home of Judge Taylor, who had presided at the trial. Taylor, who is home alone, hears a peculiar "scratching noise . . . coming from the rear of the house," and when he goes to investigate he finds "the screen door swinging open" and catches a glimpse of Ewell's "shadow on the corner of the house." His wife comes home to find Taylor sitting "with a shotgun across his lap" (*TKAM* 285). Later, in an even more disturbing incident, Ewell follows Tom Robinson's wife, Helen, as she walks to work: "All the way . . . , Helen said, she heard a soft voice behind her, crooning foul words" (*TKAM* 286). Then, of course, on a night when there is "no moon" (*TKAM* 292), Ewell actually stalks (and then assaults) Jem and Scout.

If anyone in Maycomb, then, is truly a "malevolent phantom" who goes out when "the moon [is] down" and provokes terror through "a series of morbid nocturnal events," it is Bob Ewell, not Boo Radley. By focusing on an imaginary phantom in the beginning of the novel and then shifting her attention to a genuinely malign figure as the book closes, Lee not only ties the two halves of the book together but makes an important point about the nature of evil. Real evil is not the sort of thing that exists in gothic fiction or in the imaginations of children; it is the sort of thing practiced by men like Bob Ewell who are so obsessed with themselves that they are willing to abuse not only other people in general but even children, and not only their own children but the helpless children of others.

As has already been suggested, Boo is described early in the novel in ways that make his alleged evil seem humorous and implausible:

> Jem gave a reasonable description of Boo: Boo was about six-and-a-half feet tall, judging from his tracks; he dined on raw squirrels and any cats he could catch, that's why his hands were bloodstained—if you ate any animal raw, you could never wash the blood off. There was a long jagged scar that ran across his face; what teeth he had were yellow and rotten; his eyes popped, and he drooled most of the time. (*TKAM* 14)

Even at the time this description is first offered, it seems anything but "reasonable"; rather, it is a reflection of Jem's overheated youthful imagination, and it is probably also a reflection of his exposure to gothic novels, horror films, folk wisdom, and the irrational prejudices of the local community.[4] Jem assumes that Boo is even willing to murder children ("he'll kill us each and every one, Dill Harris" [*TKAM* 15]) and that he is capable of assaulting children with a knife (*TKAM* 15)—assumptions that prove false concerning Boo but that prove all too ironically appropriate concerning the later conduct of Bob Ewell. Significantly, the only killing that Boo ever commits is a killing in defense of children—specifically protecting them from Ewell's revenge for their father's treatment of him at the Tom Robinson trial. Lee implicitly compares and contrasts Boo Radley and Bob Ewell throughout the text until she finally brings them together in a bloody nighttime confrontation in which Boo is revealed not as the villain of a gothic children's book but as the hero of a far more complicated kind of novel.

Bob Ewell's capacity for evil is foreshadowed long before he actually enters the novel as a major character. His young son Burris, for instance, is described in chapter 3 as a lice-infested truant who comes to school only on the first day of each new academic year and then rejects schooling the rest of the time. When the new young teacher decides to send him home to prevent the other children from becoming infected with his "cooties," Burris responds with a kind of vulgar anger that foreshadows the later conduct of his father, whose worst traits Burris is obviously in the process of adopting as his own: "'Ain't no snot-nosed slut of a school teacher ever born c'n make me do nothin'! You ain't makin' me go nowhere, missus. You just remember that, you ain't makin' me go nowhere!'" (*TKAM* 31). Although he is still apparently under the age of ten, Burris is already emulating some of his father's own antisocial attitudes and conduct. Burris' words and behavior this early in the novel adumbrate his father's later negative conduct during the trial and afterwards.

Thus, when Bob Ewell is called to testify at the trial of Tom Robinson, his opening words are already so vulgar and suggestive (at least by the standards of the time) that the judge must immediately warn him against making "obscene speculations" (*TKAM* 196). Whereas Boo Radley, despite his fearsome reputation, is actually a highly reserved and soft-spoken Southern gentleman, Bob Ewell is crude both in his speech and in his public conduct. He also, unlike Boo, enjoys being the center of public attention. He is described as "a little bantam cock of a man" who "rose and strutted to the stand," and when he turns to face the courtroom "his face" looks "as red as his neck" (*TKAM* 193). In height, cockiness, and complexion (he is quite literally a redneck), Bob Ewell thus contrasts pointedly with Boo Radley, who is later described as very tall, very shy, and very pale (*TKAM* 310; 318–319). In addition, Ewell shows little respect even to the district attorney who is acting on his behalf (*TKAM* 195), just as he also later shows no respect to the memory of his dead wife (*TKAM* 195). His language is consistently and persistently vulgar, as when he describes his daughter "screamin' like a stuck hog" or when alleges having seen "that black nigger yonder ruttin' on my Mayella" (*TKAM* 196). Nevertheless, despite his supposed devotion to his daughter, it soon becomes clear that he has no great love or concern for any of his children (*TKAM* 207–208) and that his treatment of Mayella in particular has been both physically and perhaps even sexually abusive (*TKAM* 207–208; 221).

Boo Radley, of course, is just the opposite of Bob Ewell in all these ways. Long before Boo ever speaks, his fundamental values become clear, especially his fundamental affection toward innocent children. He leaves gifts for the children in the knothole of a tree (*TKAM* 37); he inconspicuously sews and returns the pants Jem tore while trespassing on the Radley property (*TKAM* 66), thus preventing Jem from getting into trouble; and then later, while Scout is shivering in the winter cold while watching Miss Maudie's house burn to the ground, it is Boo Radley who quietly comes up behind her and puts a blanket around her shoulders (*TKAM* 81–82). By this point in the novel, it is clear even to the suspicious, superstitious children that Boo is a fundamentally benign figure, especially in his treatment of youngsters. He is, in some ways, as admirable a father figure as Atticus Finch himself, and indeed Lee makes this comparison between Boo and Atticus (and this contrast between Boo and Ewell) explicit near the very end of the novel in a strange, almost surrealistic passage in which Scout reminisces about the events of the year just past, recalling specific moments of significant connection between the Finch children and their loving father.

Just when we have become accustomed to her allusions to Atticus, Scout surprises us by alluding instead to Boo Radley: "Autumn again, and Boo's children needed him" (*TKAM* 321). By this point in the book, it is clear that Scout has not only become able to empathize with Boo Radley—to "stand in his shoes and walk around in them" (*TKAM* 321)—but has even become able to think of Boo as a kind of father figure, as indeed he has shown himself repeatedly toward the Finch children throughout the book. Boo, who never enjoyed an especially close or affectionate relationship with his own father, acts repeatedly as a kind of paternal figure to Scout and Jem. In this respect, as in so many others, he differs strikingly from Bob Ewell, who lacks any capacity for tenderness or affection, even toward his own genetic children. Ewell, indeed, is incapable of standing in another person's shoes. He is so obsessed with his own pride that although he has fathered numerous children in the biological sense, he is hardly a father at all in the deepest and truest senses of that word.

By implicitly and explicitly contrasting Boo and Bob throughout the novel, then, Lee not only emphasizes many of her book's key themes but also enhances the sophistication of the book's artistic design, making its structure far more subtle and solid than may seem obvious at first. The children's fear of Boo dominates the first part of the novel, but as the novel proceeds, Boo seems a far less frightening figure than he had originally appeared. In the case of Bob Ewell, the process is just the reverse: he is a major figure in the second half of the novel, and the more the novel develops, the more genuinely menacing and even evil he appears. Lee (I would argue) uses the contrasts between Boo Radley and Bob Ewell to help enhance the book's coherence and unity. *To Kill a Mockingbird* is indeed "a child's book" (to use Flannery O'Connor's reiterated description), but to say this is by no means to suggest that it is artistically immature or structurally simple. Though the narrative is seen through the eyes of a young person and reveals childlike naïveté and humor, it also demonstrates how perceptive and insightful a child's viewpoint can be, indeed sometimes achieving more skillful and penetrating observations than those attained by adults. Lee's use of Boo Radley and Bob Ewell as foils throughout the work adds to the skill and complexity of the novel's artistry and thus helps make this work appealing to a far broader audience than children alone.

Notes

1. See particularly Johnson's discussion in *Understanding*, especially pages 8–9. There she argues, for instance, that

> the novel is unified by the fact that it opens and closes with Boo Radley. Furthermore, the Tom Robinson and Boo Radley sections are integrally connected, in that two characters and what they represent are united in their identification with the mockingbird of the title. Like the mockingbird, they are vulnerable and harmless creatures who are at the mercy of an often unreasonable and cruel society. (9)

2. For an early but still helpful discussion of the design of the novel, see Schuster, who emphasizes thematic motifs.
A number of critics have noted the use of parallels and contrasts in the novel, although I have discovered no one who focuses extensively on the contrast between Boo Radley and Bob Ewell, as I intend to do. Thus, Johnson (in *Understanding*) argues that the

> characters are at times divided into opposing camps, according to age or race or social status. At times, for example, the children seem to be opposed to the adults, the African-American characters at odds with the white characters, and the lower-class Old Sarum characters set apart from the townspeople. At the same time, boundaries between these categories are often broken down momentarily, as when the children feel a kinship with the once-feared adult, Boo Radley. (Johnson 7)

These boundaries are also broken temporarily when Atticus urges Scout to step into Bob Ewell's shoes (*TKAM* 249). For interesting passing comments on "doubling" in the novel, see Fine (70, 74–75). For a comment on two recognition scenes involving Scout, see Johnson (*Threatening* 84). Johnson also mentions some other interesting parallels that help to support my basic contention that the novel is often structured around comparisons and contrasts (*Threatening* 89 and esp. 102).

For a good recent overview of much commentary on the novel, including negative criticism, see Petry ("Introduction"). For an earlier overview, see Johnson (*Threatening* 20–27).

3. I am indebted to Maggie Seligman for this suggestion.

4. Readers will remember several references to Sec'atary Hawkins's *The Grey Ghost*, Dill's viewing of film versions of *Dracula*, and the children's superstitious beliefs in Haints and Hot Steams.

Works Cited

Fine, Laura. "Structuring the Narrator's Rebellion in *To Kill a Mockingbird*." In *On Harper Lee: Essays and Reflections*. Ed. Alice Hall Petry. Knoxville: U Tennessee P, 2007. (61–77)

Johnson, Claudia. *"To Kill a Mockingbird": Threatening Boundaries*. New York: Twayne, 1994.

———. *Understanding "To Kill a Mockingbird": A Student Casebook to Issues, Sources, and Historic Documents*. Westport, CT: Greenwood, 1994.

Lee, Harper. *To Kill a Mockingbird*. 1960. New York: Harper Perennial Modern Classics, 2006.

O'Connor, Flannery. *The Habit of Being: Letters*. Ed. Sally Fitzgerald. New York: Vintage, 1979.

Petry, Alice Hall. "Introduction." In *On Harper Lee: Essays and Reflections*. Ed. Alice Hall Petry. Knoxville: U Tennessee P, 2007. (xv–xxix)

Schuster, Edgar H. "Discovering Theme and Structure in the Novel." *English Journal* 52.7 (1963): 506–511.

CHAPTER 8

On Reading *To Kill a Mockingbird*: Fifty Years Later

Angela Shaw-Thornburg

1. Reading from the Margins

It has been fifty years since the publication of Harper Lee's *To Kill a Mockingbird*, and while neither the South nor the United States as a whole has managed to unravel the knot of the complex history of racial inequality and white privilege, with the election of Barack Obama we have arrived at a moment when we can honestly say that American democracy has moved a little closer to that ideal of fairness and equality before the law. Approaching the novel so many decades after its publication, I find myself wondering, what can a novel written in the midst of the modern civil rights movement have to say to a reader of today, particularly a young person—sixteen, seventeen, eighteen—who saw Obama elected? What does the landscape of race of today—still fraught with tensions, still riddled with clear instances of lethal unfairness, but nevertheless showing signs of progress in some areas—have to do with a town in which (evidence, able defense, and an apparently impartial judge notwithstanding) an African American man can have his life eaten up by the legal system unleashed upon him by the untrustworthy word of Bob Ewell and his daughter? Add to that conundrum the question of what to do with the clearly paternalistic and downright accommodationist approach to justice of Atticus Finch, figured as mostly heroic both by Lee's characterization of him and by many critical readings of the novel, and I begin to wonder if the novel is in fact too dated to even be taught in contemporary classrooms. Although it is a commonplace of literature classes to ask students to read with an eye to historical context, is there a moment when the context of composition and publication becomes so far removed from the context of reading that the novel becomes unintelligible as such, when it becomes historical document, as opposed to literature? In short, I find myself asking what would make this novel, beloved as it may be by many American readers, worth the class days it would take to historically situate and read it in the classes I teach?

At this point, I have a confession to make: It is one thing to teach a novel that students might be resistant to reading, and quite another to teach a novel that I find *myself* deeply resistant to reading, much less teaching. Unfortunately for me (African American *and* an Americanist), I often find myself in this position when I am preparing to teach a novel or work that represents African Americans as peripheral, incapable of self-representation, monumentally passive, and positively grateful for the small compensation of white guilt over injustices done to African Americans. It is not that I naïvely expect the black citizens of 1935 Maycomb to endorse strategies that would not even begin to gain traction in Alabama and other Southern states for many decades after that. It is not that I expect Atticus Finch to suddenly acknowledge the degree to which he is complicit in the racism that undergirds the legal system in Alabama. That is not the root of my resistance at all.

What gets me are those moments of struggle or, even worse, dreadful silence when we read *Huckleberry Finn* or even a novel like *To Kill a Mockingbird*, which was certainly seen as progressive in its day, when students who are people of color try to figure out why they feel unvoiced by the literature they are reading, or ask why we are reading *this* stuff. I currently teach at a majority minority institution, so such encounters can at times overwhelm my ability to keep students engaged. The often standard response in these cases would be, for example, to retreat to formalist readings of the text, or else to do more work to historically situate the novel as a product of Harper Lee's context. I have made it clear to my students, of course, that they can expect to read literature and view films that insult and offend them. That comes with the territory, given that literature and its ideologies are as various as its readers are, and that pedagogies that acknowledge and celebrate the multiple sources of American identity and literature in the classroom are really not that old in the larger scheme of how we teach literature in the United States. Suck it up, I tell them, bracket the stuff that impedes your ability to read critically for a minute or two, then come back to that thing that bothers you and unravel it from the cold, hard distance of what you know about that thing and what the author thought about that thing.

When students finally find an entrée into texts like *To Kill a Mockingbird*— they might note, for instance, how little we see of Tom Robinson, whose life and death would presumably be at the center of this story, or that Calpurnia seems to function as a maternal figure who can be hired and fired (that is, she is something akin to a mammy)—they are often reading on the margins and reading the margins. Although Scout's coming of age or Atticus Finch's moral quandary might, in the eyes of some, be at the center of the novel and such marginal reading a distortion of that threatened thing—the author's intention—there is something to be said for this strategy, as it makes literature that may have presumably lost some of its relevance or intelligibility more teachable, more readable in certain situations. Although proponents of the canon as great works that appeal to so-called universal literary values (Harold Bloom, anyone?) might look askance at such a strategy, it is not such a bad one if it generates critical reading where only resistance or refusal to read stood before.

Students are in fact in good company when they read the margins. It is a strategy used to great effect by Toni Morrison, for example, when she re-reads American literature by being attentive to what she calls the seemingly marginal Africanist presence that exists there, or Virginia Woolf when she imagines Shakespeare's sister, or Alice Walker when she reads a history of the creative self-expression of African American women by "looking low" in focusing on quilts and gardens. We are used to this kind of critical move, in fact, but not particularly accepting of it when students attempt to deploy its cousin in a literature classroom. By *cousin* I mean that students will often question why they have to read literature that marginalizes them, or else will zero in on the small spaces in the margins that are occupied by people of color in some of the literature they are reading to the exclusion of other spaces and themes in the works—attempting to deal with books by, for, and about white people, as one student bitterly remarked as we opened up our discussion of *Huckleberry Finn*.

My training consistently leads me to push back against such readings because it is never enough to say that this text embraces a racist ideology and just stop reading; whole swaths of well-crafted literature would simply disappear if that were the litmus test of what we did and did not read. If I am honest with myself, though, I will admit that I do not read books like *Huckleberry Finn*—or *To Kill a Mockingbird*, for that matter—for pleasure in my spare time. When I begin my course prep for *To Kill a Mockingbird* by reading the novel, I finish up with a profound sense of alienation, a sense of bewilderment that Lee decentered the story of Tom Robinson so utterly. Because of that aftertaste, I only read such works because I am expected to teach them (especially in classes with students who will one day become teachers), just as my students frequently read them only because I have required them to. Parents of students in high schools have sometimes taken the stance that novels like *To Kill a Mockingbird* marginalize people of color to such a great degree that they should be removed from the curriculum. *To Kill a Mockingbird* was included in the American Library Association's list of banned books for 2008–2009 as a result of one parent's attempt to have it removed because it deprecated black people (Doyle 5). While I could never feel comfortable in preventing other people from reading a book, I am at last at a moment when I am having to consider, like those parents, whether or not I should teach a novel that neither I nor my students are interested in reading, and that endorses, with the best of intentions, ideologies and ideas about people of color that foreclose the possibility of agency.

2. Reading Whiteness

But then there is this: I am thinking about my response to the student who made the remark about *Huckleberry Finn*. I answered her by saying that yes, Twain had not necessarily envisioned an African American reader of his text, and that perhaps it would be better to think about what the novel sought to teach readers about white people, and proceed from there. The student didn't scoff as I expected but instead offered up a pretty good critical reading of Twain's continual pokes at the paradoxes of white American cultures. We got much better work done, in fact, when students focused more narrowly on what it was the novel was saying about the construction of white identity.

Although I didn't name this mode of reading as such at the time, my students were actually working through the lens of whiteness studies, a discipline that has its roots in multiple disciplines, including antiracist critiques by the likes of W. E. B. Dubois and Malcolm X and more recent work by writers such as Toni Morrison, Ruth Frankenberg, and Matt Wray. Gregory Jay and Sandra Elaine Jones have identified whiteness studies as being grounded in a "critical multiculturalism," one that I believe can help me and my students read through the paradox of *To Kill a Mockingbird*'s central message, that one has to and can walk a mile in a person's shoes to know that person, and Lee's refusal or inability to provide a conduit for the reader to acknowledge the centrality of Tom Robinson's story.

As I re-read *To Kill a Mockingbird* with an eye to what it tells me about Lee's vision of whiteness, I am particularly struck by other characters who, although identified as white, are on the boundaries because they don't conform to the dominant notion of whiteness, articulated in large part by Atticus Finch. I am not talking about Boo Radley, who seems to represent a whiteness that Atticus, at least, is content to let into the fold momentarily when he rescues his children from the threat of violence. I am thinking instead about the poor white characters in the novel, and most particularly of the story of Mayella Violet Ewell, whose big lie—that Tom Robinson raped her—putatively sets off the chain of events that leads to the death of Tom Robinson and both Scout and Jem's loss of innocence. I say *putatively* because one of the things the novel works hard to obscure is the degree to which what happens to Tom Robinson is less the result of the virulent racism of the Ewells and more the direct result of the way that white supremacy structures the legal system. Theodore and Grace-Ann Hovet have called this sleight of hand an example of "the white trash scenario," in which responsibility for the lethal racism of the South and the failure of the law to function impartially is displaced onto poor, white working-class people, thus relieving middle-class and affluent whites of culpability for the aftermaths of white supremacy (70).

In doing my preparation for reading the novel, the Hovets' insight was invaluable because it got me to look more directly at Mayella Ewell. Hovet and Hovet argue in that same essay that Lee's choice of the "'coming of age' and 'beset American justice' formulas . . . position the reader to anticipate a positive narrative closure and to read over the darker strands in the story" (68). Although the choice of the word *darker* is infelicitous here, I take their point that some of Lee's choices make it quite difficult to examine certain characters critically, the chief example of which is Mayella. Mayella is thoroughly grounded in what Wray calls the *stigmatype* ("stigmatizing stereotype") of the poor white Southern woman as a worker, barred by class from the idleness so key to the myth of the white Southern belle (Wray x, 29). In Wray's account, whiteness is socially constructed by boundary terms and boundary language that are deployed to control the threat that particularities of people identified as white pose to the concept of whiteness as positive, dominant, pure, and powerful. What is particularly noteworthy about Mayella is the degree to which everything about her poses a threat to notions of whiteness, and the degree to which her ability to claim her own whiteness is impeded by her gender and her class.

Mayella is first described when Scout sees her come to the witness stand. Scout describes her as "somehow fragile looking, but when she sat facing us in the witness chair she became what she was, a thick-bodied girl accustomed to strenuous labor" (*TKAM* 203). After watching the trial, Scout further describes Mayella as being

> as sad, I thought, as what Jem called a mixed child: white people wouldn't have anything to do with her because she lived among pigs; Negroes wouldn't have anything to do with her because she was white. She couldn't live like Mr. Dolphus Raymond, who preferred the company of Negroes, because she didn't own a riverbank and she wasn't from a fine old family. (*TKAM* 218)

What both of these descriptions have in common is a certain ambiguity that middle-class Scout feels as she tries to negotiate her relationship to the abjectly poor Mayella. Scout's recognition of the fragility of Mayella is a moment of empathy in which Scout tries to imagine her as a victim, and the turn to describing Mayella as "thick-bodied" is symptomatic of Scout's burgeoning sense of class distinctions—clearly consolidated by the time the adult narrator recounts that day in court—a sense informed not only by her Aunt Alexandra but by the many talks she has with Atticus about the Cunninghams, the Ewells, and other residents of Old Sarum. Scout is in the midst of an attempt to understand racial prejudice, true, but the novel is also about her struggle to understand her relationship with a young woman like Mayella, who, while clearly white and female, is as distant from her and her community as a "mixed child."

Simply because of Mayella's complicity in the death of Tom Robinson and the way her accusation echoes those of the women in involved in the Scottsboro and Till cases, I have always been hard-pressed to muster up the sympathy encouraged by Lee's use of Scout as the filter through which we see Mayella. There are multiple white feminine voices in the novel, but all of them are clearly marked as middle-class voices, the norm against which Scout has to define herself. Mayella occupies no such space, and it is in fact easy to skip over any focused analysis of her character given the overdetermined role she plays in the novel.

Through the lens of reading whiteness as a social construction, though, I began to ask, how is it that Mayella arrives on that stand and why is it that she tells this particular story to the judge and jurors? What made her want to touch Tom Robinson despite the racism that must have shaped her childhood? Are there any moments when we get to her authentic voice, given the degree to which so many people are invested in her telling this one particular story? How and why is it that she appears in the novel briefly and is sketched so slightly, but has such a staggering impact on the lives of the characters in the novel? What becomes apparent on re-reading is the degree to which Mayella's identity as a poor, white working-class woman actually makes her marginal to the story Lee has to tell.

3. "I'll tell you a story and maybe you'll believe me": Recovering the Voice and Body of the White, Working-class, Southern Woman

In *Two or Three Things I Know for Sure*, South Carolina native Dorothy Allison limns in searing detail what it was to grow up poor, white, and a girl in the South during the 1950s and 1960s, the significance of storytelling and personal myth-making to her survival of extraordinary physical and sexual abuse at the hands of her stepfather, and the long journey to healing she faced as she confronted the refusal of family members to accept her truth as a survivor of sexual abuse and as a woman finally ready to claim her identity as a lesbian. What makes Allison's writing germane in this context is her certainty that finding her voice and proclaiming her desire publicly are essential to her survival. In the opening pages of the memoir, Allison states,

> I'm a storyteller. I'll work to make you believe me. Throw in some real stuff, change a few details, add the certainty of outrage. I know the use of fiction in a world of hard truth, the way fiction can be a harder truth. The story of what happened, or what did not happen but should have—that story can become a curtain drawn shut, a piece of insulation, a disguise, a razor, a tool that changes every time it is used and sometimes becomes something other than we intended. . . . The story becomes the thing needed. (3)

Allison names the ability to tell stories about one's own life, not just as artistic self-expression, but as functional, a technique of survival, particularly in the case of white, working-class Southern women, who often find that the truths and stories they would tell about themselves are effaced or disbelieved by multiple actors and spaces in their worlds—by other women in their families who are themselves mired in cycles of abuse or poverty, by men inside and outside their families who may perpetrate the abuse, by outsiders such as the middle class, the legal system, or social service systems—who would name them "the lower orders, the great unwashed, the working class, the poor, the proletariat, trash, lowlife and scum"(1). Allison is acutely aware of the degree to which who she would be is overwhelmed by how other people represent poor white women. Allison frames the ability to transmute the real details of one's life as an effort to escape the very narrow visions of white working-class women available in American popular and literary culture.

One area of particular danger and continued threat of effacement is the idea that white, Southern working-class woman are neither capable of being the subject of desire nor of being the object of rape. As young women, Allison and her female relatives were "never virgins, even when [they] were," because they are always seen as sexually available to men, particularly by the boys who grow up to be middle-class men (36). Their sexual worthlessness in the eyes of these boys means that acts of rape are never claimed as such, given that there was putatively nothing sexually alluring about such girls, and that rape in these accounts is figured as the fault of the young woman who is sexually alluring or beautiful.

In the midst of grinding poverty and childrearing, these same girls grow up to be "measured, manlike, bearers of babies, burdens, and contempt." In popular and visual culture, these white working-class women are figured as laboring (as in childbearing and physical labor) bodies, in "photos taken at mining disasters, floods, fires, . . . all wide-hipped and predestined. Wide face meant stupid. Wide hands marked workhorses with dull hair and tired eyes" (32–33). The inability to be named as the object of rape and the inability to be seen as a body capable of sexual desire is part of the freight that Allison has to unload as she explores her identity and family history. She is ultimately able to name herself as object of rape and as capable of sexual desire only through her making community with other women and through her ability to tell her own story. In telling such a story in her many first-person writings and in *Bastard Out of Carolina* (1992), made into a film in 1996, Allison gave voice to women who by and large had been silenced by willful ignorance and virulent stereotypes in popular culture.

Allison's history of what it was like to be a white, working-class Southern girl or a woman is contiguous with the moment of composition of Lee's novel. Lee's drawing of Mayella would have been shaped, in other words, by a milieu in which the notion of Mayella as capable of producing or inspiring desire, be-yond the putative desire of a black men to enact racialized violence expressed in the act of rape, would have been almost inconceivable both to the people in the courtroom and then contemporary readers.

Examining Mayella less from the perspective of those men of the court, who read Mayella's defensiveness on the stand as a mark of her ignorance, and more as the reaction of women like those of Dorothy Allison's family, opens up the possibility that there is a knowingness to Mayella's defensiveness on the stand; her hostility toward the court is not so much evidence of her identity as "white trash" as it is an indication of her clear understanding that white men, regard-less of their class, do not have her interests at heart, and her recognition that the professional, middle-class identity of men like Atticus Finch will always find it necessary to figure her as less than, incapable of self-restraint. Her feeling that Atticus Finch is ridiculing her when he calls her "Ma'am" and "Miss" is not as far from the truth as the men on the jury or in that courtroom or even the reader may think. Structurally, the legal system of which Atticus is a part is devoted to disenfranchising and indeed holding up to ridicule the class of which Mayella is a part, as the putatively humorous story about the day the Cunninghams and Coninghams had their day in court (the case was thrown out) illustrates.

As a modern reader, I have always found myself extraordinarily conflicted as I read through the scene of Mayella's testimony. On the one hand, most contem-porary readers will hopefully be familiar with the involvement of white women in the trials of the Scottsboro boys and the death of Emmett Till, and the long history of assaults on and imagined affronts to white women as the premise for lynching. The novel's publication in 1960, so close in time to the lynching of Till and echoing the facts of the Scottsboro case, would have made it difficult to escape reading in the context of the history of lynching. Mayella's accusation, given what she had to have known about lynch law and the codes of race and sex in the Deep South, is virtually unpardonable, and (unfortunately) typical.

On the other hand, I read the novel on the other side of a decades-long struggle to help women claim a voice in their families, communities, and legal systems serving those communities as they confront sexual violence; all too often women have been re-victimized by the presumption that accusations of rape and incest are almost always false. Then, too, I am also reading on the other side of the culture wars waged over so-called false memory syndrome and other attacks on the character of women, theorists, and legal scholars involved in changing the culture of disbelief surrounding women's discussions of sexual abuse and rape. Ellen Bass and Laura Davis, authors of *The Courage to Heal,* a popular self-help book for survivors of sexual abuse, call this resurgence of a culture of disbelief a backlash, and some feminist critics situate this attack as a larger backlash against feminism itself.[1] So when a modern reader considers Mayella's testimony and that which is reported about her, that reader becomes acutely conscious that it is men—her father, Atticus, the judge, and the all-male jurors—who are engaged in battle over the meaning of her story, and by extension over her representation. The effect of the gendering of the law as male is that Mayella is never able to give voice to her own truth. She instead engages in constructing what Allison calls "fiction harder than truth," creating a story that becomes "the thing needed" (needed for whom?) (Allison 3). The danger of such a strategy for white, working-class Southern women, as Allison outlines it, is that the story "sometimes becomes something other than we intended."

Mayella's truth is that she has indeed been the object of rape and that despite the impediments to doing so, she has managed to become a subject who desires. The story that she tells on the stand—rape at the hand of Tom Robinson—is true only insomuch as it captures the outrage that her father's rape of her should have occasioned in the spectators. In real terms, however, the uncovering of such a story in any other context than the trial of Tom Robinson would merely have confirmed for the town of Maycomb and the reader the stigmatype of the Ewell family as "white trash." The public spectacle of telling *this* story of rape by a black man, though, is that Mayella's story is transformed into one that ultimately silences her. She is announced as a subject who desires, but does not get to make that announcement for herself.

Bracketing Mayella's big lie for a moment, one of the most notable things about Mayella is the degree to which her voice is co-opted and then silenced in the novel. We never quite get that authentic voice. The truth, presumably Tom's account of what she said to him, is this: "She says she never kissed a grown man before and she might as well kiss a nigger. She says what her papa do to her don't count. She says, 'Kiss me back nigger'" (*TKAM* 221). She touches Tom, grabbing him about the waist and kissing him on the cheek despite his protestations.

When acting of her own volition, Mayella violates racial taboos by touching the body of a black man in an intimate way. Her advances toward Tom are also violations of gendered norms for working-class women, in that she is figured as an aggressor as opposed to being the passive recipient of sexual aggression. The other content of that statement is that she names herself as having been sexually abused by her father, and that she is unwilling to count the depredations of her father as a part of what counts as sexual intimacy.

What makes this moment virtually unreadable is the status of what it is she is attempting to do with Tom, for starters. This scene can be read as a sexual assault on Tom, one that is ultimately fatal to him given the cultural context. Another way to read the scene is as a clumsy attempt at seduction, one that she ultimately denies simply because her father witnesses it. If we were to read the scene as clumsy seduction with unforeseen, lethal repercussions, Mayella's actions can be seen as her attempt to gain some sense of sexual agency, to name herself as capable of desire, in contrast to the coercion that she has apparently experienced on a regular basis in her home. Bob Ewell's insistence that Mayella was raped is not, then, just his attempt to exercise the prerogatives of white, middle-class male privilege; in propagating the story of his daughter's rape, Bob Ewell also co-opts her attempt at claiming sexual agency and expressing desire, albeit a transgressive and coercive expression of such.

He silences that voice, and it only enters the courtroom through the mouth of Tom, the person most injured by her voicing of that desire, and in Atticus' summation, in which he notes that "she is a victim of cruel poverty and ignorance, but I cannot pity her: she is white" (*TKAM* 231); he takes her to task for allowing her desires to overrun her knowledge of racial codes governing cross-racial intimacy: "She knew full well the enormity of her offense, but because her desires were stronger than the code she was breaking, she persisted in breaking it" (*TKAM* 231). Atticus seems to be arguing that she was overruled by her desire, and that in doing so, she broke one of the cardinal rules of his notion of white identity, that one must never overtly exercise power to one's advantage when dealing with people of color; it is this that is unforgivable. The inability to govern one's desires is a key element of the stigmatype of poor whites, and so it is on this basis, in addition to her complicity in the false accusation of rape that her father makes, that Atticus and probably then contemporary readers hold Mayella accountable in the first place.

Then, too, there is the issue of what happened before and after the encounter with Tom Robinson, namely, the relationship with her father. Although Atticus, the spectators in the courtroom, and probably the readers as well read the series of "no answer" statements (there are five of them on a single page) as Mayella's inability to continue lying or fabricating details of the Tom Robinson's so-called rape of her, these moments of silence can also be read as those parts of her story—desire for Tom, rape by her father—that are not remotely audible in Maycomb in 1935, because they violate the boundaries of white identity so thoroughly. Her sexual desire and Mayella as a subject of rape are both unspeakable, and she maintains her silence on these issues, perhaps in the interest of self-preservation, given that when the trial is over, she will return to the bounded space of the cabin where she lives with her father and siblings.

Although Mayella departs entirely from the novel after the courtroom scene, one of the most vivid images in the book, one that Scout returns to as she attempts to imagine what it is to be Mayella, is that of the red geraniums that Mayella (presumably) has potted in slop jars around the house. Hovet and Hovet read the geraniums as Lee's efforts to destabilize the white trash scenario. The flowers are a bit more than that, however. If we believe that Mayella is merely the product of her environment, that nothing can break through the degradation and poverty that have beaten her down in life, then how do we account for the geraniums?

Flowers in Southern literature have served multiple symbolic functions related to race, class, and gender. In her 1946 story "The Geranium," Flannery O'Connor represents the protagonist's desire for community and connection as a geranium that sits in the tenement apartment window across from him. The geranium only assumes this significance because the narrator has been uprooted from his rural Southern origins and transplanted to the city.[2] In *To Kill a Mockingbird*, the yard in which the geraniums sit is surrounded by a fence constructed of "bits of tree limbs, broomsticks and tool shafts, all tipped with rusty hammerheads, snaggle-toothed rake heads, shovels, axes, and grubbing hoes" and littered with the broken accoutrements of the lives of the middle-class town folk—"the remains of a Model T Ford (on blocks), a discarded dentist's chair, an ancient box, . . . old shoes, worn-out table radios, picture frames" (194). The fence, capped with rusted implements of the farming life and land from which poor Southern whites had been uprooted as the result of structural economic changes, could possibly represent Mayella's acute awareness of the significance of that lost connection and rootedness in rural community.

In other words, Mayella has class consciousness. Planting the geraniums in the context of that yard is a gesture of defiance, not pretension to the middle-class respectability of the town. The geraniums, "cared for as tenderly as if they belonged to Miss Maudie Atkinson" (194), "bewilder" the town folk because they gainsay the stigmatype of white, working-class Southern women as mere laboring bodies. Mayella's planting and nurturing of the geraniums are acts of self-representation, ones that express her refusal to allow the bounds of that fence, of white, working-class Southerners as surplus to the economy of the South, to determine how she will be represented. They may also be expressions of her notion of herself as a person who has access to the sensuous, as opposed to a body that merely labors.

In "In Search of Our Mothers' Gardens," Alice Walker figures the garden of her mother, who like many rural Southern black women in the early decades of the twentieth century served as "the mule of the world," as nurturing of the creative spirit, symbolic of the muted impulse for self-expression. Walker's work in this seminal essay in African American women's studies is to locate a genealogy that could account for African American women who would be artists despite cultural norms to the contrary. Mayella's circumstances in rural Alabama during the 1930s resonate with the experience of Walker's mother in terms of class, so those geraniums may perhaps also be read as the desire for creative expression on the part of Mayella.

Ultimately, if there is a narrative here of white working-class women's identity, it is one communicated by indirection, inference, silence, and symbol. Although Mayella fits into one far too familiar story of the complicity of white women in racial violence, those small elements that communicate something beyond that story are tantalizing, and highlight the different access to white privilege that working-class people and women have. The slightness of Mayella's representation, her complicity in the death of Tom Robinson, and her inability to claim an authentic voice within the novel represent significant teaching challenges, however.

4. Reading Whiteness as Marginal

Given that the novel has often been taught in the context of the history of lynching or as a coming-of-age story of the middle-class female narrator, teaching the novel with some attention to white working-class Southern identity is fraught with potential problems. Focusing on Mayella's marginal status might, for instance, serve as a first move in the historical forgetting that has become a key component of the backlash against the broadening of the canon to include marginal voices and histories such as Tom Robinson's. To Kill a Mockingbird is not truly a novel about Tom Robinson's life and death. It is characteristic of the novel that his trial and death are already somewhat obscured by the guilt and outrage of both Atticus and Scout, the two characters with whom the readers are most likely to sympathize. It is possible that an insistence on recovering Mayella's voice might only serve to marginalize Tom's story even further.

Then, too, there is the question of point of view and reader identification in the novel. Lee's use of first person to explore Scout's confrontations with the legal and cultural codes surrounding race, class, and gender make it much more likely that the reader will uncritically identify with Scout's perspective on the residents of Old Sarum. Although there are moments when Scout reveals her sympathy with Mayella—identifying her as perhaps the most lonely person in the world, a young woman who tried to keep herself clean, the person who nurtured those slop jars of geraniums—Scout ultimately reduces Mayella to a "thick-bodied girl accustomed to strenuous labor" (TKAM 203). While Scout frequently identifies with outsider or grotesque figures in the novel, there is no such identification with Mayella, who seems to be part author of a terrible miscarriage of justice. That overlay of Scout's perspective would mean that a significant task of preparing the students to read the novel with attention to what Mayella represents would be to prepare students to talk about the construction of whiteness and of white working-class women's identity in the South in particular.

Nevertheless, it is only through access to such background that students can potentially gain a greater sense of what accounts for the presence of a Mayella in the world inhabited by both Scout and Tom Robinson. As fraught with racial tension and violence are the worlds of Maycomb in 1935 and the South in 1960, they are also worlds in which boundaries of race and class have already been explicitly broken, even if the results of these fractures are tragic. Many students will be reading the novel in classrooms or at least via curriculums that are explicitly multicultural in nature. The racial, gender, and class dynamics of the novel offer an opportunity to have discussions about white paternalism and white privilege that might better equip students to navigate their communities in a more conscious way, particularly in racially homogenous classrooms.

Reading analysis of the construction of whiteness in works such as Toni Morrison's *Playing in the Dark: Whiteness and the Literary Imagination* (1992) and Ruth Frankenberg's *White Women, Race Matters: The Social Construction of Whiteness* (1993), Matt Wray's *Not Quite White: White Trash and the Boundaries of Whiteness* (mentioned earlier), Annalee Newitz and Wray's "What Is White Trash?" anthologized in *Whiteness: A Critical Reader*, Claudia Durst Johnson's *"To Kill a Mockingbird": Threatening Boundaries*, along with her contribution to the Greenhaven Understanding Literature series, would provide invaluable resources for teaching students to think about whiteness as a construction articulated by race, class, and gender. Understanding this idea might lead students to be more aware of issues of representing the Other, particularly in the case of Scout's and Atticus' decision to speak for characters such as Mayella, given the deep class divides between the Ewells and the Finches. Students would first have to recognize the non-monolithic nature of whiteness, so brief critical excerpts from the aforementioned works might be useful in this regard. In the company of thorough discussions of *Brown v. Board of Education of Topeka, Kansas*; the Emmett Till and Scottsboro cases; and the civil rights movement, such discussion might predispose students to turn a more critical eye on the ideology espoused by Atticus.

Another useful contextualizing exercise might be to bring in examples of how white Southern working-class women are represented visually. Dorothy Allison's *Two or Three Things I Know for Sure*, mentioned earlier in this essay, might prove particularly useful in this regard since she provides glosses alongside the photographs of the female members of her family. There is also a rich historical archive of pictures of Appalachian women available from sites such as the Library of Congress (http://www.loc.gov/rr/print/catalog.html), but it would be important in using these sources to emphasize the degree to which cultural representation is in the hands of the photographers.[3] Analyzing these images alongside images of working-class African American women might reveal some instructive parallels as well. Students might then be capable of identifying common stereotypes of working-class Southerners—black and white, women and men—that they have encountered in film and television, of which there are numerous examples, in order to get a better sense of the stigmatypes at work in the novel.

After students have read the novel, it would be useful to include several important passages among those generally examined when discussing the novel with an eye to thinking about how they situate white identity as well, such as Scout's discussions with Atticus and her teacher about the Cunninghams (*TKAM* 22–24, 33–34), and the narrator's summary of the court testimony about the living conditions of the Ewells (*TKAM* 193–195 and 208). One of the more telling moments in the novel is also to be found on page 218, in which Scout compares Mayella to a "mixed child." The teacher or professor might ask *why* Scout might see Mayella as someone more akin to a person of mixed racial descent than to Scout herself, and how this passage relates to the earlier discussion of "white trash" identity in the excerpts from the critical pieces.

To Kill a Mockingbird has at times been censored in schools on the basis of the subtle and not so subtle racism at work in the text, particularly the use of the word *nigger* and the representation of African Americans as cardboard cutouts, passive recipients of white violence. It is difficult to imagine Southern women's literature or working-class American literature without the ability to observe the degree to which they are in dialogue with *To Kill a Mockingbird*, however. Although some would argue that the historical moment of the novel and its unfortunate racism mean that the book is no longer relevant, I would argue that the novel can help to open up a discussion about the complexities of white identity, both in the South and in the United States as a whole.

Notes

1. See "Honoring the Truth" in *The Courage to Heal* by Laura Bass and Ellen Davis, for their discussion of the backlash against their work, and chapter 8 of Janice Haaken's *Pillar of Salt: Gender, Memory, and the Perils of Looking Back* (187–197), for a critical discussion of these issues.

2. Critic Sarah Gordon, in *Flannery O'Connor: The Obedient Imagination*, figures this flower as the hold the past has on Southern identity (75), especially in the context of

this protagonist's uprootedness as he finds himself isolated and alienated in New York, living with his daughter.

3. See chapter 4 of Katherine Henninger's *Ordering the Façade: Photography and Southern Women's Writing*, for a discussion of the way photography reinforces power structures that privilege the male gaze.

Works Cited

Allison, Dorothy. *Two or Three Things I Know for Sure*. New York: Dutton, 1995. Print.

Bass, Laura, and Ellen Davis. "Honoring the Truth." In *The Courage to Heal*. New York: Harper, 1994. (187–197)

Doyle, Robert P. "Books Challenged and Banned, 2008–09." American Library Association. Web.

Frankenberg, Ruth. *White Women, Race Matters: The Social Construction of Whiteness*. Minneapolis: U Minnesota P, 1993.

Gordon, Sarah. *Flannery O'Connor: The Obedient Imagination*. Athens: U Georgia P, 2000.

Haaken, Janice. *Pillar of Salt: Gender, Memory, and the Perils of Looking Back*. New Brunswick, NJ: Rutgers U P, 1998.

Henninger, Katherine. *Ordering the Façade: Photography and Southern Women's Writing*. Chapel Hill: U North Carolina P, 2007.

Hovet, Theodore, and Grace-Ann Hovet. "'Fine Fancy Gentlemen' and 'Yappy Folk': Contending Voices in *To Kill a Mockingbird*." *Southern Quarterly* 40.1 (2001): 67–78. Print.

Jay, Gregory with Sandra Elaine Jones. "Whiteness Studies and the Multicultural Classroom." *MELUS* 30.2 (Summer 2005): 99–121. Print.

Johnson, Claudia Durst. *To Kill a Mockingbird: Threatening Boundaries*. Twayne Masterwork series 139. New York: Twayne, 1994.

Morrison, Toni. *Playing in the Dark: Whiteness and the Literary Imagination*. Cambridge, Mass., and London: Harvard U P, 1992.

O'Connor, Flannery. *Collected Works: Wise Blood / A Good Man Is Hard to Find / The Violent Bear It Away / Everything that Rises Must Converge / Essays & Letters*. New York: Library of America/Penguin Putnam, 1988: 107–113. Print.

Walker, Alice. *In Search of Our Mothers' Gardens: Womanist Prose*. Orlando, FL: Harcourt, 1983. Print.

Wray, Matt. *Not Quite White: White Trash and the Boundaries of Whiteness*. Durham: Duke U P, 2006. Print.

Wray, Matt and Annalee Newitz. "What Is White Trash?: Stereotypes and Economic Conditions of Poor Whites in the United States." In *Whiteness: A Critical Reader*. Ed. Mike Hill. New York: New York U P, 1997. (168–184).

CHAPTER 9

Spooks, Masks, Haints, and Things That Go Bump in the Night: Fear and Halloween Imagery in *To Kill a Mockingbird*

Michael J. Meyer

In the first paragraph of his March 1933 inaugural address to Congress, Franklin Delano Roosevelt, the thirty-second president of the United States, was frank and bold in his assertion that the only thing Americans had to fear was fear itself.[1] Assessing the common difficulties faced by citizens in the deep throes of the Great Depression, FDR sought to reassure his fellow countrymen and -women that failure was not imminent and that the key to a return to success—both financial and emotional—was to rely on interdependence: being a good neighbor who respects one's self and because she does so, respects the rights of others; a neighbor who respects his obligation and respects the sanctity of his agreement in and with a world of neighbors.

Some twenty-seven years later, Harper Lee published *To Kill a Mockingbird*, a book now celebrating its fifty-year anniversary. Whether ironically or intentionally, Lee set the story in 1933, the same year that Roosevelt delivered the speech—a time that despite Roosevelt's protestations to the contrary, was rife with various fears, not the least of which were the economic conditions that brought the failure of banks and businesses and that also foreshadowed the foreclosures of homes and loss of property. At this time, individuals also worried about having enough to eat, about finding a job, and about supporting a family. It was a distressing era throughout the United States but even more so for minorities, who found these concerns compounded by racial prejudice—by unfounded fears that black people were somehow individuals who, as their skin color suggested, were allied with the forces of evil. Overseas this dark force was already evident in the racialization of Germany under the rule of Adolf Hitler, whose rise to power prefigured the fall of the Weimar Republic and the rise of the Third Reich. These Nazi goals of genetic and racial purification, of course, fostered hatred and discrimination especially against Jews, blacks, Catholics, and homosexuals while promoting a "pure" Aryan race.[2] Given these parallels to real-life events that existed within the novel's time frame, it should be no surprise that Lee decided to incorporate the very real racial tensions that had flourished in her native South since the arrival of African slaves in the 1600s, not to mention the conflict that existed even earlier with Native Americans. It was a tension that she realized was escalating in her present-day world and had culminated in the modern civil rights movement in the late 1950s and early '60s. Set in Maycomb, Alabama—a town that parallels Lee's own hometown of Monroeville, Alabama—Lee's novel clearly addresses many types of fear that flourished on the American scene both in the distant past and the more recent present. Unfortunately, the novel still reflects the concerns of current American citizens who continue to be terrified not only by such things as the supernatural but also by individuals who are labeled as "Others," those whose backgrounds and personalities are different from their own and thus seem threatening and need to be avoided or condemned.

Although several critics have assessed Lee's use of a child narrator, her employment of childlike humor and naïveté, and the accuracy of her reproduction of preadolescent language, to my knowledge no study has been made of Lee's emphasis on fearful childhood experiences and her assertion that for the most part, such fears are unfounded. While not developing this idea fully, critic Gerard Early goes so far as to label the character Boo Radley as "the strange Doppelganger of the national conscience, a madman trapped within our haunted house, the ghost of the middle class southern liberal [as well as] the rabid lower-class racist, Bob Ewell" (94). Indeed, the haunted nature of Southern culture and the fear motif that typifies Southern Gothic fiction becomes more evident, an emphasis Lee expands on as she presents scary images as a dominant concern in the novel's plotline. Claudia Durst Johnson's assessments of the novel's close connection to the Gothic tradition are helpful in this regard as she cites the theories of such scholars as Eve Sedgwick, William Patrick Day, Irving Malin, and David Punter, among others, as a reminder to readers of what the most frequent emphases in Gothic fiction include: "murder, ghosts, witches, werewolves, vampire monsters, imprisonment, ruins, nostalgia for the past, unnatural parents, haunted or decayed quarters, specters, foreboding, deformity, madness, magic, dark and forbidding secrets, sexual violence, rape, incest, insanity, mental breakdown and cultural decay" (Johnson 40). Citing Punter specifically, Johnson's chapter on the Gothic also stresses the genre's portrayal of the "terrifying, its prominent use of the supernatural, its repetition of 'horror' and 'horrible'; the total darkness and masked faces of villains, its insistence on the potential finality of imprisonment and its note of half gasping, half gloating voyeurism as commonplace traits in such fictional output" (Punter qtd. in Johnson 40). Clearly, when readers examine *Mockingbird* for the above emphases, they will discover that most of these characteristics are manifest within its pages.

While Johnson's study notes the general parallels to the genre of Gothic fiction that exist in *To Kill a Mockingbird*, it does not delve into sufficient detail to help readers see the various connections that Lee makes between how children approach fear and how adults deal with it. Although the motif seems most evident at the beginning of the novel and in its reappearance at the Halloween celebration and pageant at Jem and Scout's school that occurs as the novel draws to a close, it is my contention that the text intentionally foregrounds a number of scary things throughout the novel and that Lee frequently makes reference to such frightful elements as ghosts, masks, spirits, and darkness as indicators of things that trouble both children and adult characters in the novel. I further believe that most of the fears that occupy a central position in *To Kill a Mockingbird* are those shown as having their origins in youthful fantasies,[3] which then unfortunately extend into maturity where they are revealed as irrational and unsubstantiated. Most ironic, however, is that many of the "things that go bump in the night" in the novel are connected to the unknown, the different, or unusual—items that may prove especially unnerving and upsetting to the naïve and largely susceptible characters in the novel, but that then develop, due to ignorance, into some sort of excuse that allows mature individuals to justify their tendency to be afraid of what may be entirely normal and safe. Indeed, a close reading of the novel will substantiate the claim that the events in *To Kill a Mockingbird* reveal that for most humans there initially seems to be far more to fear than fear itself, but will also support the assertion that Roosevelt's contention was ultimately correct.

As the title of this essay indicates, my study of Lee's novel draws attention to how Lee's foregrounding of the imagery of childhood fears helps to determine and even control the novel's organizational pattern. Perhaps the first indication of Lee's interest in fear begins with the introduction of Charles Baker "Dill" Harris early in the novel (*TKAM* 8), when he is almost immediately associated with the cinematic version of *Dracula* (a 1931 film featuring Béla Lugosi), a chilling movie to have been viewed by a young child but one that endears him to ten-year-old Jem Finch, who is the brother of Lee's narrator, the precocious six-year-old Jean Louise "Scout" Finch. Dill's choice of fiction (he also enjoys the pulp novel, *The Grey Ghost* by Seckatary Hawkins [*TKAM* 15, 322]) and cinema indicates his assumed courage in the face of dangerous people and dangerous locations. Therefore, when the "malevolent phantom" of Maycomb, Boo Radley, is introduced shortly after Dill's entrance (*TKAM* 9), Jem and Scout seem motivated to discover his real personality primarily because Dill is around to support their investigation. The Radley story, which has been created and exaggerated by local legend and gossip, suggests Boo is a ghostlike individual who has been forcefully isolated from society after he committed an act of violence many years previously. After being sequestered or perhaps even incarcerated for almost fifteen years in his own home, this outsider is considered mentally deficient and dangerous after he stabs his father in the leg with scissors. As a result of this unprovoked attack, Boo has become a local "spook" (ironically, a slang term for blacks).[4] He is depicted as a strange and unusual character whose very mysterious personality creates an uncomfortable sense of anxiety and discomfort among the townsfolk of Maycomb many of whom interpret his presence as threatening. Their "othering" of Boo also accounts for Lee's development of his negative reputation by associating him with exaggerated terrifying events:

> People said he went out at night when the moon was down, and peeped in windows. When people's azaleas froze in a cold snap, it was because he breathed on them. Any stealthy small crimes committed in Maycomb were his work. Once the town was terrorized by a series of morbid nocturnal events: people's chickens and household pets were found mutilated, and people still looked at the Radley Place, unwilling to discard their initial suspicions. . . . A negro would not pass the Radley Place at night: he would cut across to the sidewalk opposite and whistle as he walked. (*TKAM* 9)

As Johnson notes, this description may just as well have been given to the actions of a coven of witches (42).

Indeed, Dill's active imagination invents an even more fantastic Boo for the trio's play/fantasy reenactment of Boo's life, speculating with Jem on Boo's monster-like appearance (*TKAM* 14) and warning his new-made friends that the Radley house smells of death (*TKAM* 40).[5] The first supernatural element, besides Dill's literary and film interests, is clearly evident in Arthur Radley's previously discussed nickname of Boo. As Johnson states in *Threatening Boundaries*, "Chief among [the predictable character types] is Scout and Jem's neighbor, Arthur Radley, whom they seem to type from their readings of horror literature, stereotyping him by renaming him Boo" (50). For the town of Maycomb, Radley has become a type of ghost, his reputation connected to a spectral scene that has been enhanced by hearsay and exaggerated beyond reality. The actions quoted here suggest a fantastical individual who exists primarily in the imagination of Maycomb residents. In short, Boo becomes someone whose unstable personality must be feared; he looms in the background as an individual who can never quite be trusted, primarily because his motives and mental stability are in question. As Laura Fine states, "Townspeople, especially the children, think

Boo is weird, ghoulish, dangerous, insane, and perhaps even dead. Whatever he is, in truth or rumored to be, the one certainty is that he is an outsider" (73). He is indeed a character who Jem and Scout and Dill are in awe of and who they quizzically try to understand. But since they fear his differences, specifically his deranged mental state and his penchant for violence, they are wary of him as someone who may indeed threaten their very safety and security.

Perhaps because the children are intrigued by adventure stories such as *Tom Swift, Tarzan,* and *The Rover Boys* (*TKAM* 8–9), they are quick to add to the Radley mystique: they even believe that the pecans from the Radley Place would kill you (*TKAM* 10) and that Boo was so dangerous "he was chained to the bed most of the time" (*TKAM* 12). In fact, the description Jem gives of Radley is right out of a horror novel: "Boo was about six-and-a-half feet tall judging from his tracks; he dined on raw squirrels and any cats he could catch. . . . There was a long jagged scar that ran across his face, what teeth he had were yellow and rotten; his eyes popped, and he drooled most of the time" (*TKAM* 14). Even though the feeling of fear is addictive and even though Boo may gouge their eyes out or even kill them, the children are fascinated by the danger he represents. For them, such fear is exhilarating. Dill even risks losing treasured possessions like *The Grey Ghost,* offering his copy to Jem and daring him to just touch the Radley house, thus possibly helping the trio of friends to find out more about Boo's true nature (*TKAM* 150). Even the description of the Radley property fits the architecture of fear, "harboring what appears to be forbidden secrets and embodying the degeneracy of the past. . . . The house and grounds are, in the minds of the children, a haunted place of palpable evil and danger" (Johnson 43).

As the mood progresses, still other characters are associated with the fear motif. For example, Burris Ewell's "cooties" scare Miss Caroline, and Mrs. Henry Lafayette Dubose is avoided as the "meanest old women who ever lived" (*TKAM* 39). Like Boo, each is misunderstood because outward masks or previous judgmental attitudes about their reputation seem to take precedence over what may be on the inside of these individuals. Another illustration of a character wearing a mask of deception would be Calpurnia's use of different language patterns since she adopts "white" language patterns when working for the Finches and uses "black" ones when interacting with her own race at church and elsewhere. But, as Atticus says in an oft-quoted section of the novel, "You never really understand a person until you consider things from his point of view . . . until you climb into his skin and walk around in it" (*TKAM* 33). Lee thus advocates all attempts by humanity to see behind the mask. Unfortunately, this method of discovering truth is ignored for most of the novel as characters prefer to foreground superstitions and exaggerated rumors rather than look beyond them.

The episode in which Dill, Jem, and Scout discuss the ability to smell death is typical of a child's tendency to believe in supernatural events that cannot be substantiated. Jem describes his belief in a type of ghost called a Hot Steam who "wallows around on lonesome roads and you walk through him when you are you'll be one too, and you'll go around at night suckin' people's breath" (*TKAM* 41). This childish belief in monsters is Lee's way of telling her readers how foolish and unfounded fear often is. She then proceeds to apply this conclusion to still other "fearful" characters and to illustrate how unfair and unwarranted our hated misgivings are of people whose masks we cannot or choose not to penetrate. Instead of seeing behind the façade, the outside cover, we choose rather to exaggerate strangeness, suggest deformities of character and personality, and continue to isolate ourselves from what is unknown and therefore frightening.

While a good number of characters in the novel wear distorting masks, so to speak, examining only a few in detail will illustrate Lee's interest in seeing beyond outward appearances. For example, both Mrs. Dubose and Mr. Dolphus *Raymond* illustrate how inaccurate initial perceptions of people may be.

Mrs. Dubose is portrayed as a cantankerous and ill old lady who Jem decides to punish after she calls Atticus a "nigger-lover" and asserts that he is "no better than the niggers and trash he works for' (*TKAM* 116–118). Jem then strikes back by cutting the tops off of the old lady's camellia bushes.[6] His revenge, however, fails to take into account either her illness or her age. He only sees her mask of anger and frustration and does not look beyond it to discover the causes of such emotions. Readers discover later that Mrs. Dubose is a morphine addict and that her struggle to overcome her addiction is a major factor in her negative emotional state. Frustrated by her problems, she strikes out at others instead. Atticus forces Jem to look beyond retribution for her supposed crime of slander by ordering him to fulfill the old woman's request that he read to her for a month. When the children arrive to carry out their "punishment," they discover that her house is like the Radley Place, "dark and creepy [with] shadows and things on the ceiling" (*TKAM* 121). It is an ominous home, which Scout describe as "having an oppressive odor . . . I had met many times in rain rotted gray houses. It always made me afraid, expectant, watchful" (*TKAM* 121). Moreover the physical description of the old woman accentuates Jem and Scout's fear of their task. Her appearance is rather reminiscent of a ghoul or a witch. Lee's portrait follows:

> She was horrible. Her face was the color of a dirty pillowcase and the corners of her mouth glistened with wet which inched like a glacier down the deep grooves enclosing her chin. Old age liver spots dotted her cheeks, and her pale eyes had black pin-point pupils. Her hands were knobby, and the cuticles were grown up over her fingernails. Her bottom plate was not in, and her upper lip protruded; from time to time she would draw her nether lips to her upper plate and carry her chin with it. . . . Cords of saliva would collect on her lips; she would draw them in then open her mouth again. Her mouth seemed to have a private existence of its own. It worked separate and apart from the rest

> of her, like a clam hole at low tide. Occasionally it would say "Pt," like
> some vicious substance coming to a boil. (*TKAM* 123)

Yet despite the fact that the house and its occupant frighten them, as time passes Jem and Scout learn to quell their fears and accept the locale and its owner. Similarly, Mr. Dolphus Raymond has a negative image in the town. His reputation as a lower-class town drunk is established (*TKAM* 182–183), and his close association with black people (he has a "colored" mistress and several mulatto children) make him someone to be feared and avoided. Later in the novel, however, readers discover that Raymond's trashy reputation is merely a sham as he confesses to Scout that his paper bag—which Maycomb residents mistakenly believe contains a bottle of whiskey—in reality just contains a bottle of Coca-Cola (*TKAM* 227–228). Raymond explains his deception in this way: "Why do I pretend? Well it's very simple. . . . I try to give 'em a reason you see. It helps folks if they can latch on to a reason . . . folks can say Dolphus Raymond's in the clutches of whiskey—that's why he won't change his ways. He can't help himself" (*TKAM* 228). Raymond removes his mask or fake identity only to the children, however, knowing that adults could not cope with the truth that his so-called negative actions (hanging with Negroes and drinking) are simply motivated by personal choice: "I live like I do because that's the way I want to live" (*TKAM* 228). Once more, readers can see Lee's message that after probing behind the obvious, we may discover that the frightening and disturbing may only be façade, concealing an inner truth. In this case, the readers discover the fact that Raymond is an insightful observer of the world rather than the trashy drunk he is assumed to be by the townspeople of Maycomb.

While other characters—including Walter Cunningham, Judge Taylor, Link Deas, and Mr. Underwood—might be examined as having similar deceptive character traits that belie their true identity, I merely suggest the possibility here and move on to a more primal use of fear that Lee incorporates into the novel: a childhood fear of the dark. Specifically, Lee relies on the fact that several psychological analysts such as Sigmund Freud and Carl Jung have probed this specific fear in their writing. For example, speaking of Infantile Anxiety, Freud writes,

> Anxiety in children is in reality nothing else than an expression of the
> fact that they are feeling the loss of the person they love. It is for that
> reason that they are afraid of every stranger. They are afraid in the dark
> because they cannot see the face of the person they love, and their fear
> is soothed if they can hold of that person's hand in the dark.[7] (289)

Lee then proceeds to employ such psychological speculation in a variety of ways.

As we have seen previously, Mrs. Dubose's house is described as dark and creepy, and the encounter with Boo Radley in chapter 6 is heightened by the fact that it occurs in the night and involves a frightening shadow silhouetted by the back porch and a disturbing jolt of a shotgun blast as the children scatter in an attempt to escape from what they assume must be innate evil (*TKAM* 59–60). A few pages later, Scout recounts the exaggerated apprehension this event caused:

> Every night sound I heard from my cot on the back porch was magnified three-fold; every scratch of feet on gravel was Boo Radley seeking revenge, every passing Negro laughing in the night was Boo Radley loose and after us; insects splashing against the screen were Boo Radley's insane finger picking the wire to pieces; the chinaberry trees were malignant, hovering alive. (*TKAM* 62)

Thus, early in the novel, Lee places the fear of the dark as an integral image, and, of course, she continues to develop it by tying external darkness (lack of light) to the dark-skinned characters of the novel, including Calpurnia, Rev. Sykes, and, of course, Tom and Helen Robinson. Significantly, critic John Carlos Rowe describes Mayella Ewell's reactions to Robinson as evidence of "racial demonization" (14), suggesting once more the position of dark men and women as othered, perhaps even supernatural and thus to be feared. The fear of the male of the Negro race is particularly linked to the unfounded childish fears of dark places, to the need for night-lights and the apprehension of monsters that live in dark closets or beneath beds waiting to prey on unsuspecting children once they have fallen asleep.

As Judge Taylor notes, people generally see what they look for and hear what they listen for (*TKAM* 198). And the fear of the dark seems to be passed down through generations. Thus, as Atticus assesses the trial's outcome in a conversation with Jem (*TKAM* 253), he attributes the verdict to fear: fear that by acquitting Tom the jury may find themselves changing the rules of their society where black men are always threats to white women—hypersexual and powerful masculine symbols who must be kept under control and restricted. Rowe points out that the fear of the dark is also mentioned in passing when the Misses Tutti and Frutti Barber suggest that their furniture (actually hidden by childish pranksters) must have been stolen (13) by "those traveling fur sellers who cam through town two days ago. . . . Da-rk they were . . . Syrians" (*TKAM* 289), thus suggesting anyone with dark skin, not just Negroes, may elicit apprehension and mistrust.

The "dark" stereotype established in Maycomb is also evident in the scene with Aunt Alexandra's Missionary Circle where the ladies discuss the poor Mrunas, African residents who are compared to jungle animals and who are considered "savages" by this "Christian" community, avoided by everyone except the saintly missionary J. Grimes Everett, who is the only white person who will go near them. This concept of the Dark Continent of Africa suggests an inferior people ("you have no conception, no conception of what we are fighting over there—" [*TKAM* 263]) and anticipates a resultant misunderstanding of African Americans that relies on similar stereotyping rather than on firsthand experience. Lee suggests that ladies of the Missionary Circle, in obvious contradiction to Christian tenets, work to alleviate the pain and deprivation experienced by an African tribe from the Dark Continent but fail to offer emotional assistance or material help to the black citizens of their own town, whom they consider unworthy of their aid and lacking the potential to develop positive character traits. These local Others are more qualified for discrimination and hate than equality and love.

As the scene develops, it becomes more and more ironic for it seems as if Christianity fosters such misinterpretation of cultural difference and sees all "strange" black cultural activities as frightful practices. Similarly, the dissatisfaction of the racial Others is also seen as scary; as Mrs. Merriweather pronounces, "There is nothing more distracting than a sulky darky" (*TKAM* 264). Indeed, in the social class battle, the search for equality seems warlike (*TKAM* 265), and no matter what the "devout" white elite do to placate African American citizens, "no lady is safe in her bed" (*TKAM* 265) when male members of the black race are around. Goodness and thoughtfulness, usually seen as positive traits, are now perceived as misguided acts of the citizenry that rile up the dark race rather than placate them (*TKAM* 265). Rather then interact with what they fear, these individuals find it preferable to hold people at bay, to isolate them, and to refuse to recognize that blacks are as good and respectable as their white neighbors. Like a child who refuses to enter a dark bedroom, these women of the missionary circle prefer to be safe in the white light rather than take the risk of what they may discover about the dark people of Africa, besides the fact that their presence stimulates an unwarranted fear of the unknown. The native Africans are eligible for the ladies' pity and compassion because they are safely distant, rather than an imminent threat, as are the blacks of Maycomb.

Other childhood fears also are subtly insinuated into the novel's pages. For example, though Scout seems immune to both of these episodes, fear of insects is mentioned in the cootie episode discussed previously and then repeated in the roly-poly (centipede) episode that begins chapter 25. Even the gifts given by Boo Radley suggest childhood superstitions, albeit of a positive nature, as the Indian head pennies are described by Jem in this manner: "They come from Indians. They're real strong magic, they make you have good luck" (*TKAM* 40). Another fear that receives prominence is seen in the Tim Johnson episode in chapter 10. A snarling dog threatening to bite can certainly make a child run in fright, and a rabid one is an even more serious threat. Last of all, Lee suggests a potential fear of isolation in an enclosed space or imprisonment. Of course, this fear is present in Jem's unwillingness to be confined in Mrs. Dubose's house as we have seen earlier. Moreover, it is further developed in the details of Boo's childhood incarceration, first in the jail and then in his own home. Citing Malin, Johnson notes that the Radley home is "a site of terror" for Boo, "a place of danger and imprisonment where some are shut in and some are shut out" (Malin qtd. in Johnson 51). We might further see such isolation and fear of enclosed space in the "cage" of race constructed for Tom Robinson and that of class that constricts the social movement and acceptance of the Cunninghams and the Ewells.

The question that seems to be posed in all these episodes is whether the children deal with fear in ways that suggest they are more wise than adults. Darkness, insects, and angry animals can be faced with courage and be seen as irrational and capable of being conquered. Given the tight structural emphasis on fear and the frequent repetition of words such as *scary, scared, frightened, frightening, terrifying, fearful,* and *afraid,* it is no wonder then that Lee returns full circle to the image as the novel draws to a close.

As chapter 1 introduces a character named Boo and suggests a Halloween figure who has white and ghostlike skin, so the final three chapters return to that same holiday celebration and to a pageant that suggests that many individuals are in disguises and/or are those who have an outward appearance that belies their inner identity: the outside (real skin color) is not an accurate prediction of reality just as a Halloween costume is merely a ruse worn by the wearer who is not really scary at all.

Chapter 28 begins the return of Lee's use of Halloween imagery by introducing a life-in-death spirit that is said to suck the breath of life from individuals it meets on a dark road (*TKAM* 293). Not surprisingly, this mention occurs in front of the Radley Place but is modified by the narrator's comment that "Haints, Hot Streams, incantations, secret signs, had vanished with our years as mist with sunrise" (*TKAM* 292). This dismissal of superstition is followed, however, by the sudden appearance of Scott's classmate, Cecil Jacobs, who surprisingly leaps from the dark to scare the children while they are on their way to the pageant. Although they have previously asserted a maturity that would nullify unwarranted fear, this interaction intensifies the unease that Jem and Scout will experience when they arrive at the auditorium. When at the Halloween celebration, the children demonstrate a developing maturity that helps them survive the House of Horrors and the ghoul guide who makes them touch normal objects that are intended to suggest severed body parts, but eventually the two siblings must face the scary walk home in the dark with Scout still encased and restricted in a ham costume (perhaps another indicator of the imprisonment/fear of enclosed spaces discussed previously). The spooky sounds of echoing footsteps cause Jem to stop briefly and motivate Scout to suggest that he is deliberately trying to scare her (*TKAM* 298). They also suspect Cecil of returning to frighten them—this time when it is pitch black. The unknown presence this time is, of course, not a child playing a prank but instead the malevolent Bob Ewell, who threatens the children and is bent on taking revenge on Atticus Finch for sullying the Ewell name during the Tom Robinson trial for the rape of Ewell's daughter, Mayella. Again relying on irony, Lee makes a white man into the dark and evil presence and, at the same time, transforms the Boo of the earlier episodes from a scary ghost into a Savior figure.

According to Robert Butler, "His [Boo's] difficult environment . . . should have made him the monster the town perceives him to be, but, in fact, he is a decent and courageous man" and can be "perceive[ed] as an innocent, even saintly figure" (*TKAM* 124). Of course, readers have been prepared for this transformation by Boo's previous actions—his kind treatment of Jem (folding and mending his pants in chapter 6) and his protection of Scout (covering her with a blanket during the fire at Miss Maudie's in Chapter 8 [*TKAM* 81]). Such kindness/generosity is also shown in the gifts of gum, carved figures, and pennies that Boo leaves for Jem and Scout in the knothole of the tree. Butler also asserts that the Boo who appears at the end of the novel is characterized by "goodness, generosity and kindness . . . a guardian angel that saves them [the children] from a man whose very name—Ewell—suggests evil" (124).

Things that go bump in the night, ghosts, masks, and supernatural dark events are all revealed as mere illusions. Even Scout's description of Boo as he cowers behind the bedroom door indicates Lee's belief that outward appearances are deceiving. It also reflects Boo's tendency to prefer darkness over light and to remain in the shadow world of Maycomb society. The description of Radley reads like a description from a horror novel. Scout's description follows:

> His face was as white as his hands, but for a shadow on his jutting chin. His cheeks were thin to hollowness; his mouth was wide; there were shallow, almost delicate indentations at his temples and his grey eyes were so colorless, I thought he was blind. His hair was dead and thin, almost feathery on the top of his head. (*TKAM* 310)

Yet somehow Scout knows this man is not a zombie, and his scary looks do not reflect a dangerous personality. Given this conclusion, it is not difficult to make the connections about not being deceived by appearance; instead, readers are invited to conclude that, even as the town's assumptions about Boo have been inaccurate, so the white citizenry's reaction to blacks is yet another unwarranted fear. Perhaps Lee really does agree with Franklin Delano Roosevelt that most fears are unfounded and are based on prejudices and undocumented assumptions. If so, then Roosevelt was right; the only thing we have to fear is fear itself.

However, as long as black men like Tom Robinson need to be afraid of white courts, white mob violence, and prejudiced white juries (see *TKAM* 232–233) and as long as the potential for lynching before a fair trial can occur exists (see the jail scene in chapter 15), race will continue as a factor in determining our assessment of intelligence, physical abilities, and human worth. Clearly, the challenge for Lee's readers and for America as a whole is to reassess the accuracy of its unwarranted fear of the dark.

As Lee seems to suggest in the novel, historical evidence indicates that contrary to what most white people might like to believe, the black race was probably the first one on the planet and was not an aberration. Indeed, if this is so, despite feelings of Caucasian superiority, it is more than likely that all whites have a drop of Negro blood in their veins. Indeed, according to paleoanthropologists, our earliest human ancestors did come from Africa, and it seems likely that they were dark skinned. More importantly, the findings of the Human Genome Project support the idea that we are, indeed, one human family.[8]

In the novel, Scout asks Jem, "How do you know we ain't Negroes?" to which Jem replies, "Uncle Jack Finch says we really don't know . . . for all he knows we mighta come straight out of Ethiopia durin' the Old Testament." When Scout protests that that time frame is so long ago it doesn't matter, Jem replies, "That's what I thought . . . but around here once you have one drop of Negro blood, that makes you all black" (*TKAM* 184). Perhaps Lee's implication is that Caucasian readers of the novel have an obligation to admit that they are similar to what Scout labels an "absolute morphodite" in chapter 8: a muddy black snowman who is merely covered with a surface-thin film of white exterior (*TKAM* 75). This pseudo-snowman is yet another example of Lee's use of masked appearances. The truth is, it is not a snowman; it is rather a collection of hampers and baskets of dirt collected from the Finches' backyard. When encased in snow borrowed from Miss Maudie's yard, the snowman only appears to be real.

Certainly, in the novel, no one can know his or her racial heritage as a certainty since as generations passed, skin color began to modify. It is also impossible to say which race was the first. But what if? What if the belief in Maycomb that one drop of Negro blood makes you black is absolutely correct (*TKAM* 184)? If that statement is taken literally, it follows that everyone must admit his or her dark-skinned heritage because somewhere in the past, each person had one chromosome from a Negro ancestor; it then also follows that in order to fear the black race, we would be forced to fear ourselves.

Furthermore, the typical Southern belief that one drop of blood tainted an individual was merely a way to keep the freed slaves and their descendents under the thumb of white supremacy and to reestablish the social balance in the South. The only hope for social power that "poor white trash" such as the Ewells had over the blacks who, in many cases, were socially and economically above them was ultimately the fact that they were white. Thus Bob Ewell's smugness and cockiness derive from the fact that he knows he will be believed over Tom, regardless of the evidence. His skin color is all that he has.[9] His anger at Atticus is in part a result of the ways in which Atticus makes it clear that skin color just may not be enough anymore.

That, of course, is the message of To Kill a Mockingbird and of FDR, and it is repeated often in the text. Instead of being scared of what appears to be different, we need to admit we are all essentially the same. Like Jem, we need to be colorblind (TKAM 134) and attempt to see all folks as folks. This exhortation toward equality is seen after the Tom Robinson trial, when Jem tells Scout, "I've got it figured out. There's four kind of folks in the world. There's the ordinary kind like us and the neighbors, there's the kind like the Cunninghams out in the woods, the kind like the Ewells down at the dump, and the Negroes" (TKAM 258). As he and Scout argue over this classification, it becomes clear that his divisions are foolish because "everybody's family is just as old as everybody else's" (TKAM 258); the idea of fine folks and old family is fantasy, and there's "just one kind of folk. Folks" (TKAM 259).

Lee reasons that if we stop hurting others who have done nothing to hurt us, we will find that stepping into another's skin allows us to discover how much like us they really are (see TKAM 33, 65, 249). Johnson reminds readers that the lure of terror is perhaps universal—especially among children who seem to relish being scared (69). But, as Edgar Allen Poe famously noted, perhaps the ideal end effect of terror is transcendence of the event rather than being defeated by it. When an individual breaks through to an understanding of his or her own psyche, such recognition is of "peculiar epiphanic importance" (Johnson 69).

The fact that most differences in people are harmless is discovered by Scout and Jem in numerous episodes in the book. As they discover Boo's friendliness, as they begin to understand the reason for Mrs. Dubose's hostile nature, as they realize the contradictions evident in the Missionary Society's failure to see their own hypocrisy, as they enjoy a heart-to-heart talk with Mr. Dolphus Raymond, and as they sit in the Negro balcony at the trial, understanding slowly develops. They have experienced the worldview of another and have gained significant knowledge that had previously been concealed by the veil of apparent otherness.

Johnson quotes Kate Ferguson Ellis as asserting the following: "Not knowing is the primary source of Gothic terror and knowing can only occur with seeing and experiencing the unknown" (Ellis qtd. in Johnson 69). Ellis also states, "Two fears dominate the Gothic world, the fear of terrible separateness and the fear of unity with some terrible Other" (22). Similarly Robert Butler's closing assessment of the novel's conclusion foregrounds what he labels the religious discovery made by Scout in the final tableaux as she "overcom[es] her initial terror and disorientation, [and] is calmed by Boo's gentleness, warmth and radiant presence" (131). Deeply touched by her close contact, she experiences her world as "transfigured" as Boo becomes a neighbor and friend rather than someone to be feared (131). Johnson seems to agree, stating, "By the novel's end, Boo has shed his horror story stereotype and becomes a fully developed, if somewhat odd human being, who discards his nickname and is called Mr. Arthur by Scout after his normalization" (50). In short, the fears we develop are mostly imaginary, born from the delusion that harm and injury will be sustained from that which is different. If we allow these frightening elements free range, they will control our lives—but only if we let them. After all, as Scout tell us, "Nothin's real scary except in books" (*TKAM* 322) and most people are real nice "when you finally see them" (*TKAM* 323).

Notes

1. Franklin D. Roosevelt, Inaugural Address, 4 March 1933 as quoted in *The Public Papers of Franklin D. Roosevelt. Volume Two: The Year of Crisis, 1933*. Ed. Samuel Roseman. New York: Random House, 1938. (11–16). Even more relevant is the fact that Lee references the speech in the novel itself, stating on page 6: "Maycomb County had recently been told that it had nothing to fear but fear itself."

2. Lee even mentions the Hitler phenomenon (which ironically also began in January 1933 with Hitler's appointment as Reich's chancellor) and suggests the supreme irony that is evident in America's fear of racial oppression abroad while it continued to practice it at home. See *TKAM* 280–283 for the discussion of Germany's policies as opposed to American democracy.

3. Dill's fantasies are shown in his account of his running away from home during the third summer of the narrative, a tale in which he claims to have been fearfully tortured, bound in chains and left to die in the basement. His account of escaping from being restrained by wrist manacles and of being forced to walk from Meridian to Maycomb clearly shows how he tends to exaggerate fears and dangers. (*TKAM* 158)

4. The *Oxford English Dictionary* offers this as the first example of the usage: "1945 L. SHELLY Hepcats Jive Talk Dict. 17/2 Spook (n), frightened negro."

5. Dill even claims, "I mean I can smell somebody an' tell if they're gonna die. An old lady taught me how" (*TKAM* 410), subsequently predicting Scout's death in three days and further fostering Jem and Scout's apprehensions over Boo's threatening personality.

6. There is no doubt a symbolic purpose in Lee's choice of white camellias and in her naming the flowers Snow on the Mountain.

7. Jung's concept of archetypes also foregrounds what he labeled "the shadow"—the unconscious negative or dark side of the personality, and he too spoke of the inevitable fear of the dark observed in most infants. Moreover, according to http://www.guideto psychology.com/identity.htm, "Quite often [Jung's] fear of the unconscious manifests

itself as a specific phobia whereby the interior terror becomes projected on to external objects, situations, or even the environment itself such as a fear of the dark."

8. For further information of the Human Genome Project, see http://www.ornl.gov/sci/techresources/Human_Genome/education/education.shtml

9. The following comment by Lee is most significant in this regard, referring to Ewell's appearance at the trial: "All the little man on the witness stand had that made him any better than his nearest neighbors was, that if scrubbed with lye soap in very hot water, his skin was white" (*TKAM* 195).

Works Cited

Butler, Robert. "The Religious Vision in *To Kill A Mockingbird*." In *On Harper Lee: Essays and Reflections*. Ed. Alice Hall Petry. Knoxville: U Tennessee P, 2007. (121–133)

Day, William Patrick. *In the Circles of Fear and Desire: A Study of Gothic Fantasy*. Chicago: U Chicago P, 1985.

Early, Gerald. "The Madness in the American House: The New Southern Gothic, and the Young Adult Novel of the 1960s: A Personal Reflection." In *On Harper Lee: Essays and Reflections*. Ed. Alice Hall Petry. Knoxville: U Tennessee P, 2007. (93–103)

Ellis, Kate Ferguson. *The Contested Castle: The Gothic Novel and the Subversion of Domestic Ideology*. Urbana: U Illinois P, 1989.

Fine, Laura. "Structuring the Narrator's Rebellion in *To Kill a Mockingbird*." In *On Harper Lee: Essays and Reflections*. Ed. Alice Hall Petry. Knoxville: U Tennessee P, 2007. (61–77)

Freud, Sigmund. *Three Essays on the Theory of Sexuality*. 1905. Reprinted in *A Freud Reader*. Ed. Peter Gay. New York: Norton, 1989.

Johnson, Claudia Durst. *"To Kill a Mockingbird": Threatening Boundaries*. New York: Twayne, 1994.

Lee, Harper. *To Kill a Mockingbird*. 1960. New York: Harper Perennial Modern Classics, 2006.

Malin, Irving. *New American Gothic*. Edwardsville: Southern Illinois U P, 1962.

Oxford English Dictionary. 2nd ed. Oxford: Oxford U P, 1989.

Petry, Alice Hall, ed. *On Harper Lee: Essays and Reflections*. Knoxville: U Tennessee P, 2007.

Punter, David. *The Literature of Horror: A History of Gothic Fictions from 1765 to the Present Day*. London: Longman, 1980.

Rowe, John Carlos. "Racism, Fetishism, and the Gift Economy in *To Kill a Mockingbird*." In *On Harper Lee: Essays and Reflections*. Ed. Alice Hall Petry. Knoxville: U Tennessee P, 2007. (1–17)

Sedgwick, Eve. *The Coherence of Gothic Conventions*. New York: Arno Press, 1980.

CHAPTER 10

"A Rigid and Time-Honored Code": Sport and Identity in *To Kill a Mockingbird*

Carl F. Miller

> When he was nearly thirteen, my brother Jem got his arm badly broken at the elbow. When it healed, and Jem's fears of never being able to play football were assuaged, he was seldom self-conscious about his injury. His left arm was somewhat shorter than his right; when he stood or walked, the back of his hand was at right angles to his body, his thumb parallel to his thigh. He couldn't have cared less, so long as he could pass and punt. (*TKAM* 3)

This opening passage from Harper Lee's classic *To Kill a Mockingbird* stands to this day as an unusual choice on Lee's part, given the paragraph's emphasis on both masculinity and sports in a novel that has traditionally (and rightfully) been lauded for its portrayal of the feminine and a series of social concerns that seemingly encapsulate everything *except* sports. Upon closer examination, however, Lee's book utilizes sports to specifically establish the identity of a number of its characters, and inversely uses the identity of several characters to solidify their relationship to sports. From the very opening of the book, *To Kill a Mockingbird* is deceptively reliant on the sporting culture of the South in its realistic depiction of the town of Maycomb, Alabama, and its citizens.

To Kill a Mockingbird is, of course, a quasi-autobiographical account of Harper Lee's own childhood, with Scout (Jean Louise) Finch representing Lee herself, Atticus portraying Lee's father, and Dill Harris serving as a memorable illustration of Lee's close friend, Truman Capote. Jem is modeled after Lee's brother, Edwin, and his fascination with sports is reflective of Edwin's own passion for all things physically competitive in his early adult years. Fiction did, however, afford Harper Lee a number of cathartic advantages that real life did not. The opening passage detailing Jem's injury essentially provides a happy ending to the resultant book, as it implies that Bob Ewell's attack on the Finch children will ultimately carry no lasting physical limitations. Lee's brother, on the other hand, died suddenly in 1951 at the age of thirty, and the cause of his death was blamed in part on sports, as "a few of the servicemen attending the funeral mentioned that Edwin had been playing a strenuous game of softball the afternoon before" (Shields 110). Whatever the veracity of these claims, it seems a bit ironic that his death be attributed to a sport decidedly less violent and dangerous than football—much the same as Jem's own injuries result not from football but rather walking home from a school pageant.

Even if Jem had been based on any number of other boys from Lee's hometown of Monroeville, Alabama, his attitude toward sports would likely have been similar. The Deep South of Lee's childhood was characterized by the phrase, "One party, one crop, one sport, and one dollar if you were lucky." The Democratic Party was the effective default vote of the South at this time (note the Barber ladies mentioned in *To Kill a Mockingbird*, who "were rumored to be Republicans" and are characterized by "their Yankee ways" [288]), and cotton was the dominant crop of the region. Poverty was widespread throughout the South; the novel begins in 1933, in the midst of the Great Depression, and even by the standards of the time, Alabama was strikingly impoverished. Scout describes the newspaper stories she would read with her father and brother: "There were sit-down strikes in Birmingham; bread lines in the city grew longer, people in the country grew poorer. But these were events remote from the world of Jem and me" (*TKAM* 132).

Perhaps most ubiquitously of all, football was the sport of choice in the South. While economic and labor developments in Birmingham are decidedly remote from the world of Maycomb, football news of any kind is equally applicable across the entire state and carries with it a degree of interest and excitement that is notably absent from accounts of the Great Depression. Scout recalls,

> That spring [of 1934] was a good one: the days grew longer and gave us more playing time. Jem's mind was occupied mostly with the vital statistics of every college football player in the nation. Every night Atticus would read us the sports pages of the newspapers. Alabama might go to the Rose Bowl again this year, judging from its prospects, not one of whose names we could pronounce. (*TKAM* 126)

Michael Oriard has theorized that "football is indeed a cultural text, that it tells a story, that this story is read differently by different groups and individuals, and that these different interpretations change through time" (17), and this interpretation is particularly applicable to the South of this time. The enthusiasm attached to football is due in part to the sport providing a source of achievement and pride, in contrast to the national perception of the South as an impoverished, socially inequitable region that had lost the Civil War (an event that a number of people could still personally remember in 1933). The University of Alabama was an institution that was so cash-strapped in the late 1920s that seniors actually had to teach freshman classes, but it was also a college football powerhouse second only to the University of Notre Dame in national reputation. Alabama would indeed go to the Rose Bowl following the 1934 season, capping their fourth national championship in a decade with a 29–13 victory over Stanford University.

The narrative appeal of football reaches beyond the regional affinity for the sport. As Christian Messenger observes, "Injuries are real, even tragic at times, as is the remote possibility of death. Careers are short; bodies are left in pain. . . . Within a known, repeatable format, there is a vast amount of play, room for the improbable, the incredible, the tragic, the absurd" (729). An interest in football also represents a significant step forward in the maturation process of Jem and Scout, who in the early part of the novel are content to busy themselves with games rather than sports. These myriad childhood games, such as "Boo Radley" (*TKAM* 43), are unique and private and clandestine, whereas sports are standardized and public and a source of civic pride. The games of Jem and Scout's youth are more akin to stage acting, and the children understand that adults like Atticus and Calpurnia will view such games suspiciously (at one point, Jem suggests changing the names of the characters in "Boo Radley," so they "couldn't be accused of playing anything" [*TKAM* 46]).

Conversely, a sport like football represents the horizon beyond childhood and the passage into adulthood, in both the physical maturity it demands and in the collective social network it enables. While Jem's participation in childhood games marks him as relatively unusual for a boy of his age, his obsession with football is an overwhelmingly ordinary pursuit and a signal of his expanding social development. There is a "fake peace that prevailed on Sundays" because, Scout explains, "Jem in his old age had taken to his room with a stack of football magazines" (*TKAM* 168). In fact, Jem's increased interest in football results in his diminished interest in being Scout's playmate, much to the bemusement of his sister, who often finds her brother "on the sofa with a football magazine in front of his face, his head turning as if its pages contained a live tennis match"[1] (*TKAM* 155).

Far from simply being extraneous references within the novel, these magazines serve as a deeper window into the children's characters and their culture. Atticus does not understand how deeply frightened Jem is about Bob Ewell's threats until "he tempted Jem with a new football magazine one night," only to have "Jem flip the pages and toss it aside" in disinterest (*TKAM* 249). When Jem seems inconsolable after cutting the tops off Mrs. Dubose's camellia bushes, Scout explains that she "picked up a football magazine, found a picture of Dixie Howell, showed it to Jem and said, 'This looks like you.' That was the nicest thing I could think to say to him" (*TKAM* 118–19). It is unclear whether this is simply the first picture of a player that Scout comes upon, or whether she knows who Dixie Howell is well enough to specifically select him. In either case, the compliment would have been exceedingly satisfactory: Millard "Dixie" Howell (figure 10.1) was the All-American quarterback on Alabama's 1934 national championship team, who was also one of the nation's best punters and punt returners. In his final college game, the 1935 Rose Bowl, Howell was named the outstanding player as he scored two touchdowns and threw two touchdown passes (to future NFL Hall of Famer Don Hutson).

As much as reading about football represents an intellectual identity for Jem, the actual playing of the sport drives his aspirations for physical and emotional maturity. Jem has always been several grades above Scout, and while his graduation to the high school building represents a notable difference between the siblings, it is his place on the football team that truly creates a deviation in their daily routines. As Scout explains,

> School started, and so did our daily trips past the Radley Place. Jem was in the seventh grade and went to high school, beyond the grammar school building; I was in the third grade, and our routines were so different I only walked to school with Jem in the mornings and saw him at mealtimes. He went out for football, but was too slender and too young yet to do anything but carry the team water buckets. This he did with enthusiasm; most afternoons he was seldom home before dark. (*TKAM* 277)

Jem is effectively stuck in maturity limbo, too old for the childhood games of Scout and too young for the playing fields of high school sports. The only way for him to break from this stasis—both literally and symbolically—is to grow older and larger and make the varsity football team, a task that he takes very seriously (if not entirely realistically). Scout describes a seemingly common scene from that fall:

> Jem was worn out from a days' water-carrying. There were at least twelve banana peels on the floor by his bed, surrounding an empty milk bottle. "Whatcha stuffin' for?" I asked.
> "Coach says if I can gain twenty-five pounds by year after next I can play," he said. "This is the quickest way." (*TKAM* 282)

Figure 10.1. Dixie Howell.[2]

While Jem finds himself on the young side of the window to play football, his father, Atticus, is instead too old to participate in the sport. Football, in accordance with Messenger's aforementioned statement, is characterized by short careers, and in the early part of the novel Jem and Scout are both apt to gauge their father's masculinity and social status in terms of his physical and recreational abilities. "Jem and I found our father satisfactory," Scout says, "he played with us, read to us, and treated us with courteous detachment" (*TKAM* 6). But while he plays *with* them, Atticus never plays *against* them—at least not to win—and never pits them against one another in competition, either. Instead, Atticus is fond of crafting scenarios in which his children "were both right" (*TKAM* 4). Since sports are designed to establish winners and losers, participating seems to run contrary to Atticus' central philosophy.

To Atticus' son, this is taken at best as a sign of old age, at worst as a sign of weakness. Jem is described as having been "football crazy. Atticus was never too tired to play keepaway, but when Jem wanted him to tackle him Atticus would say, 'I'm too old for that, son'" (*TKAM* 102). The breaking point for Jem comes when Atticus dismisses the opportunity to compete against other fathers in the South's sport of choice:

> Jem underlined it when he asked Atticus if he was going out for the Methodists and Atticus said he'd break his neck if he did, he was just too old for that sort of thing. The Methodists were trying to pay off their church mortgage, and had challenged the Baptists to a game of touch football. Everybody in town's father was playing, it seemed, except Atticus. Jem didn't even want to go, but he was unable to resist football in any form, and he stood gloomily on the sidelines with Atticus and me watching Cecil Jacobs's father make touchdowns for the Baptists. (*TKAM* 105)

Despite Atticus' impeccable reputation as both a lawyer and a state legislator, the cultural capital for fatherhood (at least in Jem's mind) is based on the ability to compete on the football field for public edification. Scout, likewise, is unimpressed that Atticus can play the Jew's harp or draw up an airtight will (both nonsporting pursuits) and is unwilling to cede that Atticus is the best checker player in town, on the grounds that she and Jem beat their father all the time—to which Miss Maudie knowingly emphasizes, "It's because he lets you win" (*TKAM* 104).

Instead, it is only when Atticus is summoned to shoot Tim Johnson, the rabid dog wobbling dangerously down their street, that Jem and Scout both take notice of their father's sporting abilities. Despite not having fired a gun in thirty years, Atticus takes down the dog in a single shot, to the amazement of both of his children. Hunting is a sport to Jem and Scout and to most of the residents of Maycomb, and when Miss Maudie reports in the wake of the shooting that Atticus' nickname growing up was "One-Shot Finch," it effectively clinches Atticus' status as a master sportsman in the eyes of his family (*TKAM* 111). The fact that he shoots out of necessity (rather than sport) only heightens their appreciation for their father's talent; in this case, the stakes are not win or lose, but rather life or death. At chapter's end, Jem declares, "Atticus is real old, but I wouldn't care if he couldn't do anything—I wouldn't care if he couldn't do a blessed thing. . . . Atticus is a gentleman, just like me!" (*TKAM* 113).

Of course, the notion of being a sporting gentleman raises the conundrum of where ladies fit into the world of sports. Harper Lee's own biography offers some insight into this query, as she was a self-described tomboy who was often willing to test the social boundaries traditionally ascribed to women. While attending the University of Alabama from 1945–1949, Lee wrote for the campus humor magazine, the *Rammer Jammer*, so named after the cheer that erupted after football victories in Denny Stadium ("Rammer jammer, yellow hammer, give 'em hell, Alabama!"). Furthermore, Charles Shields records that, while Lee was at Alabama, "one of her favorite spots to hang out was the University Supply Store, the SUPe—a combination bookstore and soda fountain—where she liked nothing better than to sit in a booth crammed with young men and talk about football" (99). In Lee's first year on campus, the football team went undefeated and again won the Rose Bowl, and by this time the fervor for playing football was no longer limited to just male students. The Honey Bowl (figure 10.2) was established to showcase female intramural football teams at Alabama, and "Nelle [Lee's given name] played on a powderpuff team of junior and senior girls— 'pigskin-packin' mamas,' the *Crimson White* [Alabama's student newspaper] called them" (Shields 99).

The social and physical boundaries of sports that Lee faced (if not overcame) in her own life are readily reflected in her writing. Michele Ware suggests that "*To Kill a Mockingbird* can be read as a feminist bildungsroman, for Scout emerges from her childhood experiences with a clear sense of her place in her community and an awareness of her potential power as the woman she will be one day" (288). But her growth also leaves Scout aware of her limitations as a

Figure 10.2. The 1948 Honey Bowl.

female and still excluded from the rites of passage into manhood—for which sports stands as the primary popular designation.

Scout's very nickname (as opposed to "Jean Louise," her given name) implies a sort of tomboyish nature and acceptance. Her desire to follow in Jem's footsteps is readily evident throughout the novel, but while she can become a lawyer (as Miss Stephanie Crawford suggests) or a nurse or an aviator (professions she considers for herself), there are two things she can never become: a man or a football player. Furthermore, this pair of concepts—manhood and football—is largely synonymous in Jem's mind, as seen in his exchange with Scout after she quarrels with Aunt Alexandra:

> His eyebrows were becoming heavier, and I noticed a new slimness about his body. He was growing taller.
>
> When he looked around, he must have thought I would start crying again, for he said, "Show you something if you won't tell anybody." I said what. He unbuttoned his shirt, grinning shyly.
>
> "Well what?"
>
> "Well can't you see it?"
>
> "Well no."
>
> "Well it's hair."
>
> "Where?"
>
> "There. Right there."
>
> He had been a comfort to me, so I said it looked lovely, but I didn't see anything. "It's real nice, Jem."
>
> "Under my arms, too," he said. "Goin' out for football next year. Scout, don't let Aunty aggravate you."
>
> It seemed only yesterday that he was telling me not to aggravate Aunty.
>
> "You know she's not used to girls," said Jem, "leastways, not girls like you. She's trying to make you a lady. Can't you take up sewin' or somethin'?" (*TKAM* 257)

The social designations evident in this conversation are, for a pair of decidedly progressive children, overwhelmingly traditional; Jem is to become a football player and subsequently a gentleman, while Scout is to engage in needlepoint on her way to becoming a lady—in short, as Jem yells at her on one occasion, "bein' a girl and acting right" (*TKAM* 131). When Jem earlier threatens to spank Scout if she antagonizes Aunt Alexandra, Scout attacks him physically. She admits that "it nearly knocked the breath out of me, but it didn't matter because I knew he was fighting, he was fighting me back. We were still equals" (*TKAM* 156–57).

Such symbolic victory proves short-lived, however, as Scout can never ascend to a position of equality in the public realm of physical competition. This realization is not lost on the narrator; Michele Ware observes that "according to Scout, power and authority are masculine attributes; to be a girl is to be marginalized and excluded" (286).

Scout and Dill are both characters who are marginalized on the grounds of their femininity. Unable to join Jem (or anyone else for that matter) in a real game of football, Scout and Dill "kicked Jem's football around the pasture for a while" before deciding that—deprived of its competitive element—it "was no fun" (*TKAM* 168). Even more revealing are Dill's parents telling him, "You're not a boy. Boys get out and play baseball with other boys, they don't hang around the house worryin' their folks" (*TKAM* 162); in this case, biological gender has no bearing upon masculinity, with sports instead serving as the primary designation of manhood. Not coincidentally, upon recollecting this statement, Dill compensates by suggesting the most masculine response he can think of: that he and Scout should have a baby together (*TKAM* 162).

Even when left to her own devices, free of her Aunt's rules and Jem's suggestions, Scout invariably (if unintentionally) chooses to conform with the sporting roles traditionally assigned to young women. She explains,

> The day after Jem's twelfth birthday . . . [he] thought he had enough to buy a miniature steam engine for himself and a twirling baton for me. I had long had my eye on that baton; it was at V. J. Elmore's, it was bedecked with sequins and tinsel, it cost seventeen cents. It was then my burning ambition to grow up to twirl with the Maycomb County High School band. (*TKAM* 116)

While Scout seeks to follow in Jem's footsteps, she does not aspire to join the Maycomb County High School football team, and she rests her desires on the realistic goal of twirling on the gridiron instead of tackling. While this may be partly attributed to the lack of any female football players to look up to, it may also be seen as a desire to engage in the same scene of social normalcy that the sport of football provides for Jem. Short of the trial of Tom Robinson, Friday night high school football is an unparalleled public event in Maycomb, one that offers competition and entertainment opportunities to both genders in a stratified manner.

It is, however, the trial of Tom Robinson that provides the starkest reminder that not every citizen of Maycomb has the same opportunities. The "Colored balcony" in the courtroom is a testament to the enduring segregation practices of the Deep South (*TKAM* 187), which are also evident in the children's earlier visit to First Purchase African M.E. Church (*TKAM* 134). Although never explicitly depicted in *To Kill a Mockingbird*, schools were among the most segregated institutions of all, assuming that individuals of color even had a school to attend. Criticism of the book has often centered on its treatment of race, to the extent that some have questioned the work's contemporary pertinence on the subject. Isaac Saney, for example, states that "the images and messages of *To Kill a Mockingbird* are [consistently] given new life, despite the reality that, as in the case of *Uncle Tom's Cabin*, these motifs have long since outlived any positive and progressive purpose" and are instead "a detriment and a regressive block" (103).

But Tom Robinson's trial highlights an even more enduring aspect of discrimination that stretches beyond legal segregation: what Scout describes as "the secret courts of men's hearts" (*TKAM* 276). For it is just such a motivation that drove every major college football program in the South to remain exclusively white,[3] despite the fact that there was never any law barring African Americans from participating. This was akin in many ways to the unspoken color barrier of major league baseball, which required the finest African American ballplayers of the time to play in the Negro leagues. Any man who dared violate this established tradition faced ostracism, in much the same way that anyone who loved someone of another race would be outcast; as Atticus says of Mayella Ewell, "She has committed no crime, she has merely broken a rigid and time-honored code of our society, a code so severe that whoever breaks it is hounded from our midst as unfit to live with" (*TKAM* 231).

Atticus stresses that this realization gives added significance to institutions like the courtroom, where "all men are created equal. . . . In this country our courts are the great levelers" (*TKAM* 233). Sports would seem to offer an equivalent institution, but the African American characters in *To Kill a Mockingbird* are more fixated on mere survival (as in Tom's case) than on recreational competition and entertainment. Even a progressive child like Jem thinks that, in Maycomb County, "there's four kinds of folks. . . . There's the ordinary kind like us and the neighbors, there's the kind like the Cunninghams out in the woods, the kind like the Ewells down at the dump, and the Negroes" (*TKAM* 258). African Americans occupy the bottom rung of the social ladder, and it is a position with seemingly little hope of advancement and leisure. The others may be equal in sports, but the last rung is barred from even participating.

Instead, the lone opportunity for an African American to utilize his athletic ability ends tragically, when Tom Robinson attempts to escape from prison. Atticus tells his family that Tom "was running. It was during their exercise period. They said he just broke into a blind raving charge at the fence and started climbing over. Right in front of them. . . . They said if he'd had two good arms he'd have made it, he was moving that fast" (*TKAM* 268). Scout, in an effort to conceptualize the how far and fast Tom would have had to run, recalls, "I had seen Enfield Prison farm, and Atticus had pointed out the exercise yard to me. It was the size of a football field" (*TKAM* 270). It is not only instructive that Scout conceptualizes size in terms of football, but also that it is Tom's (or any African American character's at the time) one chance to demonstrate his athletic prowess. However, much the same as Atticus' aforementioned shooting of Tim Johnson, the stakes of this competition are literally life and death. While Tom performs fine on the field itself, it is the fence erected around it that proves to be his undoing.

While the color barrier was broken in major league baseball in 1947 with the debut of Jackie Robinson and was also broken thereabouts in both the National Football League (1946) and the National Basketball Association (1950), major college football in the South was still a whites-only institution at the time of *To Kill a Mockingbird*'s publication in 1960. The fact that it was institutions of higher education enforcing this policy makes segregation all the more scathing and perplexing in retrospect, with some Southern universities going out of their way to avoid playing against teams that fielded African American players. By this time, Northern universities had been integrated for several years, a development that was seen in a different light in the South. At Aunt Alexandra's missionary circle meeting, Miss Merriweather refers to Northerners as "born hypocrites" (*TKAM* 267). She justifies segregation by explaining that "at least [Southerners] don't have that sin on our shoulders down here. People up there set 'em free, but you don't see 'em settin' at the table with 'em. At least we don't have the deceit to say to 'em yes you're as good as we are but stay away from us. Down here we just say live your way and we'll live ours" (*TKAM* 267).

Nevertheless, there was perhaps no better demonstration of the accelerated progress of national integration than major college football. The year after *To Kill a Mockingbird* was published, Syracuse's Ernie Davis became the first African American to win the Heisman Trophy, while Ohio State captured a share of the national championship thanks to African American stars Bob Ferguson, Paul Warfield, and Matt Snell. The other half of the national title was won by the University of Alabama (with an all-white football roster), which was coached by a former teammate of Dixie Howell's: Paul "Bear" Bryant. Bryant's playing career at Alabama (1932–1935; see figure 10.3) effectively parallels the time frame of *To Kill a Mockingbird*, when he was a second-team all-conference receiver. He would go on to win more games than any other college coach in history (figure 10.4),[4] along the way becoming one of the two most famous men in the history of the state.

The other most famous man in Alabama history is George Wallace, who is best known for his "Stand at the Schoolhouse Door," in which he attempted to block the integration of the University of Alabama in 1963. This event was hailed by many as the symbolic end of segregation in the South, as evident in E. Culpepper Clark's historical account, *The Schoolhouse Door: Segregation's Last Stand at the University of Alabama* (Oxford University Press, 1993). But there still remained the equally significant barrier of racial segregation in athletics, with even a figure as powerful as Bryant unable to break the established code.

Figure 10.3.   Paul "Bear" Bryant as a player.

As emphasized by *To Kill a Mockingbird*, such injustices can rarely be immediately rectified. When Jem expresses his displeasure with Alabama's system of letting juries determine capital punishment, he tells Atticus (an elected state representative) that he should "go up to Montgomery and change the law" (*TKAM* 251). Atticus replies, "You'd be surprised how hard that'd be. I won't

Figure 10.4. Bryant as a coach.

live to see the law changed, and if you live to see it you'll be an old man" (*TKAM* 251). The same could certainly have been said at the time about segregation in sports in the South, although its status as a "secret" law—rather than a legitimate one—made it a more readily correctible one, based more on public opinion than on outright legislation and bureaucracy.

The game between Alabama and the University of Southern California (USC) in 1970 would prove to be just such a paradigm-changing moment. Played in Birmingham, the contest saw Alabama trounced 42–21 by USC and its African American fullback Sam Cunningham, who rushed for 135 yards and two touchdowns. After the game, Bryant invited Cunningham into the Alabama locker room so he could show his players "what a real football player looks like," and Cunningham's performance convinced many in the crowd and around the state that integration was both inevitable and necessary. As a result, Alabama assistant coach Jerry Claiborne was quoted as saying, "Sam Cunningham did more to integrate the South in sixty minutes than Martin Luther King did in twenty years" (Yaeger 138). In 1970, running back Wilbur Jackson became the first black athlete to be recruited by Bear Bryant, while the following season transfer John Mitchell became the first African American to play for the Crimson Tide. The change thereafter was startlingly swift: by 1973 (a season in which Alabama won the national title for the first time in eight years) one-third of the team's starters were African American, and by Bryant's last season as coach, 54 of Alabama's 128 players were African American.

Such integration did not, however, end all racial prejudices, as the same general stereotypes about African Americans in *To Kill a Mockingbird* were still visible years later. Scout explains, "To Maycomb, Tom's death was typical. Typical of a nigger to cut and run. Typical of a nigger's mentality to have no plan, no thought for the future, just run blind first chance he saw" (*TKAM* 275). This is reflective of the thought that, even after African Americans were permitted to play major college football in the South and had demonstrated themselves as equal (if not superior) athletes, they were thought unfit to play quarterback, a position that demands superior intellect, planning, and patience. In Bryant's final two seasons as coach, this last barrier was shattered, with Walter Lewis expertly serving as Alabama's starting quarterback from 1981–1983. Just as revealing, when Bryant died in 1983 (twenty-eight days after coaching his last game), Lewis was one of the pallbearers selected to carry Bryant's coffin along with teammate Jeremiah Castille—a pair African Americans entrusted with the body of the most famous white man in what had been the most segregated state in the country (figure 10.5).

In the fifty years since its publication, *To Kill a Mockingbird* has remained an exceedingly relevant work to American culture, partly for the cultural aspects within the book that have changed, but also for those cultural aspects that have

Figure 10.5. Bryant's funeral in 1983, with Walter Lewis on the right and Jeremiah Castille on the far left carrying the coffin.

not changed. Nowhere is this uneasy relationship between progress and tradition more evident than within sports, which in spite of its peripheral status in the novel is central to both the establishment of the book's characters and the placement of the novel in relevant terms for contemporary readers. Making the varsity football team is still often seen as a rite of passage into manhood, and females are still accorded only secondary roles within high school and college football. However, the opportunities that have been generated for girls in other sports, and the overwhelming success of African American athletes at major Southern universities points to a more equitable society, one reflective of much of the progress that Lee advocates in her literary masterpiece.

Notes

1. Indeed, the only non-football magazine Jem is depicted reading in *To Kill a Mockingbird* is *Popular Mechanics* (250), another decidedly popular publication among adolescent boys.
2. All photos in this chapter are reprinted courtesy of the Paul W. Bryant Museum.
3. Instead, African American players played for either integrated teams in the North or for historically black colleges and universities in the South. Many of these schools, such as Grambling University and Southern University, consistently had teams that rivaled the larger schools of the South in terms of talent and sent comparable numbers of players to the NFL.
4. Bryant's record for all-time wins (323) has since been eclipsed on a number of occasions. The record is currently held by Penn State's Joe Paterno, with 394 wins entering the 2010 season, while Florida State's Bobby Bowden (who grew up in Birmingham, Alabama, during the years that *To Kill a Mockingbird* took place and attended the University of Alabama at the same time as Harper Lee) is currently second, with 389 wins.

Works Cited

Lee, Harper. *To Kill a Mockingbird.* 1960. New York: Harper Perennial Modern Classics, 2006.

Messenger, Christian K. "Football as Narrative." *American Literary History* 7.4 (Winter 1995): 726–39.

Oriard, Michael. *Reading Football: How the Popular Press Created an American Spectacle.* Chapel Hill: U North Carolina P, 1993.

Saney, Isaac. "The Case against *To Kill a Mockingbird.*" *Race & Class: A Journal for Black and Third World Liberation* 45.1 (July–September 2003): 99–105.

Shields, Charles J. *Mockingbird: A Portrait of Harper Lee.* New York: Henry Holt and Company, 2006.

Ware, Michele S. "'Just a Lady': Gender and Power in Harper Lee's *To Kill a Mockingbird.*" In *Women in Literature: Reading Through the Lens of Gender.* Ed. Jerilyn Fisher and Ellen S. Silber. Westport, CT: Greenwood Press, 2003. (286–88)

Yaeger, Don. *Turning of the Tide: How One Game Changed the South.* New York: Center Street, 2006.

CHAPTER 11

Symbolic Justice: Reading Symbolism in Harper Lee's *To Kill a Mockingbird*

Jochem Riesthuis

Life in Maycomb, Alabama, the archetypal Southern town that is the setting of Harper Lee's *To Kill a Mockingbird*, is rife with symbolism. Every incident and every occurrence is seen in the light of an ideal, a greater truth. Typical of this tendency to look for the moral of every story is narrator Scout's Aunt Alexandra:

> Aunt Alexandra, in underlining the moral of young Sam Merriweather's suicide, said it was caused by a morbid streak in the family. Let a sixteen-year-old girl giggle in the choir and Aunty would say, "It just goes to show you, all the Penfield women are flighty." Everybody in Maycomb, it seemed, had a Streak: a Drinking Streak, a Gambling Streak, a Mean Streak, a Funny Streak. (*TKAM* 147)

In this manner, each adventure of Scout Finch seems to express some essential truth about the characters, Southern society, morality, or humanity at large. Yet, as the quote above highlights, the truth of the claim "All the Penfield women are flighty" lies as much in the eye of the beholder as in actual occurrences. Since many of the townspeople view life in Maycomb similarly to Aunt Alexandra, life begins to conform itself to those truisms, and thus the truisms seem all the more true. *To Kill a Mockingbird* upsets this delicate cycle by introducing the possibility of seeing things differently.

What Scout slowly learns—from Atticus, from her uncle Jack Finch, from her brother Jem, from Calpurnia, and even from Aunt Alexandra—is not merely tolerance and empathy, to "climb into [another's] skin and walk around in it"

(*TKAM* 33), but, more importantly, to look beyond the so-called tried and true toward new meaning and new ideas of honor and justice. She is learning to question the truth of seeing life in symbols and "streaks." As readers accompany her on this journey of discovery, they observe how Scout comes to see the constructedness of social conventions. While the novel shows Southern life changing toward what, to the reader of 1961, would seem social justice, it is also, in a similarly 1950s–1960s move, "deconstructing" some of the myths and truths supporting the old social order. Such questioning of images, stories, and old truths is echoed in French literary theory of the period, most notably in Roland Barthes' 1957 *Mythologies*.

This essay examines three specific episodes in *To Kill a Mockingbird*: the Tim Johnson episode (part 1, chapter 10), where Atticus shoots a mad dog; Scout's first day of school (part 1, chapters 2 and 3), which highlights the role of reading in the narrative and also introduces the Ewells; and the Dolphus Raymond episode (part 2, chapters 16 and 20), which shows how Mr. Dolphus Raymond uses and deliberately encourages his scandalous reputation. This essay explores the role of each episode in order to determine its function within the larger narrative. Hopefully, this examination will foreground how these episodes enhance or challenge preconceived notions of symbolism, of reading meaning into everyday occurrences, itself.

The Tim Johnson Episode (part 1, chapter 10)

Chapter 10 starts with Scout's description of her father, Atticus Finch, as she compares him to other fathers in Maycomb: "Our father didn't do anything. He worked in an office, not in a drugstore. Atticus did not drive a dump-truck for the county, he was not the sheriff, he did not farm, work in a garage, or do anything that could possibly arouse the admiration of anyone" (*TKAM* 102). What Atticus doesn't do, here, is work in plain sight of everyone, nor does he perform physical labor with his hands. Yet the real problem seems to be not his profession, which is honorable enough, nor his work as a state legislator, for which he is returned in several elections. No, the real problem is with what Atticus does when he is not working or what he does not do: "He did not do the things our schoolmates' fathers did: he never went hunting, he did not play poker or fish or drink or smoke. He sat in the livingroom and read" (*TKAM* 102–103).

Through the embarrassment of his children, Atticus is portrayed as less than a full man. He is described as feeble, blind in one eye, and with glasses, yet at the same time as an intellectual: "Our father didn't do anything. . . . He sat in the livingroom and read." There are echoes here not only of Oblomov, the lethargic central character of Russian author Ivan Goncharov's novel of the same name,[1] but also of Baudelaire's flaneur and modernism's anti-hero. Yet this anti-hero is not some aristocratic Russian on his estate or an independent artist as a young man, wandering the streets of the modern city. However atypical for Maycomb, Atticus is a father and a respected member of Maycomb society.

Thus one of the objectives of chapter 10 is to place Atticus in an unfamiliar role, to show him taking responsibility and presenting himself, however reluctantly, as a man of the South. When Tim Johnson, the mad dog, comes up the road and sheriff Heck Tate forces his gun on Atticus, the latter can no longer hide his innate ability to kill:

> "Take him, Mr. Finch." Mr. Tate handed the rifle to Atticus; Jem and I nearly fainted.
> "Don't waste time, Heck," said Atticus. "Go on."
> "Mr. Finch, this is a one-shot job."
> Atticus shook his head vehemently: "Don't just stand there, Heck! He won't wait all day for you—"
> "For God's sake, Mr. Finch, look where he is! Miss and you'll go straight into the Radley house! I can't shoot that well and you know it!"
> "I haven't shot a gun in thirty years—"
> Mr. Tate almost threw the rifle at Atticus. "I'd feel mighty comfortable if you did now," he said.
> In a fog, Jem and I watched our father take the gun and walk out into the middle of the street. (*TKAM* 109)

In a setting reminiscent of the classic Western, the lone hero steps out into the street to meet his enemy and eliminate him permanently. Never mind the contradictions to heroism that appear in the rather embarrassing scene preceding it, where both Heck Tate and Atticus seem less than manly in their eagerness to pass up this confrontation, each downplaying any ability with a gun they might have. Indeed, Atticus's willingness to leave this one to the "proper authorities" would seem to indicate a lack of belief in himself.

Yet when he gets out in to the street, and the crucial moment arises, he is in control and his body moves seamlessly to his command: "With movements so swift they seemed simultaneous, Atticus's hand yanked a ball-tipped lever as he brought the gun to his shoulder. The rifle cracked" (*TKAM* 110). In the killing of the "beast," but even more in the ability to do so in one shot, Atticus is reaffirming his credentials as a Finch, that is, as a Southern gentleman. In the same swift movements, his action also reaffirms his loyalty to the town of Maycomb by putting his life on the line to protect its citizens.

At the crucial moment, the "movements so swift they seemed simultaneous" (*TKAM* 110) emphasize Atticus's physical being, his masculinity. Unsurprising, then, that we see him discard the symbol of his intellect, his glasses, just before those movements: "Atticus pushed his glasses to his forehead; they slipped down, and he dropped them in the street. In the silence, I heard them crack" (*TKAM* 110). It is not his mind, or even his enhanced vision, that he needs for this task, but his inherent being, his "Finchness" and his body. And yet, when it is all over and the killing is done, Atticus stoops and picks up his glasses, merely grinding the broken lenses to powder. He realizes that he will still need glasses in order to exercise that other side of his personality, his intellect. If one of the messages of this chapter is that Atticus has the inclination of a Southern gentleman as well as the physical courage needed for the coming legal battle, the saving of the specs' frame also shows his determination to keep his ground and symbolizes his belief in his intellect and the rule of law.

Atticus's prowess with a gun astonishes Jem and Scout, much to the amusement of both Heck Tate and Miss Maudie. Yet when Heck starts to expound on Atticus's talent as a marksman, Atticus is quick to silence him. "Hush, Heck," said Atticus, "let's go back to town" (*TKAM* 111). With this, Atticus is deflecting the glory of the kill, leaving it to Miss Maudie to explain both his talent and his behavior in denying it.

> "Maybe I can tell you," said Miss Maudie. "If your father's anything, he's civilized in his heart. Marksmanship's a gift of God, a talent— oh, you have to practice to make it perfect, but shootin's different from playing the piano or the like. I think maybe he put his gun down when he realized God had given him an unfair advantage over most living things. I guess he decided he wouldn't shoot till he had to, and he had to today."
>
> "Look's like he'd be proud of it," I said.
>
> "People in their right minds never take pride in their talents," said Miss Maudie. (*TKAM* 112)

The description of marksmanship as a God-given talent might slightly rattle our postwar sensibilities, but it does seem to accurately describe the general view of Maycomb's residents. In fact, marksmanship is a prerequisite to Atticus's civilization: he needs to be at an unfair advantage to be able to repudiate it. The refusal to take pride in his God-given talent is, at the very least in Miss Maudie's mind, a mere sign of Atticus's sanity. By tying his uncanny marksmanship—considered by society as an aspect of his masculine body—to civilization and right-mindedness, Miss Maudie weds the two divergent aspects of Atticus's persona—his intellectual behavior and his physical courage—into one, a union suitably expressed by his son: "[Jem] called back: 'Atticus is a gentleman, just like me!'" (*TKAM* 113).

While chapter 10 thus serves to establish Atticus as a Southern gentleman, albeit of an unusual cut, it is also a chapter full of foreboding, where danger, disease, mania, and death invade the quiet street where Scout lives. All of this is encapsulated in the figure of Tim Johnson, the old dog walking erratically toward the Radley Place. In the rabies-infected dog, two symbols are combined: on the one hand the well-known Tim Johnson, "the pet of Maycomb" (*TKAM* 105); on the other hand, a mortal danger to any warm-blooded being that crosses his path.

The slow movement of the dog and the way in which Scout rarely describes the dog's behavior itself—she only does so for fourteen sentences in the entire chapter—focusing instead on the reaction his behavior provokes in Jem, Calpurnia, the neighborhood, Heck, and Atticus, increases the symbolic stature of the animal. As with the Albatross in Coleridge's *Rime of the Ancient Mariner*, it is not so much the dog itself, or even the disease he carries, that strikes fear in men's hearts; it is the fact that death itself is in sight. Thus Jem's squinting takes on added significance: "We had gone about five hundred yards beyond the Radley Place when I noticed Jem squinting at something down the street. He had turned his head to one side and was looking out of the corners of his eyes" (*TKAM* 105). "Looking out of the corners of his eyes" may even imply that he considered Tim Johnson as some sort of canine Medusa, which even the tough and cool Jem would not dare look at directly.

The reactions of the adults are even more disturbing. Calpurnia's easy dismissal of Jem's concerns seems to dissipate when he relates what disturbed him so much about Tim Johnson's behavior. In fact, it is not until Calpurnia sees Tim Johnson with her own eyes that the fear grips her: "Calpurnia stared, then grabbed us by the shoulders and ran us home. She shut the wood door behind us, went to the telephone and shouted "Gimme Mr. Finch's office!'" (*TKAM* 106). The immediacy of her response, getting the children out of harm's way and referring the case up to a higher authority, shows just how great her fear of rabies is. Her further actions—shouting at Atticus; talking back to Miss Eula May, the operator; yelling at Scout and Jem; and running over to warn the Radleys of the approaching threat—also demonstrate how truly panicked she is. Similarly, the back and forth between Heck Tate and Atticus about who is going to shoot the dog is highly disturbing. These two towering figures of authority in Scout's narrative are both scared of shooting an old dog. That none of this fear disappears with Tim Johnson's death, as seen in the warnings of Atticus and Zeebo (TKAM 112), makes the diseased dog all the more ominous.

The classic suspense building structure of this chapter, in which description of the response to the danger take precedence over descriptions of the danger itself, is intended to increase the reader's emotional reaction to the episode. Yet by continuing to focus on the response of the neighborhood rather than on the danger they all face, Scout uses a narrative style that at first serves to heighten the tension and then is equally important in dispelling it. The bickering between Miss Maudie and Miss Stephanie that follows the violence and the wicked fun Miss Maudie has in informing Atticus's children of his prowess with a gun serve to reduce a truly frightening episode into just another specimen of Maycomb lore. The symbolic quality of the lone dog confronted by the Law, in the figure of Atticus who takes over when the authorities fail to take responsibility, is thus minimized and reduced to an episode that is merely illustrative of the Finches' Social Conscience Streak. Aunt Alexandra would be proud.

Part 1, chapter 10, then, creates two symbols. First, it depicts the portrayal of Atticus as the Southern gentleman, the title bestowed upon him by his son, an almost Homeric epithet, which endows him with a whole range of heroic qualities. Second, the mad dog Tim Johnson is a sinister reminder of the death, fear, and panic to come. Like Tim Johnson, the town of Maycomb will seem to be moving toward death and destruction, urged on by an invisible force it cannot ignore, nor yet recognize. Ultimately, this episode sets up the coming battle for the soul of Maycomb as a mythical battle between an Homeric hero and the unstoppable force of prejudice and racism. For all the deflating gesturing at the end of the chapter, the image that remains is that of Atticus, standing in the road, waiting for Tim Johnson to move.

Scout's First Day of School (part 1, chapters 2 and 3)

Scout's first day at school, as described in part 1, chapters 2 and 3, is full of confrontation, most notably between Scout and the new teacher, Miss Caroline Fisher. Even if Miss Fischer is just from upstate Alabama, she might as well have been from another country:

> Miss Caroline printed her name on the blackboard and said, "This says I am Miss Caroline Fisher. I am from North Alabama, from Winston County." The class murmured apprehensively, should she prove to harbor her share of the peculiarities indigenous to that region. (When Alabama seceded from the Union on January 11, 1861, Winston County seceded from Alabama, and every child in Maycomb County knew it.) North Alabama was full of Liquor Interests, Big Mules, steel companies, Republicans, professors, and other persons of no background. (*TKAM* 18)

What is interesting in Scout's description of the peculiarities of that region is that it begins with Liquor Interests and Big Mules, two elements of the Alabama political scene that Scout might be familiar with as the daughter of a representative, but that might not be common knowledge to "every child in Maycomb County." Nonetheless, what is represented in the apprehension of the whole student body in their first encounter with Miss Caroline is the distaste of the farmer for industry and of the countryside for the city. Winston County may have been on the side of victory and may indeed represent the future, but that doesn't stop Maycomb from resenting the area and all it stands for. Thus, its residents are "othered" and considered suspicious and untrustworthy. Yet while Winston County may be just a stand-in for the hated North, it is also a force in state politics and a rival one at that. In fact, Scout's inadvertent slipping in of terms from the *Maycomb Tribune*'s editorial page betrays a political rivalry between the industrial bourgeoisie of the big cities and the agricultural "aristocracy" of the rural communities.

At the same time, Miss Caroline Fisher represents the future, the change that is coming. As Jem describes it,

> Our teacher says Miss Caroline's introducing a new way of teaching. She learned about it in college. It'll be in all the grades soon. You don't have to learn much out of books that way—it's like if you wanta learn about cows, you go milk one, see? . . .
> I'm just trying to tell you the new way they're teaching the first grade stubborn. It's the Dewey Decimal System." *(TKAM* 20)

For all of his misunderstanding and mixing up John and Melvil Dewey, Jem's grasp of the change occurring in their school is accurate, much to the Scout's chagrin: "As I inched sluggishly along the treadmill of the Maycomb County school system, I could not help receiving the impression that I was being cheated out of something" (*TKAM* 37). In her rejection of the new way of teaching, Scout seems to be rejecting modernity itself and expressing a wish to return to a time before public schooling reached the depths of Maycomb County. As she explains it to her father, "You never went to school and you do all right, so I'll just stay home too. You can teach me like Grandaddy taught you 'n' Uncle Jack" (*TKAM* 32).

Yet the main reason for Scout's rejection of Miss Caroline Fisher and her version of John Dewey's ideas lies primarily in their confrontation over literacy on Scout's first day in a public school classroom. Hoping to teach the children something about writing and written language, Miss Caroline prints the alphabet on the blackboard. As most of the class is repeating the first grade, she's not showing them anything new, though she is unaware of this fact. When Miss

Carline then chooses Scout to read aloud what it says on the blackboard, the trouble starts:

> I suppose she chose me because she knew my name; as I read the alphabet a faint line appeared between her eyebrows, and after making me read most of *My First Reader* and the stock-market quotations from *The Mobile Register* aloud, she discovered that I was literate and looked at me with more than faint distaste. Miss Caroline told me to tell my father not to teach me any more, it would interfere with my reading. (*TKAM* 19)

Rather than accepting Scout's precocious ability as a given, Miss Caroline sees her as an abnormal freak and as a threat to her dream of lifting her schoolchildren out of ignorance. After all, by already being able to read, Scout is not only separate from the other children in her class, but she is also closed to the influence of the new teaching method, which requires children to have an open mind. In the same way that Miss Caroline is symbolic of Scout's inevitable disappointment with formal learning, Scout becomes symbolic of Miss Caroline's disgust with the haphazard educational system in Maycomb that produces both the ignorant children she sees before her and this highly literate Scout.

Reading, which had seemed an innate ability to Scout, suddenly turns out to be something learned, an acquired ability. According to Miss Caroline and the Maycomb County school system, Scout has acquired this ability not only illegally but also somehow "wrongly." As noted previously, Scout discovers that reading with Atticus apparently "would interfere with my reading" (*TKAM* 19). Thus, the introduction of a "foreigner" into Scout's world-perspective produces a new way of seeing the world as a whole. Unfortunately, it is a way in which what was natural and unfettered becomes bound by rules and restrictions. Thus, Scout's remedy for the long hours of church—the innocent reading of hymns—becomes an illegal activity. Similarly, Calpurnia's strict writing instruction—"In Calpurnia's teaching, there was no sentimentality: I seldom pleased her and she seldom rewarded me" (*TKAM* 21)—becomes the overindulgence of a peculiar child's unnatural interests.

However, Scout is not quite ready to give up her enjoyment of the written word. Instead, she appeals to Atticus, "And she said you taught me all wrong, so we can't ever read anymore, ever. Please don't send me back, please sir" (*TKAM* 33). Atticus's responses to this plea is to teach Scout how to compromise with the authority's rules, rather than either obeying or directly disobeying, and thus they strike a deal: "If you'll concede the necessity of going to school, we'll go on reading every night just as we always have. Is it a bargain?" (*TKAM* 35). The line Atticus takes, where the rules about going to school do not entail following all of its prescriptions in one's private life, teaches Scout that there's no need to bend one's convictions, even in the light of overwhelming authority.

Scout learns that Maycomb's ways are not natural, but merely a set of conventions, as arbitrary as those of Winston County. Suddenly, convictions are one's own and are beyond any stricture, yet any claims of Truth, Intelligence, and Naturalness can rest on no more than local customs or family traditions. In other words, if Miss Caroline with all her education is not necessarily right, neither is Atticus with all his experience. The main difference between the two, the narrative implies, is that Atticus is aware of this.

Scout's ability to read is not limited to her literacy, as she is also, in this description of her first day, able to accurately "read" her classmates, as shown in the example of Walter Cunningham. When Miss Caroline tries to lend Walter a quarter to buy lunch downtown and he refuses, it is clear to everyone but Miss Caroline why he does so. Scout, after some prodding by her classmates, decides to provide her teacher with an explanation:

> I rose graciously on Walter's behalf: "Ah—Miss Caroline?"
> "What is it, Jean Louise?"
> "Miss Caroline, he's a Cunningham."
> I sat back down.
> "What, Jean Louise?"
> I thought I had made things sufficiently clear. It was clear enough to the rest of us: Walter Cunningham was sitting there lying his head off. He didn't forget his lunch, he didn't have any. He had none today nor would he have any tomorrow or the next day. He had probably never seen three quarters together at the same time in his life. (*TKAM* 22)

While accepting the responsibility of explaining Walter's predicament, Scout is also taking on a role as spokesperson for the district. Yet even while Scout is able to quickly read Walter's predicament, the new element of Miss Caroline has Scout stumped. The phrase "he's a Cunningham" means nothing to Miss Caroline, and Scout does not quite understand why it doesn't explain everything, as it does for her and "the rest of us." Although she tries again to explain, she realizes that she is not up to the task—"it was beyond my ability to explain things as well as Atticus" (*TKAM* 24)—and Miss Caroline duly punishes her. That punishment may seem unjust since Scout was merely trying to help, but it does bring home the message that reading, whether of texts or of people, is not without danger, and if one gets it wrong, there is a price to pay.

Scout's first day of school also brings the introduction of the Ewells, another tribe from the outskirts of Maycomb, like the Cunninghams, but without the scruples. Burris Ewell, the specimen in Scout's class, may be only be in first grade, yet the danger he poses is clear:

> Miss Caroline said, "Sit back down, please, Burris," and the moment she said it I knew she had made a serious mistake. The boy's condescension flashed to anger.
> "You try and make me, missus."
> Little Chuck Little got to his feet. "Let him go, ma'am," he said. "He's a mean one, a hard-down mean one. He's liable to start somethin', and there's some little folks here."
> He was amongst the most diminutive of men, but when Burris Ewell turned toward him, Little Chuck's right hand went to his pocket. "Watch your step, Burris," he said. "I'd soon's kill you as look at you. Now go home."
> Burris seemed to be afraid of a child half his height, and Miss Caroline took advantage of his indecision: "Burris, go home. If you don't I'll call the principal." . . . Safely out of range, [Burris] turned and shouted: "Report and be damned to ye! Ain't no snot-nosed slut of a schoolteacher ever born c'n make me do notin'!" (*TKAM* 30–31)

The Ewells are the classic villains of *To Kill a Mockingbird*, with Mayella Ewell as Tom Robinson's accuser and her father, Bob Ewell, as the attacker of Jem and Scout in the final episode. Burris here lives up to the type, menacing and hateful, but easily scared and cowed by any genuine resistance, even from the "most diminutive of men." Burris Ewell—and by extension all of the Ewells, who "had been the disgrace of Maycomb for three generations" (*TKAM* 33)—is shown to be repulsive physically as well as morally. Yet Burris is also a pitiful figure, who lacks a mother and whose "paw's right contentious" (*TKAM* 30). There is no one to take care of Burris or to show him any kindness. Indeed, there is no one even to wash him, and Scout relates that he is "the filthiest human I had ever seen" (*TKAM* 29). While Miss Caroline is eager to see Burris wash himself—and especially his hair, which is crawling with lice—she also lets her repulsion and her fear inform her view of the boy. Thus, when Chuck Little threatens to kill Burris, there's surprisingly not a word of protest from their mutual teacher, cowering behind her desk. Thus, this little episode shows the ugly side of Maycomb, not just in the Ewells, but also in the complete rejection of them by the rest of the town. It is as if no one would mind if one or all of the Ewells got killed or hurt, as long as it was done by another white person.

Only Atticus seems aware of the tragedy as well as the horror of the Ewells: "They were people, but they lived like animals" (*TKAM* 33). Unfortunately, his attitude is similar to the rest of the "common folk" who "allowed them certain privileges by the simple method of becoming blind to some of the Ewells' activities" (*TKAM* 34). Yet, unlike most of the town, Atticus does not become blind to their common humanity, as witnessed both in his explanation to Scout and in his cross-examination of Mayella Ewell during Tom Robinson's trial.

The Dolphus Raymond Episode (part 2, chapters 16 and 20)

Mr. Dolphus Raymond is first introduced in chapter 16, as part of the crowd that comes to town to watch the spectacle of Tom Robinson's trial and, indeed, to observe Atticus's defense of him. Among the Mennonites, Mr. X Billups— "X's his name, not his initial" (*TKAM* 180)—Mr. Tensaw Jones, Miss Emily Davis, Mr. Byron Waller, Mr. Jake Slade, and the foot-washing Baptists that confront Miss Maudie over her flowers, Mr. Raymond hardly stands out. It is only his drinking that gets noticed: "Mr. Dolphus Raymond lurched by on his thoroughbred. 'Don't see how he stays in the saddle,' murmured Jem. 'How c'n you stand to get drunk 'fore eight in the morning?'" (*TKAM* 180). Yet, even here, long before the whole story of Mr. Raymond gets presented, there is the curious mismatch between the drunken lurching and riding a thoroughbred, seeming to indicate degeneration in a wealthy family.

At the "gala occasion" (*TKAM* 182) of the trial, Mr. Dolphus Raymond is seen again, sitting with the Negroes in the far corner of the square, drinking through two yellow straws out of a paper bag. That in itself is enough to raise Dill's curiosity: "'Ain't ever seen anybody do that,' murmured Dill. 'How does he keep what's in it in it?' (*TKAM* 182). When Jem explains there is a Coca-Cola bottle inside, full of whiskey, Dill moves on to the next question: "Why's he sittin' with the colored folks?" (*TKAM* 183). Again, Jem explains, first by saying that Mr. Raymond likes "'em better'n he likes us" (*TKAM* 183), before giving a full history of his life. Thus Dill's curiosity leads to a fuller picture of Mr. Dolphus Raymond. Yet since all the explanation comes from Jem, without the usual commentary from either Atticus or Miss Maudie to take down the drama a peg or two, the emphasis is on how Raymond's erstwhile bride killed herself, rather than any choices Mr. Raymond made since that moment.

Still, the romantic figure of Mr. Dolphus Raymond that emerges from Jem's narrative is in itself symbolic of the harshness of life, and especially of life in a small Southern town, where condemnation and interference are never far away. Jem's tale of Mr. Raymond suggests that he is primarily a tragic figure, who lives with the Negroes because his history makes him unfit to live in harmony with so-called normal society, and more tragic yet is the fact that his children are sent up North because neither "colored" nor "white folk" will have them. Thus, Mr.

Dolphus Raymond represents a warning to those who would cross the color line: banishment from one's own society and condemnation to an uneasy life among the colored folk.

Yet, this is not all there is to Mr. Dolphus, as becomes clear when Scout makes his acquaintance personally after taking the crying Dill away from the hustle and bustle of the courtroom. As Mr. Raymond offers Dill a sip from his paper sack, it is discovered that in fact it contains "nothing but Coca-Cola" (*TKAM* 227). But Mr. Raymond does more than simply expose his paper sack trick; he also explains why he does it:

> "You mean why do I pretend? Well, it's very simple," he said. "Some folks don't—like the way I live. Now I could say the hell with 'em, I don't care if they don't like it. I do say I don't care if they don't like it, right enough-but I don't say the hell with 'em, see? . . . I try to give 'em a reason, you see. It helps folks if they can latch onto a reason. When I come to town, which is seldom, if I weave a little and drink out of this sack, folks can say Dolphus Raymond's in the clutches of whiskey—that's why he won't change his ways. He can't help himself, that's why he lives the way he does." (*TKAM* 228)

It is interesting that Mr. Raymond's description of what "they" say of him, matches reasonably closely what Jem reported at the pre-trial "gala occasion." Therefore Mr. Raymond seems to have a pretty astute view of the way Maycomb works, and his final reason for pretending to be a drunk—"They could never, never understand that I live like do because that's the way I want to live" (*TKAM* 228)—would then also be the truth. The ugliness that the trial has already shown, and is yet to bring, is rooted in the same opinion that caused Mr. Dolphus Raymond's expulsion from Maycomb's polite society. As Atticus describes it when he explains "nigger-lover" to Scout, "Ignorant, trashy people use it [the term] when they think somebody's favoring Negroes over and above themselves. It's slipped into usage with some people like ourselves, when they want a common, ugly term to label somebody" (*TKAM* 124).

Yet what Mr. Raymond's example shows is a rejection of favoring Negroes over whites by the whole town, not just by "ignorant trashy people." Thus Mr. Raymond's example, more than the actions of the mob that want to run the jail, the name-calling, or even Ewell's attack on Jem and Scout, symbolizes Maycomb's belief, however much hidden in Maycomb truths, in what Atticus calls "the evil assumption—that *all* Negroes lie, that *all* Negroes are basically immoral beings, that *all* Negro men are not to be trusted around our women" (*TKAM* 232). It is in Mr. Dolphus Raymond that Harper Lee confronts her readers with how much further they may yet have to travel before they are able to truly reject Atticus's "evil assumption."

Mr. Dolphus Raymond seems, however, to be less tragic than Jem originally represents him. He chooses to reject the life that was planned for him because he likes living the way he does. Rather than being ostracized over drinking and his bad behavior, Mr. Raymond uses his Coca-Cola to trick the town into giving him the freedom he craves.

Yet even Coca-Cola is not innocent in the complicated caste system that is Maycomb County: only the "more affluent chased their food with drug-store Coca-Cola" (*TKAM* 182), while others drink warm milk from fruit jars, and the Negroes, sitting together with Mr. Dolphus Raymond, drink "the more vivid flavors of Nehi Cola" (*TKAM* 182). Even in his rejection of the upper crust of Maycomb society, Mr. Raymond's tastes still reflect theirs, as symbolized by his choice of an "innocent" beverage.

More importantly, in his defense of his behavior, Mr. Raymond never seems to wonder what the effect of his choices are on the people he chooses to live among. From Jem's story, for what it is worth, there is some indication that there is a long and loving relationship with the African American woman he is living with, but how much can we rely on that? And even if Mr. Raymond has such long-lasting loving feelings for her, how much freedom does she ever feel to reject him? All such questions remain unexplored by the text, as Mr. Dolphus Raymond, for all his fascinating position and behavior, is no more than a minor character in a large cast.

Yet, as an unreformed sinner who flaunts his drinking and lives with a Negro woman and their children, Mr. Dolphus Raymond represents the most blatant, visible rejection of Maycomb's mores and truths. No wonder, then, that once Scout makes contact with this mythical degenerate, she is loath to leave him, even for the spectacle of Atticus's closing arguments: "Between two fires, I could not decide which I wanted to jump into: Mr. Raymond or the 5th Judicial Circuit Court" (*TKAM* 229).

Conclusion

In *To Kill a Mockingbird* these three episodes are not the pivotal points in the narrative. For that we would have to look at the scene outside the jailhouse or examine the trial and the eventual murder of Tom Robinson. Yet the three episodes show the development of Scout's ability to challenge the conventions of Maycomb, to see her father in a new light, and to "play the system." Thus they constitute essential elements in *To Kill a Mockingbird* that establish it as a bildungsroman as well as a social commentary.

The three scenes question the status quo in 1930s Alabama and interrogate the present-day world as well. In these episodes, the narrative does not avoid the difficult questions that lie beyond the good/bad equation. In the Tim Johnson episode, notions about masculinity, Southern honor, and premonitions are challenged, while during Scout's first day of school, she and the reader are confronted by the fact that conventional wisdom doesn't travel very well when it is given close, firsthand inspection. Finally, the Mr. Dolphus Raymond episode shows ways to play the system, but be warned: you cannot fool all of the people all the time.

Thus *To Kill a Mockingbird* creates and uses symbols to great effect, while at the same time drawing our attention to how these myths are little more that social constructions, and are not to be confused with actual truth. Lee's novel posits uncomfortable questions and positions and demands attention, not just to convince us to do the right thing but to challenge the ease with which we reject individuals and whole peoples.

Note

1. Oblomov is a young, generous nobleman who seems incapable of making important decisions or undertaking any significant actions. Throughout the novel, he rarely leaves his room and famously fails to leave his bed for the first 150 pages of the novel of the same name The book was considered a satire of Russian nobility whose social and economic function was increasingly in question in mid-nineteenth-century Russia.

Works Cited

Barthes, Roland. *Mythologies*. Trans. Annette Lavers. New York: Hill and Wang Farrar, Straus and Giroux, 1999.

Goncharov, Ivan. *Oblomov*. Trans. David Magarshack. London: Penguin Books, 1996.

Lee, Harper. *To Kill a Mockingbird*. 1960. New York: Harper Perennial Modern Classics, 2006.

CHAPTER 12

Walking in Another's Skin: Failure of Empathy in *To Kill a Mockingbird*

Katie Rose Guest Pryal

Early in Harper Lee's 1960 novel *To Kill a Mockingbird*, Atticus Finch gives his daughter Scout some advice, advice that frames the entire story: "You never really understand a person until you consider things from his point of view . . . until you climb into his skin and walk around in it" (*TKAM* 33). Because racial conflict plays a central role in *Mockingbird*, this advice to try on another's "skin" takes on great significance. Arguably, the jurors convict the innocent black man, Tom Robinson, for the rape of the white Mayella Ewell because they refuse to walk around in a black person's skin. Thus they fail to follow Atticus's admonition to practice empathy. Indeed, scholars often point to empathy as the central theme of the novel. For example, Mary Ellen Maatman suggests that *Mockingbird* "emphasizes the significance of empathy in moral development" (210–11). Still other scholars point to Atticus as the model of an empathetic character. Robin Winter writes that Finch possesses "the unwavering powers of courage, empathy, and moral fortitude to fight against racial prejudice" (548), while Maatman suggests that "Atticus Finch repeatedly emphasizes the importance of empathy for others" (211). But this praise of Atticus—and of the novel—is not universal among its readers.

Indeed, respondents have critiqued both the character Atticus and *Mockingbird* itself for a lack of empathetic qualities. Most recently, author Malcolm Gladwell addressed this point in the August 2009 issue of the *New Yorker*. According to Gladwell, Atticus does not take on Tom Robinson's case because he empathizes with the plight of black people in Alabama; rather, Gladwell argues,

Finch practices "old-style Southern liberalism" that was "gradual and paternalistic" (para. 7). He goes on to argue that Finch refuses to "look at the problem of racism outside of the immediate context" of his friends and neighbors in Maycomb (para. 15), and that Atticus was not a civil rights worker at all, despite how he has been cast in America's popular imagination. For Gladwell, Atticus takes a "hearts-and-minds approach" to Tom's rape charge, and this approach Gladwell considers to be basically "accommodation, not reform" (para. 13). As his essay continues, Gladwell calls Atticus to task for not fighting against the injustice of Tom's conviction and for failing to mount an appeal in Tom's defense. Drawing a connection with Charles Dickens, Gladwell demonstrates how Lee's portrayal of Atticus (and perhaps even the novel itself) suggests that systemic injustices in the legal system "could be tamed through small moments of justice" and through "changing hearts" (para. 27). By contending that Atticus has no desire to "endanger the status quo" (para. 27), Gladwell reveals that while Atticus might have felt sympathy for Tom and the other black people of Maycomb, he does not practice the empathy that so many associate with the novel's thematic emphasis.

Empathy—how it is discussed and deployed by both the characters in *Mockingbird* and by the author, Lee—is a useful lens to view the depictions of racial injustice in *Mockingbird*, because empathy is the moral fulcrum on which the narrative turns. In fact, each moment of tension in the book is driven by attempts to practice empathy: Jem's relationship with the dying Mrs. Dubose, the late-night confrontation at the jail in which Scout forces the group to empathize with Atticus (if not with Tom), and even the moment when Atticus shoots the rabid dog and mourns the passing of the sick animal. In particular, empathy across racial lines poses a challenge to the judge and jury in Tom's case. The scenes in and around the courtroom best reveal the power that empathy holds over us as individuals and as a society. All citizens implicitly endorse our legal system and believe that it acts on our behalf. Since this system sends some individuals to prison and others to their death, it follows that we must take responsibility for these punishments. Developing this sense of responsibility, I believe, is a central message of Lee's novel.

In this essay, I argue that *To Kill a Mockingbird* fails to aptly demonstrate the practice of cross-racial empathy. As a consequence, readers cannot empathize with the (largely silent) black characters of the novel. In order to examine the concept of empathy, I have developed a critical framework derived from Kenneth Burke's theory of identification and then used this framework to examine some ways in which empathy manifests itself in our legal system, manifestations that help reveal the failings of *Mockingbird*. Three scenes from Lee's novel are relevant—the standoff at the jail, the trial of Tom Robinson, and the Finch children's trip to Calpurnia's church—to ask whether Lee's novel successfully persuades its audience to practice cross-racial empathy, to "walk in another's skin." Although I ultimately conclude that *Mockingbird* fails in this task, there is at least one moment in the text that offers the potential to build a bridge of cross-racial empathy.

Defining Empathy

The disagreement among scholars over whether *Mockingbird* demonstrates empathy arises, at least in part, from the lack of an agreed-upon understanding of the term. "Empathy," as defined by the *Oxford English Dictionary*, is "the power of projecting one's personality into (and so fully comprehending) the object of contemplation" ("Empathy"). This definition aligns with the metaphor Atticus uses in his advice to Scout, to place one's mind inside the skin of another. Practicing empathy, however, is a risky endeavor for both the empathizers and the objects of empathy. The empathizers must leave themselves and inhabit, if only briefly, the skin (body, life) of the objects. The objects, in turn, must allow this projection to occur, opening themselves to a kind of invasion. For example, for a jury member sitting in a criminal trial, especially a trial of a violent crime, empathizing with a defendant might mean stepping inside the mind of a monster, a terrifying prospect.

Another type of fear might prevent jurors from empathizing with a defendant, especially in a trial like the one in *Mockingbird*. White jurors might fear that viewing the world—and themselves—from a black defendant's point of view will reveal ugly characteristics about themselves that the jurors would rather ignore, unwilling to face what I will call a "fear of revelation." The U.S. Supreme Court has addressed the problem of the all-white jury as recently as 1985 and lower courts even more recently. Given this context, fear of revelation and cross-racial empathy in the courtroom are important subjects of scrutiny. Just as fear of revelation stifles the possibility of empathy between white jurors and black defendants, it also plagues *Mockingbird*'s efforts to inspire cross-racial empathy in its readers. Rarely do the black characters in the novel express how they feel about Maycomb's culture of white supremacy; nor do white citizens express interest in hearing about these feelings. This disinterest, mingled with fear, ultimately stands in the way of cross-racial empathy.

Often, "empathy" is confused with "sympathy." Empathy entails the desire and ability to understand the plight of another person *from that person's point of view*. Sympathy does not require employing another's perspective. To practice sympathy only requires the feeling of pity for another's plight. It requires none of the projection required by empathy and therefore creates none of the psychic risk. In *Mockingbird*, Atticus suggests that we should empathize with others, but what he most often models, I suggest, is merely sympathy. For example, were

Atticus to walk around in Tom's skin after Tom was found guilty, he would, as Gladwell writes, "be brimming with rage at the unjust verdict" (para. 11).

In order to understand how *Mockingbird* fails to demonstrate empathy, we need a full understanding of how empathy works in practice. I suggest that empathy is something we must *do*, not merely something we feel. In *A Rhetoric of Motives*, Kenneth Burke provides a way to think about the practice and effects of empathy. Burke's term for empathetic practice is "identification." Identification occurs when one's "interests are joined" with another's interests (Burke 20). Even when two parties are identified, however, they retain the power of their separate selves: "In being identified with B, A is 'substantially one' with a person other than himself. Yet at the same time he remains unique, an individual locus of motives. Thus he is both joined and separate, at once a distinct substance and consubstantial with another" (21). The practice of identification can be powerful because the parties draw from their combined strength *and* from the strength of their individual identities.

As I will show, rather than identifying—empathizing—with Tom, Atticus merely sympathizes. Worse, he subsumes Tom within his own identity when he takes on legal representation of Tom. Were Atticus to empathize, he would have to believe that what is at stake for Tom is substantially similar to what is at stake for himself were he in Tom's skin. One might question whether a white lawyer in the Jim Crow South could ever identify with a black person because black people and white people were in substantially different positions in the eyes of the law. For example, Mayella Ewell would never have been able to bring such empty charges of rape against Atticus for reasons of both class and race. Similarly, within the confines of the novel, it is nearly inconceivable that Atticus could ever encounter a situation where he would stand in a position substantially similar to that of Tom. At its best moments, *Mockingbird* raises these kinds of questions about the roles of lawyers and judges. Can a lawyer identify with his client? Should he? Can a judge identify with the parties to a case? Should she?

Empathy and Our Legal System

In order to answer these questions, we must explore what role empathy plays in the delivery of justice in the United States. An examination of two moments of legal debate in which empathy came to the fore will be helpful in developing a framework for examining the practice of empathy in *Mockingbird*.

The first instance of empathy in law that will be examined occurred in the Supreme Court race discrimination case *McCleskey v. Kemp* (1987). In his dissenting opinion in *McCleskey*, Justice William Brennan attempted to describe the role that empathy should play in criminal sentencing, particularly death penalty sentencing.[1] Justice Brennan suggested that a lack of cross-racial empathy enables the majority of U.S. society to endorse capital punishment despite the proven existence of racism in capital sentencing.[2] After declaring that capital punishment is cruel and unusual punishment, Brennan writes,

> It is tempting to pretend that minorities on death row share a fate in no way connected to our own, that our treatment of them sounds no echoes beyond the chambers in which they die. Such an illusion is ultimately corrosive, for the reverberations of injustice are not so easily confined . . . the way in which we choose those who will die reveals the depth of moral commitment among the living. (McCleskey 345)

Justice Brennan chastised those who ignore the suffering of black death row inmates such as Warren McCleskey because of an unwillingness to see any human connection with them. Justice Brennan implied that this unwillingness to connect—to empathize—is a willful blindness, a "pretending." One might suggest further that this blindness is driven by fear: fear that our safe position of superiority might crumble if we recognize the agonistic humanity of the supposed monster before us. This is a prime example of a fear of revelation: we would rather ignore the accused than view ourselves through his eyes. Justice Brennan's words remind us that our fates are indeed tied to those of inmates on death row; we are interconnected despite our reluctance to admit it.

Brennan's words might have been directed at the very jurors that convicted Tom Robinson in *Mockingbird*: "It is tempting to pretend that minorities [who are criminal defendants] share a fate in no way connected to our own." But this argument for empathy, for interconnection, is not the argument Atticus makes. He does not suggest that the lives of the jurors have anything to do with the life of Tom Robinson. Instead, he suggests that (1) the Ewells are untrustworthy; (2) that Tom is "honest"; and (3) that the courts are the only "human institution that makes a pauper the equal of a Rockefeller" (*TKAM* 233) and, by implication, a black man the equal of a white man. Instead of evoking empathy and compassion, Atticus tells the jury that he is "confident that you gentlemen will review without passion the evidence you have heard" (233). He appeals to reason and logic rather than emotion, fearing that emotion will lead to a conviction. Perhaps Atticus's strategy would be the most likely and the most effective one for earning an acquittal in a case like Tom's. Be that as it may, however, it was not a strategy driven by empathy.

The second instance of empathy in law occurred more recently, upon the retirement of Supreme Court Justice William Souter in April 2009. After Souter announced that he would be leaving the Court, President Obama described how he would select his Supreme Court nominee. Obama's speech has spawned what pundits called "the empathy standard" (Brown para. 1). Obama declared, "I will seek someone who understands that justice isn't about some abstract legal theory or footnote in a case book. It is also about how our laws affect the daily realities of people's lives—whether they can make a living and care for their families; whether they feel safe in their homes and welcome in their own nation" (Obama para. 5). For Obama, empathy means recognizing how the abstract rules of law affect particular people and adjusting those rules to reach a just outcome. Obama's critics suggest that judges who practice empathy may deliver judicial decisions contrary to law.

According to Stanley Fish, the problem lies in the difference between decisions that are "just" and those that are "legal." Fish writes, "Just outcomes would be nice and let's hope we have some, but [Obama's critics argue that] what courts should deliver is legal outcomes" (para. 3). Critics fear that empathy will result in results-oriented judging that sets aside legal precedent if need be. Given the call by Amnon Reichman and other legal scholars to study how all people— not just judges—make "empathetic judgments," understanding the relationship between empathy and judging takes on a greater importance (303). For these legal scholars, and for Obama, real justice is empathetic, not abstract or blind. Using Obama's empathy standard to look at Atticus's closing arguments, we see once again that he has not appealed to empathy. Instead, Atticus requests blind justice from the jurors.

From what we have examined here, we see that there are at least two aspects of empathy important to law. First, there is Justice Brennan's "interconnectedness," that is, recognizing the connections between ourselves and even the most despicable criminals, since we are all members of the same community. Second, there is Obama's demand that judges be able to recognize how the great power of the law affects each person in a unique way, to be able to climb inside the skin of each party that stands before a judge. Reichman and others modify this demand by claiming that all people, not just judges, should practice empathic judging.[3] For Reichman, empathy can "enhance our ability of understanding the nuanced significance of [a legal] conclusion" (308).

The need for this nuanced understanding of the effects of law on those different from ourselves is greatest when we are faced with moments of deep social upheaval. *To Kill a Mockingbird* (1960) was published at the height of the American civil rights movement. The federal Civil Rights Act was passed four years later in 1964; the Voting Rights Act in 1965. Significantly, the novel is set in the 1930s, at the depths of America's economic depression, in Alabama, one of the most economically depressed states in the United States. Given this historical context, *Mockingbird* can be read as a means for white, middle-class people of the 1960s to engage emotionally—but peripherally—with America's racial injustice. Because the novel rarely encourages readers to empathize with Tom or the other black characters, white readers do not have to view this injustice through the eyes of black folks; in other words, for white readers, there is no risk of revelation. Furthermore, the novel depicts the "bad old days" of egregious racism and racial violence, when lynch mobs operated with the implicit endorsement of the state. Compared to the bad old days of the novel, twenty-first-century racism is nigh invisible.

Atticus tells Scout that she should strive to empathize with the folks she encounters in everyday life. But he often fails to follow his own advice. In the episodes of the novel examined in the following pages, readers can observe moments in *To Kill a Mockingbird* in which the characters might practice empathy. These studies reveal that, for the most part, the novel fails to model cross-racial empathy and further suggest that this failure can be attributed to fear of revelation. I will examine these scenes for moments when the novel (1) demonstrates interconnectedness; (2) privileges empathetic judging over "blind" judging; and (3) overcomes white fear of revelation in order to more honestly portray black characters. These three "elements" of empathy, however, cannot truly be considered as separate practices, as the readings that follow will show.

The Face-Off at the Jail

An examination of the lynch mob scene at the Maycomb jail using the three-part framework just described reveals that Scout helps the mob to recognize its interconnectedness with Atticus, revealing a bond that results in the mob's dispersal. This recognition saves the Finches and the man they have come to protect, Tom. The empathetic judgment demonstrated by the lynch mob, however, is limited to the white characters, and therefore the scene never truly challenges white fear of revelation. In fact, Tom is invisible in the scene, nearly voiceless. This scene ultimately treats Tom as a bone over which the white people fight rather than as a full-blown character.

The face-off occurs the night before Tom's trial begins. Earlier that day, Tom is moved to the jail in downtown Maycomb. When Maycomb county sheriff Heck Tate comes to warn Atticus about the risk of violence against Tom, Atticus responds by diminishing Heck's warning: "Don't be foolish, Heck. . . . This is Maycomb" (*TKAM* 165). When Heck says that he is "uneasy," Atticus replies, "I don't think anybody in Maycomb'll begrudge me a client, with times this hard" (165). Atticus seems to rely upon the small-town good will that other citizens feel toward him to protect his black client from being lynched. Atticus implies that lynching Tom, when the economy is rocky, would be impolite to Atticus. As Gladwell points out, Atticus displays a surprising nonchalance toward racial violence; Gladwell attributes this nonchalance to insularity: "Finch will stand up to racists. He'll use his moral authority to shame them into silence.

. . . What he will not do is look at the problem of racism outside the immediate context of . . . the island community of Maycomb" (para. 15). I believe that Atticus's inability or unwillingness to see racism as a large-scale problem is yet another manifestation of his failure of empathy. He cannot see the connections between the unsuccessful lynch mob in Maycomb and the horrific lynchings that took place in other parts of the South.

Despite his skepticism that a lynch mob will come after Tom, Atticus goes to the jail the evening before the trial. He brings a chair, a lamp, and a newspaper and sits outside the jail, reading. Scout, the narrator; her older brother, Jem; and their friend Dill sneak downtown to check on Atticus. Jem, knowing a little more about racial politics, is worried about his father. As the children watch from a hiding place, four cars pull up in front of the jail. A large group of white men, mostly rural and poor, emerge from the cars. Scout describes the scene:

> "He in there, Mr. Finch?" a man said.
> "He is," we heard Atticus answer, "and he's asleep. Don't wake him up."
> In obedience to my father, there followed what I later realized was a sickening comic aspect of an unfunny situation: the men talked in near-whispers.
> "You know what we want," another man said. "Get aside from the door, Mr. Finch." (*TKAM* 171–72)

Atticus appears calm while facing the lynch mob. Maintaining a tone of authority, he relies upon his superiority of class and education to gain control of the mob. They are poor; he is wealthy. They are farmers who work with their hands; he is a lawyer who works with his mind. They live in the country; he lives in the city. They are largely illiterate and speak ungrammatical English; he reads while waiting for them and speaks perfect English during the confrontation.

Although Atticus's power successfully keeps the men quiet and forces them to pause in their mission, it is Scout who convinces them to leave. The man who commands Atticus to step aside is Walter Cunningham, a man known to the Finch family. Walter is a client of Atticus, and his son, Walter Jr., is a schoolmate of Scout. Recognizing Mr. Cunningham, Scout emerges from her hiding place to speak to him, disrupting the standoff. She treats the man with respect, calling him "Mr. Cunningham," and attempts to discuss his legal problems with him. She persists even though he ignores her at first. Eventually he responds to her kindly:

> Then he did a peculiar thing. He squatted down and took me by both shoulders.
> "I'll tell him [Walter Jr.] you said hey, little lady," he said.

> Then he straightened up and waved a big paw. "Let's clear out,"
> he called. "Let's get going, boys." (*TKAM* 175)

Cunningham rounds up the lynch mob and they depart. Earlier in the novel readers learn that this same individual trades hickory nuts and greens for Atticus's legal services because the Cunninghams are too poor to pay cash. With her words at the jail, Scout reminds Cunningham of his indebtedness to Atticus, thereby shaming him. Thus, the lynch mob is defeated not by brute force—which they embody—but by language and education: by Scout's words and Atticus's legal knowledge. When Scout reminds Cunningham of the services Atticus provided to him, he recognizes the interconnectedness between her family and his own. This is a moment of judgment: at first, the mob judges Atticus as a lawyer protecting a suspected black rapist. After Scout's words, however, the mob—through Walter—sees Atticus as a white man, a father of children who are similar to their own children, and a lawyer willing to share his skills with the poorest of farmers. The next day, Atticus points out this moment of empathy: "So it took an eight-year-old child to bring 'em to their senses . . . you children last night made Walter Cunningham stand in my shoes for a minute. That was enough" (179). Notably, however, Scout's words at the jail did nothing to create cross-racial empathy: no one was standing in Tom Robinson's shoes.

During the standoff with the mob, it is easy to forget whose life is on the line: that of Tom, who remains invisible inside the jail and silent during the confrontation. After the standoff ends, readers learn that Tom has not been asleep, contrary to Atticus's words. Because the readers are unaware of Tom's conscious presence, we are able to ignore his needs and fears during the standoff. Readers are able to forget the person whose life is really threatened by the mob and instead focus on the physical threat to Atticus and to his children. When Jem stands by Atticus in the standoff, "a burly man," one of the mob, "yanked Jem nearly off his feet" (*TKAM* 173). After the standoff ends, Atticus reveals his fear when he "produced his handkerchief, gave his face a going-over and blew his nose violently" (175). Readers only learn of Tom's presence after the standoff, when Atticus speaks to him through the window of the jail:

> "Mr. Finch?"
> A soft husky voice came from the darkness above: "They gone?"
> Atticus stepped back and looked up. "They've gone," he said. "Get
> some sleep, Tom. They won't bother you any more." (*TKAM* 175)

It is important to note that during the standoff, Tom not only cannot defend himself; he cannot even speak on his own behalf. Atticus, and Scout, must speak for him. Although Tom is a grown man, he must be saved by an older white lawyer and his eight-year-old daughter. He is both helpless and, when Atticus tells him to get some sleep, childlike. His helplessness at the jail, combined with his helplessness at trial and his shriveled arm, render Tom powerless as a character and therefore safe for white audiences to engage with. Unlike, say, Wright's Bigger Thomas (from *Native Son*), Tom Robinson presents no risk of revelation to white audiences of the novel.

The Trial

As previously discussed, the standoff is just one of many moments in which Tom is presented as weak and nonthreatening, thereby creating sympathy and pity, rather than empathy, in the novel's audience. A second scene occurs in the courtroom during the trial. The trial scenes also demonstrate an emphasis on interconnectedness, instances of empathetic judging, and moments when characters overcome the fear of revelation. Yet Atticus does not try to prove that Tom and the white people of Maycomb are interconnected; instead, he shows that the Ewells are *dis*connected, impeaching Tom's accusers. Furthermore, Atticus does not ask the jurors to empathize with Tom when they pass judgment, but rather to empathize with Atticus and *sympathize* with Tom. Thus, in the end, the jurors are not asked to overcome their fear of revelation and engage in cross-racial empathy.

The trial of Tom Robinson takes place in the span of one day. Readers watch the trial from the perspective of Scout and the other children, who sit in the balcony with the black citizens of Maycomb. The prosecutor's witnesses are the sheriff, Heck Tate; the father of the alleged victim, Bob Ewell; and the alleged victim, Mayella Ewell. Heck Tate testifies that the victim was beaten on the right side of her face. Bob Ewell claims to have seen the attack through the window of his home. Mayella accuses Tom of raping, beating, and choking her. During cross-examination, Atticus establishes that the majority of Mayella's injuries were to the right side of her face and that Bob Ewell is left-handed. Once the prosecution rests its case, Atticus calls only one witness: the defendant, Tom. When Tom testifies, the jurors learn some important facts, including the detail that Tom's left arm had been severely damaged in a childhood injury. Tom testifies that Mayella tried to seduce him and may even have planned this seduction by saving money to send her younger siblings to town for ice cream.

During his cross-examination of Mayella, Atticus further demonstrates the Ewells' disconnectedness from the rest of Maycomb. Scout describes the cross-examination:

> Atticus was quietly building up before the jury a picture of the Ewells' home life. The jury learned the following things: their

relief check was far from enough to feed the family, and there was a strong suspicion that Papa drank it up anyway—he sometimes went off in the swamp for days and came home sick; the weather was seldom cold enough to require shoes, but when it was, you could make dandy ones from strips of old tires; the family hauled its water in buckets from a spring that ran out at one end of the dump. (*TKAM* 208)

Clearly, Mayella's life is depressing, nearly horrifying, for Scout and for the rest of the residents of Maycomb. With this description, Atticus hopes to show that, because her life is so horrible, it is plausible that Mayella Ewell, although white, would have tried to seduce Tom Robinson. Thus, the evidence about the Ewells that Atticus puts before the jury is primarily designed to disconnect, to squash empathy between the jurors and the accusers.

Atticus's next task is to prove that Tom could not have harmed Mayella in the ways that she claims. He implies that with his injured arm, Tom could not have beaten Mayella's face or choked her. Given the inconsistencies of the Ewells' testimony, Atticus hopes that the jury will then believe Tom's version of events: that he felt sorry for Mayella so he helped her with her chores on a regular basis (*TKAM* 218); that *she* tried to seduce *him* (220); that he ran away because he was afraid he would get in trouble even though he did not do anything wrong (222). When Atticus asks Tom why he was afraid, Tom replies, "Mr. Finch, if you was a nigger like me, you'd be scared, too" (222). This testimony seems to go a long way to creating cross-racial understanding. The last line might even provoke fear of revelation in some white listeners, because it gives a small glimpse of the brutality that haunts black people in Maycomb.

Consequently, it may appear as if Atticus's closing statement does work toward rendering Tom human in the eyes of the white jury, creating a person that they can empathize with. In fact, Atticus explicitly calls Tom a human being. Closer examination of his closing statement, however, reveals that he focuses little on Tom and far more on the Ewells. In the first place, Atticus hardly mentions Tom in his closing statement. Rather, he talks about Mayella: "The defendant is not guilty, but somebody in this courtroom is" (*TKAM* 231). She is guilty because she "broke a rigid and time-honored code of our society" when she "tempted a Negro" (231). But Tom is not an "Uncle," he is "a quiet, respectable, humble Negro who had the unmitigated temerity to 'feel sorry' for a white woman" (232).

In general terms, Atticus describes the racial politics at play in this trial, arguing that the word of white folks should not win over the word of a black man simply because of race. He further suggests that a courtroom should be the one place where all people are "equal" (233). At the end of his closing statement, Atticus commands the jury, "In the name of God, do your duty. . . . In the name of God, believe him" (233–34). But, how can the jury be expected to "believe" Tom Robinson when they have no idea who he is? Neither the fictional jury nor the audience of the novel have learned anything about Tom: where he lives, what his family is like, how he treats his wife and children and others in his daily life. Instead, readers learn these things about Atticus: we get to know his house and his family and see that he treats others with respect, most of the time. The jury in Tom's trial would have known these things about Atticus, too. So, at the end of the closing statement, when Atticus tells the jury to believe Tom Robinson, he is actually commanding the jury—and readers—to believe Atticus Finch.

Atticus relies on the fact that Tom is physically damaged, with a left arm destroyed by a cotton gin; although Tom claims otherwise, the audience of the trial surely doubts whether he could have raped Mayella Ewell, even if he'd wanted to. Tom's damaged body means that he is nonthreatening: to Mayella or to any white person that may be afraid of a young black man. Atticus tries to move the jurors to pity with this emphasis on the injured arm, but not to empathy. It is curious that after impeaching the character of the Ewells, Atticus does not call a character witness on Tom's behalf. Link Deas, Tom's former employer, interrupts the trial to announce, "I just want the whole lot of you to know one thing right now. That boy's worked for me eight years an' I ain't had a speck o' trouble outa him. Not a speck" (*TKAM* 222). Had Atticus wanted to create a full picture of Tom's character for the jury, he could have called Link, Tom's wife, and probably many others who would have testified that Tom was a good person. But creating a full picture of Tom was not Atticus's goal.

During the trial, Tom's life is on the line, but Atticus is the warrior. Never do they stand together as equals, fighting together for Tom's life. They are not identified with each other, to use Burke's term. Instead, Atticus subsumes Tom's identity into his own. Like he did at the jail with the mob, Atticus counts on the white jurors' respect for Atticus to save Tom from punishment. In fact, Atticus says as much after the trial, when discussing the jury selection with the children. When Atticus reveals that he put a member of Tom's lynch mob, one of the Cunningham clan, on the jury, Scout describes her father's explanation for such an action: "He said the other thing about [the Cunninghams] was, once you earned their respect they were for you tooth and nail. Atticus said he had a feeling . . . that they left the jail that night with considerable respect for the Finches" (*TKAM* 254). This detail suggests that, for Atticus, whether the jurors felt respect for Tom was irrelevant.

Unlike during the standoff with the lynch mob, Atticus's strategy of relying on respect for himself does not work at trial. The white jurors do not overcome differences in skin color to see Tom as a courteous and honest man—to see him the way in which they see Atticus. For the jurors, Tom is a cipher: faceless, even mindless. Atticus's dilemma is one faced by many defense attorneys: how to craft the persona of a criminal defendant so that he can garner a jury's empathy. In this task, Atticus fails.

The Voice of Lula

There is one notable scene in *To Kill a Mockingbird* in which the novel risks revelation, creating a moment of cross-racial empathy. This moment of revelation occurs about halfway through the novel, long before the lynch mob comes to the jail. One Sunday morning, Atticus has been called to an emergency meeting of the state legislature. In order to avoid leaving the children alone, Calpurnia, the Finches' black housekeeper, invites Scout and Jem to come to church with her. When they arrive at Calpurnia's all-black church, one woman, Lula, confronts them in the church yard and challenges the presence of the white children. I suggest that the complaints of Lula represent one of the few scenes in the novel that could inspire cross-racial empathy in readers.

Calpurnia brings Scout and Jem to First Purchase African M.E. Church, located "in the Quarters outside the southern town limits" (*TKAM* 134). "The Quarters" is the name of a black neighborhood of Maycomb. Its name refers to the former dwellings of slaves; its location ensures that its residents do not receive town services. Once the children enter the church, Scout describes one of the most striking confrontations of the novel. When the white children first enter, "the men stepped back and took off their hats; the women crossed their arms at their waists, weekday gestures of respectful attention" (135). The black members of First Purchase thus perform the typical, "weekday" interracial behaviors dictated by white supremacy in Maycomb. But not all of the black folks in church accept the presence of the white children. Scout describes the standoff between Calpurnia and Lula, another member of First Purchase:

> "What you up to, Miss Cal?" said a voice behind us.
> Calpurnia's hands went to our shoulders and we stopped and looked around: standing in the path behind us was a tall Negro woman. Her weight was on one leg; she rested her left elbow in the curve of her hip, pointing at us with an upturned palm. She was bullet-headed with strange almond-shaped eyes, straight nose, and an Indian-bow mouth. She seemed seven feet high.
> I felt Calpurnia's hand dig into my shoulder. "What you want, Lula?" she asked, in tones I had never heard her use. She spoke quietly, contemptuously.

"I wants to know why you bringin' white chillun to nigger church."

"They's my comp'ny," said Calpurnia. . . .

"Yeah, an' I reckon you's comp'ny at the Finch house durin' the week. . . . You ain't got no business bringin' white chillun here—they got their church, we got our'n. It is our church, ain't it, Miss Cal?" (*TKAM* 135)

Unlike the other black members of First Purchase, who allow the presence of the Finch children to push them into a position of weekday servility, Lula rebels against their presence in what has been, up until that moment, a black space, safe from white supremacy. In this way, Lula's is one of the few voices in the novel that presents the unfiltered point of view of a black person. The discomfort Scout describes is that of revelation, upon first learning that black people do not necessarily want white people around. Just as the Finches do not treat Calpurnia as "company" when she comes to work during the week, Lula does not want to treat the Finch children as company at First Purchase. She is angry that white people have invaded the church sanctuary, which had also functioned as a metaphorical sanctuary from white regulations of black behavior.

The novel cuts short the empathetic possibilities of this confrontation, however. The power of Lula's observations are limited by the voices of Calpurnia and her son, Zeebo, whom Scout recognizes as the garbage collector. After Lula departs, Zeebo says, "Mister Jem . . . we're mighty glad to have you all here. Don't pay no 'tention to Lula. . . . She's a troublemaker from way back, got fancy ideas an' haughty ways—we're mighty glad to have you all" (*TKAM* 136). Zeebo discredits Lula's truth-telling as mere troublemaking. And, indeed, he is correct—Lula's words do create trouble, a conflict between the white children and the black people of the church. Although Zeebo's words are meant to reassure that the black members are "glad to have you all here," Lula's words cannot be unspoken. Scout—and the readers of *Mockingbird*—now know that there are black spaces in which white people are not welcome.

Underlying Lula's words is the implication that *all* demonstrations of black respect, such as the crossed arms and tipped hats of the other members of First Purchase, are performed only because white regulations require it. Lula's challenge to Scout and Jem has the potential to shock white readers into a position of cross-racial empathy in which they must wonder what exactly black people think of white people, and, by implication, what it is like to be a black person in our society. Unfortunately, by reassuring us that Lula is simply a disgruntled outlier rather than a prophet, Zeebo weakens the effects of the shock of Lula's words.

Conclusion

To Kill a Mockingbird, rather than creating empathy between readers and the victims of racial injustice, creates emotional distance. Readers of *Mockingbird* can point to the 1930s setting and claim that the novel represents the "bad old days." They might also speculate that, had they been around back then, they would be like Atticus. In addition, *Mockingbird* establishes faith in the contemporary U.S. justice system—even the justice system of the 1960s when the book was released—because the novel suggests that the system has changed. For example, 1960s readers could argue that *Brown v. Board of Education* (1954) represents great progress made against racism since the time of *Mockingbird*. After all, Scout Finch attends an all-white school, and school segregation is over now. Furthermore, most white people, do not (any longer) resemble the racist "bad guys" of the story—the lynch mob and Bob Ewell.

In the end, readers of *Mockingbird* can read comfortably because the novel does not disturb America's racial caste system. The defendant Tom Robinson is still a "Negro," in Atticus's words; furthermore, by the end of the novel, he is dead. Readers are not forced to empathize with Tom; they need only empathize with Atticus. Unfortunately, despite moments of cross-racial revelation such as the confrontation with Lula, in the end, Lee's novel does not force white readers to overcome their fear of revelation. Instead, *To Kill a Mockingbird* allows them to resist empathizing with Tom, the black townspeople of Maycomb, and in Justice Brennan's words, "those who will die" on death row because of race.

Notes

1. In *McCleskey v. Kemp*, the Supreme Court held that, despite rock-solid evidence that race plays a major role in deciding whether a murderer is sentenced to death (rather than life in prison), capital punishment does not violate the Eighth Amendment's ban on cruel and unusual punishment.

2. Recent polls show that Americans give popular support to the death penalty. According to a 2008 poll, the "Harris Poll," 63 percent of Americans supported capital punishment (PollingReport.com).

3. Reichman writes in the context of "law and literature," a field of interdisciplinary study that some scholars, like Reichman, suggest can create more empathetic lawyers and judges.

Works Cited

Brown. *Brown v. Board of Education.* 347 U.S. 483. Supreme Court of the United States, 1954.

Brown, Carrie Budoff. "Jeff Sessions Takes Aim at 'Empathy Standard.'" Politico.com, 6 Jun 2009. Web. 2 November 2009.

Burke, Kenneth. *A Rhetoric of Motives.* Berkeley: U of California P, 1969.

"Empathy." *Oxford English Dictionary Online.* New York: Oxford U P. Web. 23 November 2009.

Fish, Stanley. "Empathy and the Law." *New York Times: Stanley Fish Blog,* 24 May 2009. Web. 17 October 2009.

Gladwell, Malcolm. "The Courthouse Ring: Atticus Finch and Southern Liberalism." *The New Yorker,* 10 August 2009. Web. 15 October 2009.

Lee, Harper. *To Kill a Mockingbird.* 1960. New York: Harper Perennial Modern Classics, 2006.

Maatman, Mary Ellen. "Justice Formation from Generation to Generation: Atticus Finch and the Stories Lawyers Tell Their Children." *Legal Writing: The Journal of the Legal Writing Institute* 14.1 (2008): 207–48.

McCleskey v. Kemp. 481 U.S. 279. Supreme Court of the United States, 1987. Justia. Web. 23 November 2009.

Obama, Barack. "The President's Remarks on Justice Souter." *The White House Blog,* 1 May 2009. Web. 15 October 2009.

PollingReport.com. "The Harris Poll." *Crime/Law Enforcement,* 5 February 2008. Web. 15 October 2009.

Reichman, Amnon. "Law, Literature, and Empathy: Between Withholding and Reserving Judgment." *Journal of Legal Education* 56.2 (2006): 296–319.

Winter, Robin. "To Save a Mockingbird." *Family Medicine* 40.8 (2008): 548–50.

Part 4

SOCIAL CONCERNS

CHAPTER 13

"Enable Us to Look Back": Performance and Disability in *To Kill a Mockingbird*

Lisa Detweiler Miller

> We live immersed in narrative, recounting and reassessing
> the meaning of our past actions, anticipating the outcome
> of our future projects, situating ourselves at the intersection
> of several stories not yet completed.
>
> —Peter Brooks, *Reading for the Plot*, 1992

To Kill a Mockingbird is most often remembered for Atticus Finch's humbling observation that "you never really understand a person until you consider things from his point of view . . . until you climb in his skin and walk around in it" (*TKAM* 33). To walk around in the skin of the members of Maycomb, Alabama, would mean participating in the community as a disabled individual. As David Mitchell and Sharon Snyder have noted in *Narrative Prosthesis*, "Disability issues proliferate in the novel: Jem's 'deformed' arm provides pretext for the story; Atticus is blind in one eye; Tom Robinson's 'useless' right arm proves his innocence during the rape trial and is the reason for his death; Mrs. DuBose taunts neighbors from a wheelchair perch on her front porch" (173). Boo Radley, in his construction as a "feebleminded" individual, to replicate the eugenic language of the day, can certainly be added to the list of the disabled members of Maycomb, as can the Ewells and the lower planter class whose illiteracy marks their limited cognitive ability.

As Mitchell and Snyder have argued, disability has emerged in literature as a mode of characterization as well as a "metaphorical device" to stand in for a larger critique of a social condition (47). Their "narrative prosthesis," then, points to the role of disability as "a crutch upon which literary narratives lean for their representational power, disruptive potentiality, and analytical insight" (49). There is no doubt that Harper Lee places disability on center stage of the novel. In the opening sentence, Scout mentions Jem's deformed arm, pairing it with an acknowledgement of her act of remembering: "When enough years had gone by to enable us to look back on them, we sometimes discussed the events leading to his accident" (*TKAM* 3). Scout continues to explain that it really all began with Andrew Jackson and proceeds to stumble through the family lineage. At first glance, Scout's narrative voice can be read simply as a display of Southern identity and as an introduction to a narrator, who although older, still embodies much of her younger excitable self. However, considering the centrality of disability in the novel, it is striking and deliberate that a line would be drawn between one site of disability, Jem's arm, and a much larger "enabling" task.

In traditional readings, Atticus Finch as the moral beacon of the novel becomes the enabler of Maycomb. His defense of Tom Robinson, a black man accused of raping Mayella Ewell, a member of a poor and uneducated family, forces the town to reflect on the depths of its prejudice. As this plotline develops, a parallel story affects Scout and Jem, who are forced to confront their own prejudice, specifically their misconceptions of Arthur Radley, the town recluse who they construct as a monster in their imaginations and nickname "Boo." These two plotlines intersect after Atticus confronts Maycomb's racist assumptions and makes a case for Tom's innocence by drawing attention to Tom's disability. Angered by Atticus's cleverness, and unwilling to break from a racist tradition, Mayella's father, Bob Ewell, attacks Jem and Scout in retaliation. Surprisingly, it is Boo Radley who steps outside the comfort zone of his home to save Jem and Scout, revealing himself to be quite the opposite of the monster the children had imagined.

Despite Boo's brave act, it is Atticus's actions that in most interpretations of the text are seen as more significant for ushering Maycomb into a new phase of self-awareness. In this regard, Atticus becomes the crutch of the novel, the representative of this enabling process, though "it is just a baby-step" (*TKAM* 246). My purpose in this essay is to suggest that enabling a community like Maycomb means moving beyond a simple recognition of how cultural values are formed to embrace a lived and performed collective effort that addresses these formations of difference, particularly in terms of disability and race. This means relying less on Atticus as the ethical figure to do Maycomb's "unpleasant jobs" (*TKAM* 245) and instead expanding the scope of readers' attention to include precisely those figures who are pushed to the peripheries of the community and designated as misfits. For this reason, I have chosen to focus on Boo Radley and Tom Robinson (representatives of medical and minority disabilities) as figures that we can "lean on," not for their metaphorical significance as disabled bodies, but as figures who move the narrative of social progress forward in their subtle subversion of cultural norms and by the way they communicate by *performing* outside the prescribed stereotypes of Maycomb.

This reading, with its focus on the performances in the narrative, centers on the text as an embodied network of communication and requires that the narrative as a genre be destabilized. It demands that the novel be read not as a series of multiple events collapsed into one single linear cause and effect with a clear beginning and end, but as a form that "emerges from the lived realities of bodily conduct" (Peterson and Langellier 174). This reading also requires that the narrative be positioned as a location "for engaging the pleasures and power of discourse for challenging and confirming possible experiences and identities" (Peterson and Langellier 174). This shift toward performance takes note of the way Scout's narration situates the readers within a web of competing socio-ideological discourses, both able-bodied and disabled.

From Story to Narrative: Scout's Verbal Performance

As narrator, Scout is not simply retelling a story, but rather molding and sculpting her own artistic and creative use of language. Her opening line reads, "When he was nearly thirteen, my brother Jem got his arm badly broken at the elbow" (*TKAM* 3). While Jem's injury is a part of the story, or the list of events as they occurred, the narrative involves Scout's choices, her conscious decision to forefront this disability in the text, to remind readers of how young she and Jem were and to inform them that she is moving back and forth from past to present in her sharing of this experience. Her admission that it was years before they were "enabled to look back" on these events further highlights this shift from story to narrative, as she simultaneously and implicitly directs readers to a time when they were first enabled to look forward. Each time Scout moves between the past and present in her language she carries with her the values of that time. Mikhail Bakhtin takes note of this dual nature of language, referring to it as a "heteroglot" in the way that it represents "the co-existence of socio-ideological contradictions between the present and past" ("Discourse in the Novel" 291). He explains that both are always present "first and foremost, in the creative consciousness of people who write novels" (292) and asserts that it is not that one replaces the other but that they both exist simultaneously as one is privileged and one is silenced. In Scout's introduction to the text, when she draws our attention to looking back, it is that implicit nod to looking forward that is silenced.

Scout's silencing and privileging of language discourses is a means of inhabiting her language or imbuing it with meaning. Bakhtin refers to this as "taste," or the way words have the mark of a "profession, a genre, a tendency . . . a generation, an age group" ("Discourse in the Novel" 293). In the opening of the novel, Scout reveals her particular Southern "taste" of history in her recounting of her family genealogy. Additionally, she also identifies herself as part of the Depression generation when she mentions that it was a "time of vague optimism for some of the people: Maycomb County had recently been told that it has nothing to fear but fear itself" (*TKAM* 6). As Scout discusses her family history and the Depression, it is evident that there is a shift in tone. She moves from her refreshing matter-of-fact manner, explaining that "all we had was Simon Finch," and spirals into a long mechanical explanation of who Simon Finch was, while making use of language that significantly breaks from her previous casual approach. Scout explains, "In England, Simon was irritated by the persecution of those who called themselves Methodists at the hands of their more liberal brethren, and as Simon called himself a Methodist, he worked his way across the Atlantic to Philadelphia, thence to Jamaica, thence to Mobile, and up the Saint Stephens" (*TKAM* 4). Her use of politically charged language such as "persecution," the apparent distrust at the core of the phrase "those who called themselves Methodist," as well as the repetition of words like "hence," clearly identify this genealogy as an inherited story. The sentiments being expressed and the nearly epic quality of its delivery are not an accurate reflection of Scout's present. Similarly, rather than explaining the economic hardships of the Depression that affected the Deep South more so than other parts of the country, Scout relies on the words of President Roosevelt's 1932 Inaugural Address to acknowledge the anxiety that plagued towns like Maycomb.

Both instances reveal the way Scout has embodied the language of others and reproduced that language in her narrative. Her narrative is double-voiced in its repeating of other's words, further pointing to the heteroglot of languages that operate and perform in this text. In these moments, Scout's use of language very much reflects a view of the generative process of language shared by Bakhtin and V. N. Voloshinov, whose *Marxism and the Philosophy of Language* explains that "social intercourse is generated (stemming from the basis); in it verbal communication and interaction are generated; and in the latter, forms of speech performances are generated; finally, this generative process is reflected in the change of language forms" (96). As this process of language highlights, Scout draws our attention to the inherently social nature of language rooted in verbal communication and interaction, as well as the reproduction of these performances that surface immediately in the opening of the text.

Therefore, when Scout invites readers into the polyphony of voices that construct the ideologies of Maycomb, we are drawn not into a linear story, but into a narrative in which the languages behave, or perform; a narrative in which the embodied languages and communicative practices are reproduced and constantly informed by the othered, silenced voices. In this regard, Scout as narrator can be thought of as a director who sets the stage and provides readers access to a much larger community performance that might allow them to remember the past and to recognize the present in a more accurate manner.

Behavioral Language: The Physical Performance of Narrative

Bakhtin emphasizes, in a rather able-ist assumption, that "the human being in the novel is first, foremost and always a speaking human being" ("Discourse in the Novel" 332), that all language transmission and evaluation on a primary level depends on the body. Similar to the way Scout absorbs different language discourses and reproduces them in her narrative voice, so too are these languages absorbed by the body and performed quite literally by Jem, Scout, and Charles Baker Harris (aka Dill), a young visitor who resides with his aunt in Maycomb for the summers. The children's performances circulate around their construction of Boo Radley and are informed by what other members of Maycomb have to say not only about Boo, but the entire Radley family. While Atticus remains particularly quiet about the Radleys, Calpurnia, the Finchs's cook, refers to Boo's father as the "meanest man ever God blew breath into" (*TKAM* 13), and Jem, Scout, and Dill's curiosity about Boo's nature culminates in Ms. Stephanie Crawford's explanation that Boo once drove a pair of scissors into his father's leg. These independent stories as they are verbally communicated to Jem, Scout, and Dill act as different languages informed by different ideologies. Atticus's silence about Boo conveys his strong belief as a lawyer in respecting another's privacy. In their assessment of Calpurnia, who Jem and Scout perceive as a kind of link between the black and white communities of Maycomb, the children find harsh unsolicited comment about Mr. Radley to be out of character, further validating their curiosity. The comments of Miss Stephanie, an older woman of the town known for her gossipy nature, clearly stem from her desire to shock her audience as she proceeds to exaggerate and frighten Jem, Scout, and Dill with the more violent disturbing imagery of Boo's identity. What Jem, Scout, and Dill are left with are three very opposing languages to negotiate—one rooted in a sense of fairness, another rooted in personal perception, and a third rooted in personal interest.

Jem, Scout, and Dill decide to work through the tensions of Boo Radley's identity by searching for their own story to add to the collection of information borrowed from other sources in Maycomb. In a moment of mutual curiosity about Boo, Jem and Dill strike a bet. If Jem touches the Radley house, Dill will reward him with his copy of *The Gray Ghost*, a popular children's adventure story series of the day. Jem confidently replies, "Touch the house, that's all?" (*TKAM* 15). In this discussion, Jem and Dill agree to exchange a narrative for what Jem believes to be a rather simple task. The presence of *The Gray Ghost* narrative within the larger narrative is particularly significant in three ways. On the most practical level, it draws attention to the way in which Jem, Scout, and Dill understand the materiality of narrative, in the way it is embodied through the act of reading. On another level, it makes a connection between narrative and the performance of touching the Radley home. Lastly, in the way it inserts another language layer to those already at work in Maycomb, it reproduces the fundamental tension between languages that is at the root of Bakhtin's generative process.[1]

Just as Scout's narrative voice is a negotiation of the many languages that characterize Maycomb, Jem, Scout, and Dill together find themselves drawing from each of the stories around them in a desire to be part of their own adventure narrative, very much like the characters in *The Gray Ghost*. Their understanding of the materiality of narrative urges them in their creative process to produce their own material text through physical performance. The playacting draws upon the stories as they have been relayed by the members of Maycomb, or "woven from bits and scraps of gossip and neighborhood legend" (*TKAM* 44), and quickly grows from just a simple game into a more complete immersion in the imaginative process when "every scratch of feet on gravel was Boo Radley seeking revenge, every passing Negro laughing in the night was Boo Radley" (*TKAM* 62). Each utterance from someone in Maycomb is an embodied language, and Jem, Scout, and Dill take that embodied language and act it out not only in their initial dare to touch the Radley home but also in a more elaborate staging. In the culmination of the children's fascination with Boo Radley, Dill announces emphatically one day, "I know what we are going to play . . . Boo Radley" (*TKAM* 43). Quite literally their playing becomes a performance piece. Scout explains that

> Jem parceled out the roles: I was Mrs. Radley, and all I had to do was
> come out and sweep the porch. Dill was old Mr. Radley; he walked
> up and down the sidewalk and coughed when Jem spoke to him.
> Jem, naturally was Boo: he went under the front steps and shrieked
> and howled from time to time. As the summer progressed, so did our
> game. We polished and perfected it, added dialogue and plot until
> we had manufactured a small play upon which we rang changes every
> day. (*TKAM* 43)

In this moment, the staging by Scout as narrator becomes a true physical staging as Jem, Scout, and Dill elevate Boo Radley from a character to the title of a dramatic game, thus drawing attention to the complex interplay of his identity as they understand it. Their performance of their characters is firstly mimetic in the way they reproduce the actions these individuals perform in their daily routines. This performance undergoes further transformation as they add their own violent episodes to those relayed by Miss Crawford's graphic tales, imagining Boo biting the forefinger of Mr. Radley, for example. At one point, Scout refers to their game as "playing Chapter XXV, Book II of One Man's Family" (*TKAM* 44). What Jem, Scout, and Dill manage to create is a kind of hybrid form that mixes "two speech manners, two styles, two 'languages,'" as Bakhtin explains ("Discourse in the Novel" 304). Informed by stories from multiple individuals, the children create a narrative, which they even title by using the correct genre conventions of their day. Simultaneously, the dialogues they imagine in their narrative, *One Man's Family*, become reconceived and reproduced as the lines of a script that is then performed.

Reading *To Kill a Mockingbird* as a performance text allows a fuller interpretation of the novel, one that considers narrative in all of its rich complexities. In its construction of language as something that behaves, *To Kill a Mockingbird* forces readers to consider the way the verbal performance of discourse informs a physical performance. More importantly, as Bakhtin suggests, it provides a means for characters to shock the author as they seem to develop outside of the author's control—in the way they become characterized by an "inner unfinalizability, their capacity to outgrow, as it were, from within and render *untrue* any externalizing and finalizing definition of them" (*Dostoevsky's Poetics* 59). In other words, as long as a character is living, he or she will continue to participate and negotiate the language discourse, continue to add his or her voice to the many.

This unfinalizability, however, poses an important question regarding the characters of Boo Radley and Tom Robinson. If, according to Bakhtin, being alive means to always participate in the tension between discourses and evolve as a character, what becomes of Boo, who after his brave act of saving Jem and Scout, is walked back to his house, returned to the institution of his home, and essentially silenced? At the end of the narrative, Boo's status is returned to that of a disabled individual, a figure incapable of fully participating in the everyday life of Maycomb. Similarly, what becomes of Tom's voice when he is killed in an attempt to escape prison? Tom's escape is dismissed by many members of Maycomb as "typical of a nigger's mentality to have no plan, no thought, for the future" (*TKAM* 247). Like Boo, Tom's racial identity, which functions in a town like Maycomb as a disability, also means his voice will be silenced, while another voice is privileged. As previously discussed, the voice of Atticus is the one that emerges most prominently out of the text as the spokesperson for Maycomb's enabling, as it is privileged over that of two disabled figures. If enabling a community means carving out a space for all members to contribute their voices to the whole, it is our responsibility to listen to the text a bit more closely—to see the way these figures grow, speak, and perform despite their silencing.

Tom Robinson: Breaching the Contract

"Self expression and political change" are at the root of community performance, and unlike tightly scripted performances, the end result is flexible, with room for individuals to alter the energy of the space and insert themselves into the performance. Community performances then emerge as acts of experimentation that unfold layer by layer, revealing the weight of the words and actions of the performance that leave impressions in the walls of the dominant discourse (Kuppers 4, 5). One of the largest performance scenes in *To Kill a Mockingbird* is the trial of Tom Robinson, where Tom's testimony invites members of the community to surrender their bodies to a non-scripted performance.

As Jem, Dill, and Scout prepare to go to the courthouse to watch the trial, Miss Maudie describes the masses of people moving to the courthouse as "a Roman carnival" (*TKAM* 181), immediately establishing the event as a spectacle and highlighting the politics of seeing. Very much like a stage, where audiences are searching for meaning in the props and gestures of the actors, the courtroom draws spectators into a similar meaning-making process of searching for the truth by reading each detail of a witness's testimony. Miss Maudie's observation of the masses asks readers to consider when a spectator becomes a spectator; and it would be false to believe that this role is only assumed as the curtain is raised or, in this case, as Judge Taylor invites the opening comments from Atticus and Mr. Gilmer, the prosecuting attorney. Rather, the performance begins immediately in the ritualistic movement to the courthouse, where the bodies physically moving to that space grow together in order to form a community collective. This collective, however, is marked by division.

Jem, Dill, and Scout observe the procession from Miss Maudie's porch, each group keeping to their own—the prominent figures ride by in their wagons, the Mennonites who lived in the woods drive by in their bonnets and long dresses, and the African Americans of the community congregate in the corner of the town square. As each group moves into the courthouse, crammed together with little standing room, the space comes to life. As the stage of this performance, the courthouse represents democracy symbolized by the Greek revival style complete with characteristic columns that "clashed with a big nineteenth-century clock tower housing a rusty unreliable instrument, a view indicating people determined to preserve every physical scrap of the past" (*TKAM* 185). Just as the rusty clock interrupts the architectural cohesiveness of the democratic space, the community that Scout observes to be one of exclusion interrupts the definition of a community. As the members of Maycomb enter into that space, the disjointedness of the structure serves to represent their own disconnect.

The courthouse also informs the audience's expectation of what will take place in the courtroom, and as the trial reveals, the terms "justice" and "equality" are highly subjective. To the majority of the white audience members, equality would mean maintaining white supremacy, holding tightly onto their secured position within society that essentially denies African Americans their humanity. To African American audience members, these terms would mean finally being recognized as citizens. Similar to the way that someone may attend a performance with a certain expectation about its ending, each member of the audience comes with the anticipation, or at the very least the hope, of seeing their understanding of equality fulfilled. Trusting in their expectations, they watch and listen passively as one unit. Susan Bennett, who traces audience reception in theater history, argues that this kind of passive participation is part of a social contract audience members make, agreeing to give themselves up to the performance. This contract is usually marked with the purchase of a ticket, and although there is no such exchange before entering the courthouse, the members of Maycomb nonetheless enter into the same agreement.

Scout observes this passivity in the beginning of the trial, noting that "all the spectators were as relaxed as Judge Taylor" (*TKAM* 193). Despite their passive nature, as Bennett argues, audience members have the right to breach the contract by leaving the performance (165). As the expectations of the trial seem to resist this outcome, some members of the community begin to break this contract, not by leaving, but rather by throwing themselves into the performance, by openly responding to the proceedings of the court with displays of their disapproval that blur the line between stage and audience. Clearly, it is the performance of Bob Ewell that first invites this breach. As he falsely explains that he saw Tom forcing himself upon Mayella, he stands up, and while pointing his finger at Tom Robinson, exclaims, "I seen that black nigger yonder ruttin' on my Mayella" (*TKAM* 196). After this dramatic performance, Judge Taylor is forced to violently hammer his gavel as "happy picknickers" were turned "into a sulky, tense, murmuring crowd" (*TKAM* 197). Outraged at both the display and the response, Judge Taylor explains, "People generally see what they look for, and hear what they listen for" and firmly reminds the spectators, "I can assure you of one thing; you will receive what you see and hear in silence or you will leave this courtroom" (*TKAM* 198). To some in the crowd, their murmuring is an affirmation that their assumptions about race were correct; to others it is an expression of disgust and suspicion at Bob Ewell's testimony. Of most importance, though, is Judge Taylor's statement that reinforces this space as contractual, where the audience comes equipped with assumptions and expectations.

Following the testimonies of Bob and Mayella Ewell, Tom is called to the stand, and Scout observes that "he stood oddly off balance, but it was not from the way he was standing. His left arm was twelve inches shorter than his right, and hung dead at his side. It ended in a small shriveled hand, and from as far away as the balcony I could see that it was no use to him" (*TKAM* 211). Scout's observation reveals that while Bob or Mayella's testimony elicits a politics of seeing, Tom's physical disability invites a politics of staring. As Rosemarie Garland Thomson explains, staring is "a kind of potent social choreography that marks bodies by enacting a dynamic visual exchange between a spectator and a spectacle" (30). Tom's performance under this gaze begins even prior to sitting down at the witness stand, as he struggles to place his left hand on the Bible to swear the oath.

> Tom Robinson reached around, ran his fingers under his left arm and lifted it. He guided his arm to the Bible and his rubber-like left hand sought contact with the black binding. As he raised his right hand, the useless one slipped off the Bible and hit the clerk's table. He was trying again when Judge Taylor growled, "That'll do Tom." (*TKAM* 216)

Rhetoricians often forget that control of an audience means control not only over one's voice but also over one's body (Brueggemann 19). It may seem that Tom has very little control over his body, as seen by the slipping of his arm, and while it is true that his control is very different from that of Bob Ewell, who stands up and points, Tom is just as successful at sparking an audience reaction. This audience reaction seems to stem partly from Judge Taylor's own discomfort with watching Tom struggle with his injured arm, indicated by his growl. Staring at a disabled figure is often a way for an audience to confirm their own able-bodiedness, but in this moment, as Tom struggles with his arm, the aesthetic space that is usually maintained between able-bodied and disabled is closed. By closing this gap, Tom's performance invites audiences to watch and opens a space for critique that disturbs the "cultural prescription against staring at once exposing the impairments and oppressive narratives" (Thomson 32). Tom's refocusing of the stare on his physical disability reveals that his oppressive narrative is tied not only to disability but also to his race, what is truly responsible for the indictment against him. Anne Stubblefield, who has done extensive work on disability politics, explains the intersection of race and disability:

> Turning to the past, chattel slavery was a conspicuous producer of disability. Loss of limbs, vision, and hearing were common results of corporal punishment and physical hardship. Poor maternal health and healthcare led to physical and cognitive impairments in children,

as did accidents and disease. Beginning in the nineteenth century, the project of supposedly measuring intelligences, upon which the classi-fication of cognitive disability continues to rest, developed as a means to justify the exclusion of nonwhite and not-quite-white people from the social contract. (108)

Tom's injured arm, disabled in a cotton gin accident, should be read as an injury like that of chattel slavery that highlights Maycomb's unwillingness to part with a history so deeply rooted in a white supremacist hierarchy. This hier-archy is further highlighted by Judge Taylor's dismissal of Tom's repeated effort to complete the oath. By allowing Tom to complete the oath without his hand resting completely on the text, Judge Taylor prevents him from participating fully in this performance of citizenship. It may seem out of character that Judge Taylor would growl at Tom. However, it is important to understand that Judge Taylor is a paradoxical character caught between his own personal awareness of the inequality of the law and understanding himself as the embodiment of the white supremacist legal system. The social contract that Stubblefield refers to is underscored by what Charles W. Mills calls the Racial Contract, the creation of "a racial polity, a racial state, and a racial juridical system" (13–14) that classifies nonwhites as subpersons, and functions to protect the "privileges and advantages of the full white citizens" (14). Mills refers to this contract as an "epistemol-ogy of ignorance" (18), or a willful "misunderstanding" (19) of the world that would otherwise result in a jarring confrontation with the systems as they truly operate. For whites, this confrontation is often avoided since it would threaten their secure position within this system (19).[2] In Judge Taylor's case, it is more comfortable for readers to believe that his dismissal of Tom's efforts is a gesture of kindness. After all, Judge Taylor did appoint Atticus as Tom's defense attor-ney. Yet, Scout also introduces Judge Taylor as "a man learned in the law, and although he seemed to take his job casually, in reality he kept a firm grip on any proceedings that came before him" (*TKAM* 187). This introduction, particularly in the context of Mills, implies that Judge Taylor, although he may recognize the inequality of the law, will nonetheless uphold the law despite its support of white supremacy. As the representative of the law, perhaps he believes he cannot be the man to point out its inequality.[3]

As Atticus begins his examination of Tom, he asks if Tom had been to the Ewell home before the instance when Mayella claimed she was raped. Tom hon-estly replies, "Well, I went lots of times" (*TKAM* 217). At this response, Judge Taylor picks up his gavel, expecting a similar reaction to that of Bob Ewell's performance but is shocked to find quite the opposite—silence. Nonetheless, this silence performs to the same degree as the outcries of disapproval heard ear-lier during the trial and is a sign that the spectators are meditating on the events unfolding before them.

The silencing of the audience is broken with the sound of Tom's voice. Following some calming reminders from Atticus that he swore to tell the truth, Tom rubs his hands nervously over his mouth, and proceeds to explain that he did not rape Mayella, that Mayella in fact kissed him. At this point, the audience erupts, and Judge Taylor is forced to violently bang his gavel. It is almost as if Tom, a figure denied any voice in the community, suddenly becomes the mouthpiece for disrupting the racialized sexual narrative that constructed black men as deviants and white women as the inevitable victims of their sexual passes. Tom's gesture of rubbing his hand over his mouth is a physical performance of coaxing himself to speak. It is a way of helping him "overcome the internalization of subpersonhood" to bring what he has been forced to censor for white audiences—his voice—to the surface (Mills 118). The white audience's response is expected, as the performance begins to unfold beyond their comfortable expectations. The unlocking of Tom's voice disrupts not only the accepted social discourses but also the contract of the space. After Atticus's examination of Tom and before Mr. Gilmer can make it to the witness stand, the contract is breached, as Mr. Link Deas, Tom's employer, stands in outrage and addresses the audience saying, "I just want the whole lot of you to know one thing right now. That boy's worked for me eight years an' I ain't had a speck o'trouble outa him. Not a speck!" (*TKAM* 222). As Mr. Deas addresses the audience, he creates a space for other members of Maycomb to also reach the contract. Outraged by another outburst, Judge Taylor demands that the court reporter delete anything past Tom's last statement. If we think of the court report as a kind of script to the case, it is significant that Mr. Deas's account is deleted from the record. Deleting the voice of Mr. Deas is a way of shaping the dominant discourse, asserting control over the memory of the case, imagining that there was no community opposition. However, it is simultaneously a gesture that recognizes the power of the audience to change a situation, an acknowledgement Judge Taylor is reluctant to give.[4]

Despite this deletion, Mr. Deas is not the only member of the community whose physical performance imprints itself on the memory of each person in the courtroom. Dill, angered with Mr. Gilmer's examination, is unable to control himself from bursting into tears. As Tom explains that he was motivated by pity to help Mayella with her chores, Mr. Gilmer's examination, which Dill calls "acting" (*TKAM* 226), assumes an arrogant and defensive tone as he begins to feel his own position as a white man disrupted. Both Mr. Deas and Dill have reactions that seem involuntary. Mr. Deas seems unable to control himself and abruptly stands up from his seat, and Dill's tears are spontaneous and sudden. It is this spontaneity that creates this space as a community performance, where unpredictability works against the scripting or acting out of social roles. In short, it is Tom's assertion of self, seen in his control over his body and of his voice, that invites the remarkable response and performance from the audience.

The Post-Performance: Getting to Know Boo Radley's English

Audience participation in a performance does not end as soon as the performance ends. Often audience members will take the performance with them.[5] Jem and Scout have a particularly difficult task as they continue to make sense of the outcome of the trial with the democratic rhetoric they learn in the classroom. Bob Ewell, who holds a grudge against Atticus after the trial, clearly carries that performance with him, and in a drunken rage, he targets Jem and Scout as they return from a school Halloween function. Boo Radley, having heard the struggle, saves Jem and Scout by stabbing Bob Ewell and proceeds to carry the unconscious Jem back to the Finch house, as Scout, struggling to see through her costume, follows shortly behind. After Dr. Reynolds arrives at the Finch residence to check on Jem and Scout, Heck Tate, Maycomb's sheriff, begins to question Scout about the events. As she communicates to Mr. Tate that "Mr. Ewell was tryin' to squeeze me to death," she states that Ewell was suddenly pulled away from her as she heard someone "coughing fit to die" (*TKAM* 309). When Mr. Tate asks Atticus to tell him who it was, Scout tells Mr. Tate that he can ask the man himself, and in a pointing gesture, draws attention to the man, who, Scout explains, "was still leaning against the wall. He had been leaning against the wall when I came into the room, his arms folded across his chest"—Boo Radley (*TKAM* 310).

Unlike Tom, who speaks in the novel, Boo Radley's performance relies solely on his body language. While Tom represents the minority model of disability, Boo is identified as the medical model[6] by the familiar greeting he receives from Dr. Reynolds while at the Finch home and by Scout's description of him at the scene of the attack as someone "coughing fit to die." As a representative of the medical model, Boo is subjected to a scrutinizing medical gaze that constructs his body as "abnormal." Even Scout, who is quick to admit her wrongdoing for pointing at Boo, is unable to entirely remove herself from social constructions of normality. When she is properly introduced to him, her eyes move methodically from "his hands to his sand-stained khaki pants . . . up his thin frame to his torn denim shirt" and finally to his face (*TKAM* 310). When observing the features of his face, Scout takes note primarily of what is *absent* from his features, including his cheeks, which "were thin to hollowness"; gray eyes so light in color, she thought he was blind; and his "dead and thin" hair (*TKAM* 310). It is Scout's notice of what, to her mind, is missing from Boo's physical form that highlights the way he is constructed by the dominant social discourses.

Boo's personal story reaffirms that his disability was constructed. As a youth, Boo fell in "with the wrong crowd" (*TKAM* 11), traveling with the Cunninghams from Old Sarum, who were "the nearest thing to a gang ever seen in Maycomb" (*TKAM* 10). Although the boys did no real damage, they were the topic of discussion both in town and from church pulpits. After an "excessive spurt of high spirits" when they borrowed a car for a ride in the square and "resisted arrest by Maycomb's ancient beadle Mr. Connor," the boys were brought up on a number of serious charges (*TKAM* 11). Boo's father, Mr. Radley, who was "so upright he took the word of God as his only law" (*TKAM* 12) was so mortified by his son's behavior that he chose to lock him in the house, never opening the doors and windows to the outside as he used to do. While the other boys attended school, Boo was refused the experiences of growing up by his father. When Boo did make a reappearance in Maycomb County gossip, it was for having apparently stabbed his father in the leg with a pair of scissors. Despite these seemingly wild actions, "Boo wasn't crazy, he was high-strung at times" and Mr. Radley refused to press charges or send him to an asylum, although "Nobody knew what form of intimidation Mr. Radley employed to keep Boo out of sight" (*TKAM* 12). The pieces of Boo's history reveal that his behavior is a result of his victimization, not of any inherent disability.[7] Under the judgmental gaze of his father and as the speculative gossip from curious town members, it is no surprise that Boo becomes "high-strung." His social anxiety is a symptom of his isolation, and he stays in his home to avoid the diagnostic gaze that he would experience outside.

Despite Mr. Radley's wish to keep Boo out of an asylum or a juvenile detention facility, Boo's home effectively functions like an institution. It is a place known for its signature coldness of closed doors and windows that keep Boo from moving beyond its perimeters into a new social space. Moreover, Boo is still judged and diagnosed by his family as being unfit for society. The way Boo chooses to occupy the corner in the Finch home, the place in the room that has the most borders, similarly mirrors the borders that have been built around him and that have situated him on the periphery of the community. When outside the space of his home, Boo seeks similar borders, hoping to escape notice. In a protective gesture, Boo stands with his hands crossed. It is only when Scout points her finger in his direction[8] that his protective shell is cracked, and he reacts by anchoring his body and placing his arms flat against the wall.

As Boo stands awkwardly in the corner, Scout notices that "his palms slipped slightly, leaving greasy sweat streaks on the wall, and he hooked his thumbs in his belt. A strange spasm shook him, as if he heard fingernails scrape slate, but as I gazed at him in wonder the tension slowly drained from his face"

(*TKAM* 310). Boo holds onto the wall and then onto the loops of his pants in an effort to gain control of his visceral reaction to fear. Those instances when he seems to be losing control—when his hands slip and when he experiences some kind of spasm—stand as important performance moments. Just as Tom had to lose control of his hand in front of the courtroom to gain some control of the space, Boo has to allow himself to lose control under a discerning gaze in order to re-familiarize himself with his own body in this context. In other words, only by *losing control* of his body does Boo *regain* control. In his subtle removal of his hands from the wall, his spasm, and his slight smile to Scout, he comes to recognizes that Scout's gaze is not one of judgment or negative diagnosis but rather reflects a gesture of friendship and acceptance.

After Dr. Reynolds leaves the room, having given Jem some medication to relive his pain and enable him to rest, Scout observes that Boo, still lingering in the corner, stood with his "chin up peering from a distance at Jem" (*TKAM* 319). It seems Boo tries to maintain a distance between himself and Jem, perhaps a reproduction of the aesthetic space that most members of the town maintained with him. Scout invites Boo to approach the bed and look more closely at Jem, as "an expression of timid curiosity was on his face, as though he had never seen a boy before. His mouth was slightly open, and he looked at Jem from head to foot" (*TKAM* 319).[9] In the expression of curiosity that comes over Boo's face and in the way he looks at Jem, his gaze moving from head to foot, Boo reproduces his own version of the diagnostic gaze that is both curious and methodical. Suddenly, he inverts the politics of staring and the medical model of disability, and with the comfort of Scout, performs this inversion in a location that is also the stage of his own community performance. To Boo, a community performance exists on the smaller scale in the home of Atticus Finch, where Mr. Tate, Atticus, Jem, Scout, and Dr. Reynolds represent the whole. In a final moment before asking Scout to take him home, Boo, while looking at Jem, reaches out to stroke his hair but then lets his hand fall to his side in a gesture that reflects his reluctance to have a close involvement with others. Assured by Scout that it is alright, Boo gently touches Jem's head. The tenderness that Boo brings to Jem is also a final inversion of the medical model that so often separates the person from the body. Boo's short performance outside of the borders of his home requires a re-scripting of the medical model that relies not on a diagnostic gaze but on gentleness. More importantly it requires understanding the languages that Boo speaks. As Boo and Scout sit in the shadows of the porch listening to Atticus and Mr. Tate discuss the best way to handle the events, Boo indicates to Scout with a squeeze of her hand that he wants to return home. In this moment, as Scout begins to lead Boo back to his home, she embraces a gentleness similar to that exhibited by Boo toward Jem. Most importantly, Scout begins to understand "his body English" (*TKAM* 319). As readers, we are also being invited to learn this language.

Reading as Performance: Reading Deeply

Learning Boo's language requires that, as readers, we understand the way reading overlaps with performance. Peter Kivy's work on this subject, which focuses on the act of silent reading as it intersects with aesthetics, draws attention to the way reading is performed both in our imaginative creation of the text as well as our interpretive work. Scholarship on *To Kill a Mockingbird* has only begun to touch on the role of disability, and with the recent work on the intersection of disability and performance studies, it is time to continue our imaginative and interpretive task. *To Kill a Mockingbird* lends itself to a reading that focuses on the self-representation of disabled figures and places it within the context of the community that has historically denied them access. As readers, we are part of this community, and while we cannot change the unsettling ending that leads Boo back to the institution of his home and Tom Robinson to his death, we are nonetheless part of the audience expected to read and perform. The silencing of Tom and Boo would seem to remove their voices from the polyphony of the novel, but as reading performers we can relocate their agency. The enabling task proposed by Scout in the introduction then becomes an act of reading performance that demands we approach the definition of performance with new flexibility. While novels are so often viewed as a display of linearity, reading a text through a performance lens allows readers to connect our own understanding of performance as a lived experience and to attach it to the characters of the novel. This allows us to see them not merely as the metaphors that Mitchell and Snyder discuss or as purposeful plot propellers, but as complex human beings, with narratives that are part of a much larger whole. What we are confronted with in *To Kill a Mockingbird* is the opportunity to become a translator of the languages that function and push against the dominant discourse. Bakhtin argues that an understanding of the heteroglot of language is present in the minds of those who write novels. I would argue that this is equally present in the minds of those who read. As readers, we become members of the Maycomb community as well as part of the generative process of language that requires recognizing its different forms. For Tom and Boo, these languages surround the performance of their bodies, not only as they speak, but as they move and as they lose control in order to regain control. In that generative process, we can see the political progressions quietly at work beneath and begin to search for the dustings of change.

As one of the townspeople said before the trial, "Atticus Finch's a deep reader, a mighty deep reader" (*TKAM* 185). *To Kill a Mockingbird* not only *asks* that we read deeply but also *demands* that we read deeply. In addition to challenging the dominant social discourses, this reading invites a critique of the pedagogical discourses associated with the text. As a text that is first introduced on the grade school level, it is an ethical mistake to simplify the novel's message as just a statement about tolerance without addressing all the voices and bodies that perform within that space or without reassigning Tom and Boo their proper agency. Narratives and performances come with obligations to listen. The whispers, as equally as the shouts, enable us as readers and as cultural critics. Reading a little more deeply means we enable characters to then enable the communities of the text—communities not unlike our own.

Notes

1. It is important to note that this generative process is highlighted again in the closing of the novel when Scout falls asleep while Atticus reads a chapter from *The Gray Ghost*. In an effort to convince her father she is awake, Scout begins to repeat the events of the story he just read. In her exhausted state, however, her own story of meeting Boo becomes part of *The Gray Ghost*, as discussions of Three-Fingered Fred and Stoner's Boy transforms to "An they chased him 'n' never could catch him 'cause they didn't know what he looked like, an' Atticus, when they finally saw him, why he hadn't done any of those things. . . . Atticus, he was real nice"(*TKAM* 323). This scene once again highlights the move from verbal interaction, to performance, and change of language form as Scout's words become part of the narrative.

2. When Uncle Jack comes to visit, Atticus confides, "You know, I'd hoped to get through life without a case of this kind, but John Taylor pointed at me and said, 'You're It'" (*TKAM* 100). In this moment, Atticus reveals himself to also be a willing participant in this epistemology.

3. I believe Judge Taylor's growl speaks to his discomfort not only with the aesthetic closeness of Tom's disability but also to his confrontation with his own participation in the "epistemology of ignorance." It is far more comfortable for a man like Judge Taylor, whose life has revolved around the study of the law, to ignore its cracks. While this interpretation may seem too harsh to some readers, it is impossible to reassign agency to Tom if as readers we continue to construct more white characters, like Atticus, as heroes.

4. I would again argue that, in this moment, Judge Taylor's choice to strike Mr. Deas's comments from the record points to his fear of any confrontation with the truth of the system. Mr. Deas's comments not only breach the social contract of the space but also the Racial Contract. For more on the tension between race and citizenship in American courtrooms, see Ariela J. Gross's *What Blood Won't Tell: A History of Race on Trial in America* (Cambridge: Harvard U P, 2008).

5. I borrow the term and concept of the post-performance from Susan Bennett (174).

6. The medical model of disability locates an individual's inability to participate "normally" in everyday life within the individual as opposed to society and relies on the

medical field for diagnosis and treatment. This model, then, sometimes rather arbitrarily, relies on the surveying of the body. For a discussion of disability models, see Tom Shakespeare's *Disability Rights and Wrongs* (New York: Routledge, 2006).

7. Although Boo is represented as the medical model of disability, his story also points to the limitations of this model over the social model that addresses culture's role and culpability in creating impairments.

8. In this moment, we are reminded of Bob Ewell's dramatic finger-pointing gesture to Tom in court.

9. It is significant to note that the manner in which Boo inspects the body of Jem is not unlike the methodical observation of Boo by Scout.

Works Cited

Bakhtin, M. Mikhail. "Discourse in the Novel." In *The Dialogic Imagination: Four Essays by M. M. Bakhtin.* Ed. Michael Holquist. Trans. Caryl Emerson and Michael Holquist. Austin: U Texas P, 1981. (259–422)

———. *Problems of Dostoevsky's Poetics.* Trans. and ed. Caryl Emerson. Minneapolis: U Minnesota P, 1984.

Bennett, Susan. *Theatre Audience: A Theory of Production and Reception.* New York: Routledge, 1990.

Brooks, Peter. *Reading for Plot: Design and Intention in Narrative.* Cambridge, MA: Harvard U P, 1992.

Brueggemann, Brenda Jo. "Delivering Disability, Willing Speech." In *Bodies in Commotion.* Ed. Carrie Sandahl and Philip Auslander. Ann Arbor: U Michigan P, 2005. (17–29)

Gross, Ariela J. *What Blood Won't Tell: A History of Race on Trial in America.* Cambridge, MA: Harvard U P, 2008.

Kivy, Peter. *The Performance of Reading.* Oxford: Blackwell, 2006.

Kuppers, Petra. *Community Performance.* New York: Routledge, 2007.

Lee, Harper. *To Kill a Mockingbird.* 1960. New York: Harper Perennial Modern Classics, 2006.

Mills, Charles W. *The Racial Contract.* Ithaca, NY: Cornell U P, 1997.

Mitchell, David T., and Sharon L. Snyder. *Narrative Prosthesis: Disability and the Dependencies of Discourse.* Ann Arbor: U Michigan P, 2000.

Peterson, Eric E., and Kristin M. Langellier. "The Performance Turn in Narrative Studies." *Narrative Inquiry* 16.1 (2006): 173–180.

Shakespeare, Tom. *Disability Rights and Wrongs.* New York: Routledge, 2006.

Stubblefield, Anne. "Race, Disability, and the Social Contract." *The Southern Journal of Philosophy* 157 (2009): 104–111.

Thomson, Rosemarie Garland. "Dares to Stares, Disabled Women Performance Artists and the Dynamics of Staring." In *Bodies in Commotion.* Ed. Carrie Sandahl and Philip Auslander. Ann Arbor: U Michigan P, 2005. (30–41)

Voloshinov, V. N. *Marxism and the Philosophy of Language.* 1929. Trans. Ladislav Matejka and I. R. Titunik. Cambridge, MA: Harvard U P, 1986.

CHAPTER 14

"Just One Kind of Folks:" The Normalizing Power of Disability in *To Kill a Mockingbird*

Hugh McElaney

"We like to have all our comforts and familiars about us," Harper Lee remarked in the course of her address to West Point cadets in March of 1965, "and tend to push away that which is different, and worrisome" (Shields 244). The perception of "difference" and the persistent, pervasive anxiety it causes in the community of Maycomb, Alabama, have informed a variety of critical readings of *To Kill a Mockingbird*. Such readings have focused principally on issues of race, class, gender, and even the suggestion of queered identity in the text. Less commonly, scholars have attended to the actual and constructed varieties of disability that attach themselves to each and all of these marginalized identities, even though, as David T. Mitchell and Sharon L. Snyder have noted, the book "is *directly about* making the terrain of disability and disabled people less alien" (*Negative Prosthesis* 173).[1]

Reading *To Kill a Mockingbird* "disconstructively"—that is, by holding the construction of disability within the novel to be centrally informative—is in no way intended to call into question the lasting merit of other interpretations. As a story about race and social justice, in particular, it has continued to inspire both admiration and controversy. Theodore and Grace-Ann Hovet have elegantly argued for an understanding of "the way the novel links racism to gender and class oppression" (68). And, more daringly perhaps, Gary Richards has suggested that the novel's "symbolic representation of closetedness [and] a destabilization of heterosexuality" (151) in the individualized and social character of Maycomb help explain why *To Kill a Mockingbird* has been ranked among the most influential gay-themed novels produced in America.

211

The disability reading of the story I intend to offer here is not a leeward tack away from these more familiar, mainstream critical excursions, but rather a deliberate effort to moor them with a different kind of anchor. For if, as Mitchell and Snyder have contended, "disability is the master trope of human disqualification" (*Cultural Locations* 125), such a reading can provide us with a unified way of examining the myriad presentations of human difference within the story, fragmenting distinctions rooted in notions of biological fitness that Lee seeks to resolve in a fundamentally disconstructive fashion. And this, it seems to me, is arguably what *To Kill a Mockingbird* is about—an exploration of both the stigmatizing power of difference and its transformation into something privileged.

To this end, I will look first at two "different and worrisome" characters— Boo Radley and Tom Robinson—whose disability-coded presences compel the attention of both the general reader and Scout as cultural reader. Then I will look, more extensively, at the disabling way in which the biological determinism of eugenics influences comfortable community assumptions about family and folks in Maycomb. Finally, I will examine how these influences are interrogated in the text in order to invest disability with normalizing power.

"On all sides, madness fascinates man," Michel Foucault once said (23). In Maycomb, a town assiduously observant of the boundaries, visible and invisible, that separate and define its mixed populations, Boo Radley surely fascinates us—in no small part because he occupies, in counterintuitive fashion, centered space. The decaying Radley house with its "malevolent phantom" does not lie on the dusky fringe of Maycomb, but in its heart, three doors south from the Finch house and adjoining the schoolyard (*TKAM* 7). Boo's private confinement has endured for years in the midst of normal daily life all around it; but while inaccessible and *shut* away, he has never truly *gone* away, and it is this paradox that seizes upon the imagination of Scout, Jem, and Dill, who devote so much of their time together in trying to make Boo "come out." Yet another paradox serves to oppose their interests; for the rest of the town, Boo Radley's constant presence is bound up in a tacit social understanding that he cannot be acknowledged. In some sense, then, the invisible Boo exercises a dual kind of secret authority. Boo's mythic self, true to his nickname, terrifies the children, even as it compels their wakeful attention—yet Boo induces a forgetfulness on the rest of the town for whom he has largely disappeared as a living entity, "stigmatized as non-being" (Foucault 116).

To terrify, to fascinate, to be rendered invisible . . . all these masquerades are well-known among the disabled everywhere, for whom closeted confinement—whether self-imposed or imposed by others—has a complex signifying power akin to, but not derived from, that felt by queer folk. As Tobin Siebers points out,

> The closet often holds secrets that either cannot be told or are being kept by those who do not want to know the truth about the closeted person. Some people keep secrets; other people are secrets. Some people hide in the closet, but others are locked in the closet. There is a long history, of course, of locking away people with disabilities in attics, basements, and backrooms. (98)

In fact, the closeted Boo seems to so comfortably fit this profile of disability that we may be tempted not to question the reality of his mental illness; after all, most critical readings of the character don't. But as a good lawyer like Atticus Finch would surely remind his jury, such a conclusion would call on us to assume facts not in evidence.

Disability is, after all—as Lennard Davis reminds us—a phenomenon that is located in the observer (50), and Boo's disability is not so much a verifiable impairment as it is a construction of community narratives about him. The circumstances leading to Boo's home confinement are the product of "neighborhood legend" (*TKAM* 10), and Jem "received most of his information [about Boo] from Stephanie Crawford" (*TKAM* 11), a notorious gossip, who unreliably claims to have seen his "skull" peering through her window one night. Sudden cold snaps that kill azaleas are believed to be Boo's doing,[2] as is a rash of nocturnal animal killings, later discovered to be the work of another—a fact that does not disturb the town's crafted discourse of his monstrosity, the man-beast Jem translates into "reasonable" profile:

> Boo was about six-and-a-half feet tall, judging from his tracks; he dined on raw squirrels and any cats he could catch. . . . There was a long jagged scar that ran across his face; what teeth he had were yellow and rotten; his eyes popped, and he drooled most of the time (*TKAM* 14).

The felt need to codify difference through "the invocation of monstrosity should alert us to the inclination for creating fantastical landscapes where we encounter only our own ignorance and grotesquerie" (Mitchell and Snyder, *Narrative Prosthesis* 70–71), but this is a lesson lost on Maycomb's adults and not yet meaningful to the children. So they build on and perpetuate these stories by creating one of their own, "One Man's Family," a drama in which Jem, Scout, and Dill publicly reenact the lurid details of Stephanie Crawford's foundational tales.

The cumulative effect of these narratives is to create what Erving Goffman has termed a "spoiled identity" for Boo, his phantom status an essential part of the stigma by which he is "reduced . . . from a whole and usual person to a tainted, discounted one" (3). Or to put it in a disconstructive fashion, Boo's persistent invisibility creates a vacuum of anxiety that is readily filled by communal texts that collectively shape him into disabled form. But despite their own contribution to these texts, the children are unwilling to settle for the uncritical reading of Boo that more or less satisfies the adults in Maycomb, as they probe the alien space inscribed around Boo through a series of childish pranks.

While their behavior at some level can be seen as thoughtless, even taunting—a furious Atticus demands they stop "tormenting" Boo—Jem, Scout, and Dill also act to tease out Boo's humanity, to reconcile what Goffman calls the "discrepancy between an individual's actual social identity and his virtual one" (41). And it is to this impulse that Boo responds. He does not look to negotiate a socially acceptable status by "coming out" generally to Maycomb's adults; rather, he seeks a connection—selectively and furtively—to its children. Goffman notes the phenomenon of "discreditable" (for which read "disabled") people exercising information control of their identities, deciding "to display or not display; to tell or not to tell; to let on or not to let on . . . and in each case to whom, how, when, or where" (42). And so Boo, from time to time, leaves tokens for Jem and Scout in the knothole of the tree, suggesting a desire to establish familiarity, if not an almost familial bond.[3] He also ventures out to retrieve Jem's pants and fold them over the fence after the young boy's misadventure in the Radley garden. Unbeknownst to Scout, he later slips a blanket over her shoulders as Maudie's house burns down shortly after a rare winter storm (*TKAM* 77). And he emerges one last time to save the children's lives when they are attacked by Bob Ewell.

Each act bears directly upon Boo's socially constructed disability and simultaneously confounds it. He comes out only at night when he is least likely to disrupt the field of community observation—and most likely to elude its stigmatizing gaze. His gifts, on the other hand, extend an offer of symbolic kinship. Instead of requiring the solicitude of others, he assumes the role of surrogate parent, caring for and protecting Jem and Scout when both care and protection are wanting from others.[4] He also displays an unexpected reserve of physical strength in his encounter with Bob Ewell. And he shows a more figurative, but equally important, kind of strength by acting autonomously and independently. Boo *chooses*. He does not depend upon the kindness of strangers or the approval of familiars. Not only does he defy the stereotypes of weakness and victimization associated with disability, but for the Finches—some of whom are embarrassed by their lack of recorded ancestors at the Battle of Hastings—he is, as Laura Fine observes, "a knight in shining armor" (74). Without speaking a word, shorn of alien status at the story's most critical juncture, he attains a moral stature in the novel that is just as articulate in its way as that demonstrated by Atticus himself.

Most critically, Boo Radley compels us to reconsider what is normal and what is aberrant in Maycomb. Disappearing into his home for the last time, Boo may not be behaving in the fashion deemed appropriate historically for disabled people—a social contaminant best hidden from view. His decision may come, rather, from an understanding that the society itself is contaminated and disabling, an insight not lost on the children. Boo doesn't have to stay inside, Jem comes to realize—he *wants* to stay inside (*TKAM* 259). And Scout, who walks arm in arm with Boo at the story's end, seems to walk just as comfortably in isolation: "I came to the conclusion that people were just peculiar. I withdrew from them, and never thought about them until I was forced to" (*TKAM* 279).

Peculiar people in Maycomb, we come to see, are the products of peculiar institutions and thus particularly susceptible to infection from the town's "usual disease."

Nathan Radley "bought cotton" for a living, just as the male descendants of Simon Finch tended to do. As sure as the coursing of the Alabama River from Finch's Landing to the sea, the ebb and flow of Maycomb County's fortunes are morally encumbered by their historical tethering to the institution of slavery. Three score and more years after the Emancipation Proclamation, that dark entailment serves as the backdrop against which the tragic drama of Tom Robinson unfolds. But while virulent small-town racism is brought most prominently to trial in *To Kill a Mockingbird* and the book's examination of its tributary injustices have dominated critical discourse over the last fifty years, a consideration of the way race and disability conflate in the novel—or more specifically, the way notions of disability inform racialized thinking—may offer us better access to Lee's broader literary purpose.

Mitchell and Snyder have speculated that "an idea about biologically inferior bodies preceded the belief in a racially degraded body," explaining "the degree to which racial marginalization depends on concepts of in-built biological inferiority" (*Cultural Locations* 106). A generation before General Jackson ran the Creeks up the creek opening the way for Dr. Simon Finch, Dr. Benjamin Rush had argued that black skin was a form of leprosy (Baynton 40). And a hundred years later, Tom Robinson is culturally marked as a figure of disability more by virtue of his racial identity than by virtue of his damaged left arm.

The ideological justification for racism began to assume "scientific" dimension in eighteenth-century Europe, as Stephen Jay Gould cogently recounts in *The Mismeasure of Man*. Gould notes that the Swedish naturalist Carl Linnaeus proposed a racial taxonomy (as early as 1758, in *Systema naturae*) that "mixed character with anatomy" (35) in such a way as to suggest a pervasive degeneracy inherent in blackness; similarly, in 1812, the French paleontologist George Cuvier "read" in the bones of Africans a text that revealed "the most degraded of human races whose form approaches that of the beast" (Gould 36); while the Swiss biologist Louis Agassiz, after emigrating to America, extended scientific racism in 1850 by arguing the merits of polygeny, a theory that categorized blacks and other non-white people as members of distinct (and inferior) species

(Gould 42–46). Agassiz spawned a host of American disciples, notably in the medical community, among them Joseph Nott, author of *Types of Mankind* (1854), renowned for touring the South to offer self-proclaimed "lectures on niggerology" (Gould 69). The works of Nott and others—indeed the growing acceptance of scientific racism as indisputable fact—translated directly and easily into the nineteenth century's culture of mass entertainment, when freak shows burgeoned in popularity. Along with the presentation of nonnormative bodies of all kinds, a prominent feature of the freak show was the exhibition of black bodies staged to suggest atavistic or subhuman characteristics.

Other tacks were employed. Dr. Samuel Cartwright, a prominent physician and member of Jefferson Davis' Confederate cabinet, identified "diseases" peculiar to slaves. *Dysaethesia aethiopica*, a respiratory ailment, revealed itself symptomatically in sloppy, careless labor habits and was best treated, according to Cartwright, by oiling the skin, slapping it in "with a broad leather strap," then "put[ting] the patient to some hard kind of work" (Gould 71). *Draeptomania*, on the other hand, was a mental illness that irrationally compelled its sufferers to *run away*, caused by masters who "had made themselves too familiar with" their slaves, interfering with the African's natural desire to be subservient, as "written in the physical structure of his knees, being more flexed or bent, than any other kind of man" (Baynton 38). With the abolition of slavery, the pernicious arguments of scientific racism were restaged from the late nineteenth century into the early twentieth. The potential of inferior black blood mingling with and corrupting the white race led to the passage of strict anti-miscegenation statutes in nearly two dozen states; "'one drop of negro blood makes the negro' is no longer a theory," warned the Anglo-Saxon Club of Virginia, "but a logically induced scientific fact" that in the absence of restrictive marriage laws threatened white supremacy (Black 166).[5] Neither freedom nor education offered hope to African Americans in the eyes of those swayed by racist theories of biological determinism. Dr. John Van Evrie opined that "an 'educated' negro, like a 'free' negro, is a social monstrosity" (Baynton 38), whose body would be further damaged by intellectual activity. Moreover, Dr. J. F. Miller claimed that freed blacks, constitutionally unsuitable for liberty, had higher incidences of tuberculosis, mental illness, and congenital defects (Baynton 38–39).

To view the underlying nature of racism historically as a kind of disability construct is valuable in coming to a fuller understanding of "Maycomb's usual disease." In its most extreme form, the contagion triggers an outbreak of unabashed hatred from Bob Ewell, the simmering violence of the Old Sarum mob that threatens to lynch Tom, and the sputtering, dyspeptic rage of Miss Dubose. It also infects the Missionary Circle, whose purported interest in the salvation of the Mrunas in Africa stands in stark contrast with its intolerance for black folk in its own town, as well as the hypocritical Miss Gates, who guides her class through a lesson on the evils of Nazi Germany (and its campaign to exterminate those literally and figuratively disabled) and then is overheard by Scout wishing another sort of lesson could be visited on uppity Negroes.

It is a malady from which no member of the community is truly immune, even its best citizens. Maudie bemoans the fact that there are only a "handful of people with enough humility to think, when they look at a Negro, there but for the Lord's kindness am I" (*TKAM* 270), a phrase replete with the sort of degrading pity (masquerading as enlightened empathy) that is all too familiar to people with disabilities. Even Atticus himself is not without fault. His sense of history is naïve (or disingenuous) when he dismisses the Ku Klux Klan as a mere "political organization" (*TKAM* 167). He is frankly paternalistic, too. According to Scout, for example, "Atticus says cheatin' a colored man is ten times worse than cheatin' a white man" (*TKAM* 229); in addition, he esteems Tom for being a "quiet, respectable, humble Negro" (*TKAM* 231); and he despises "a low-grade white man who'll take advantage of a Negro's ignorance" (*TKAM* 252). In characterizing stereotypes about black men as "a lie as black as Tom Robinson's skin" (231), he indulges in a stigmatizing metaphor that adds linguistic weight to that very stereotype. And when he chastises Scout for using the word "nigger," he does so not because the term is hateful and degrading, but because "that's common" (*TKAM* 85), a mere breach of etiquette reflecting poorly upon the speaker's social status. Given his moral stature in the novel, Atticus' parental correction is surprising for it both lacks moral force and fails to provide insight for his child; "I ain't very sure what it means," to be a "nigger-lover" she admits later to Uncle Jack (*TKAM* 98).

Which is why, perhaps, Scout *does not* stop using the word, most egregiously employing it when she asks Calpurnia why she sometimes uses "nigger-talk" (*TKAM* 143). It is not just a word she must struggle to free herself from using, but the disabling representations of a collective past of which that word is token. Just as she learns to reject false community narratives about Boo (and mental illness), Scout must unlearn the burden of deeply embedded, false narratives about Tom (and race-as-biological-defect) that are also part of her legacy. And as a descendant of Simon Finch—the doctor-turned-enslaver—she must do so not simply through firsthand encounter, but by discovering a new historical model to replace the one created and sustained, in large measure, by medical men in the service of scientific racism.

The most visceral, personal experience that alters Scout's view of both race and disability is the revelation at trial of Tom's withered left arm, a cathartic event that Ato Quayson has called "disability as epiphany" (45). At one level, Tom's impairment encodes his unique status. It is a cotton gin, that critical engine of the slave economy, that disables Tom; the singular cripple brings into sharper relief the more generalized, historical damage inflicted on the black body, and vice versa, each marker signifying and fusing with the other. At a second level, Quayson notes, "the sudden disclosure of the disability is meant not to raise doubts about the moral stature of the disabled character, but to dispel them" (45). While Boo Radley attains stature by coming out at a moment of crisis and belying his purported disability, the conviction and fatal shooting of Tom Robinson after he comes out tragically clarifies for the Finch children the consequences of the community's persistent impulse to eradicate culturally discredited difference from the social body.

The other event, which moves Scout to an even broader reevaluation of racial identity, occurs before the trial when she meets Dolphus Raymond. Raymond, a white man, is reviled by most of Maycomb because, as Jem says, "he's got a colored woman and all sorts of mixed chillun" (*TKAM* 183), in violation of established taboo, if not law. What puzzles Scout most is Jem's insistence that "mixed chillun" are readily identifiable, even if they appear to be black. How can Jem tell?

> "You can't sometimes, not unless you know who they are. But he's half Raymond, all right."
> "But how can you *tell?*" I asked.
> "I told you, Scout, you just hafta know who they are."
> "Well how do you know we ain't Negroes?"
> "Uncle Jack says we really don't know . . . for all he knows we mighta *come straight out* of Ethiopia durin' the Old Testament."
> "Well if we *came out* durin' the Old Testament, it's too long ago to matter." (*TKAM* 184, my emphasis)

"The vision of the novel," Gerald Early has argued, "is ultimately a miscegenated one" (103); put another way, it is a vision that contests the prevailing and disabling discourse about racial distinctiveness. The possibility that the Finches—or all white people, for that matter—could trace their lineage to black ancestry is more than mere revelation to Scout. It is another in a series of coming-out moments in the story, one that ultimately leads Scout to challenge the historical model of scientific racism and replace it with a new model that abolishes imputed racial difference as a rationale for human disqualification.[6]

Tom Robinson and Boo Radley are both figures who first appear beyond Maycomb's horizon of the normal that Scout reads into normalcy through active disconstruction of their alleged differences.[7] Inoculation against one strain of Maycomb's usual disease, however, does not provide immunity against all. Scout must similarly be exposed to another insidious pathogen, the alienating tribal suppositions about kith and kin that reside comfortably and largely unchallenged in the community's core. These troubling assumptions about the nature of families found ready support from a controversial new "science" that emerged on the cusp of the twentieth century.

Eugenics, a term coined by Sir Francis Galton in 1883, arose as a conflicted social response to Darwin's theory of evolution. On the one hand, "the prevailing ideology—that those who achieved social dominance were biologically superior—seemed to fit remarkably well with Darwin's theory of natural selection in the animal kingdom" (Wray 69). The notion that economic hierarchies operated in accordance with natural law seemed particularly reassuring to those privileged with capital in America. On the other hand, there was a gnawing anxiety over the proliferation of prisons, hospitals, and asylums, as well as an increasing number of unconfined homeless, unemployed and impoverished people. A permanent working underclass was necessary, perhaps, for capitalism to function in optimal fashion, but a growing population of unproductive and institutionalized citizens was an onerous economic and social burden. If evolution promised improvement for humanity, its workings seemed frustratingly slow at best in such an environment, or gone terribly awry at worst.

Eugenics offered the promise of exerting human control over evolution to hasten its pace. Though Galton was neither a scientist nor a doctor (his special interest was statistics), he and those who followed in his steps developed a hypothesis with the trappings of both science and medicine. Human heredity, they theorized, did not simply play out in the transmission of physical characteristics like eye color or height. Superior blood lines, or "germ plasm" (as the biological unit of heritable transmission was popularly called), produced offspring of superior intelligence, industriousness, moral character, emotional soundness, and social fitness; conversely, inferior, "dysgenic" blood lines produced feeble-mindedness, shiftlessness, delinquency, poverty, and social unfitness. As a matter of social policy, eugenicists urged, histories of families should be collected and analyzed to determine their biological fitness. Those of superior breeding might then be incentivized, or even required, to marry others with superior germ plasm; those with inferior germ plasm could be de-incentivized (or legally compelled through sterilization) from continuing their blood line, since in Galton's words, "a stop should be put to the production of families of children likely to include degenerates" (Black 18).

As a practical matter, the eugenic dream did not reach full flower until it was put to earnest use in Nazi Germany to exterminate disabled people and "degenerate" Jewish stock— what Cecil Jacobs artlessly calls "washin' all the feeble-minded" (*TKAM* 280). Its application in the United States during the late nineteenth and early twentieth century was less brutal, but the involuntary sterilization of seventy thousand Americans in the twentieth century (Black 398) hardly qualifies as benign.[8] While the campaign to eliminate the reproductive capacity of unfit Americans spanned all regions of the country, much of its attention focused on the South, an area of the nation viewed as peculiarly diseased. And the particular situation of a young white Virginian woman, Carrie Buck, served, in the 1927 Supreme Court case of *Buck v. Bell*, as a constitutional test of involuntary, state-mandated sterilization as eugenic policy. Virginia's decision to sterilize Buck and members of her family was couched in terms of her alleged mental retardation, but was actually a more broadly targeted attack on a type of citizen deemed "socially inadequate," those culturally located as *white trash*, who "belong to the shiftless, ignorant, and worthless class of anti-social whites of the South" (Wray 92).

Popular objects of derision as human refuse in antebellum literary works by authors like John Pendleton Kennedy and Daniel Hundley, white trash were pathologically characterized. In his novel *Horseshoe Robinson* (1835), for example, Kennedy called readers' attention to "the corporeal stigma marks— sinewy, distorted, asymmetrical bodies, for example—that suggested lineal degeneracy and biological inferiority were the root of the poor white trash problem" (Wray 56). Anticipating eugenic rhetoric, Hundley's sociological tract *Social Relations in Our Southern States* (1860), located trash at the lowest level of hierarchical whiteness, permanently consigned to such station as the product of tainted bloodlines (Wray 60–61), with a reputed penchant for sexual immorality in general and incest in particular. The conflation of class, disability, and hereditary defect constituted the enduring image of poor Southern whites into the twentieth century, reasserting itself most famously in the Supreme Court's decision upholding the constitutionality of Virginia's sterilization of Carrie Buck when Oliver Wendell Holmes declared that "three generations of imbeciles are enough" (Wray 93).

Inhabiting the villainous fringe of Lee's novel, "the Ewells had been the disgrace of Maycomb for three generations" (*TKAM* 33). Etymologically, "ewell" trickles down from an Old English word meaning *river source* or *spring*,[9] in *To Kill a Mockingbird*, the Ewells are both the wellspring of figured contamination that flows through Maycomb's social blood and among those most explicitly contaminated by its waters. In her classic examination of the cultural phenomenon of "Africanism" in white America, Toni Morrison interrogates the "disabling virus" (7) of racism, not simply for its pathological impact on black identity, but for its concomitant and consequential effects on the host body, "the impact of racism on those who perpetuate it" (11).

The racial status of the Ewells, as victimizers and victims, is repeatedly problematized in the story. Only a "fist-sized clean space" (*TKAM* 29) in a blackened face identifies Burris Ewell as white; Bob Ewell's whiteness is revealed only by a soap scrubbing (*TKAM* 195); Mayella reminds Scout of a mixed-race child (*TKAM* 218). Concurrently, the most explicit images of degradation, disease, and disability in the story are reserved for the Ewells. Not only is Burris Ewell "the filthiest human I had ever seen" (*TKAM* 29), but his body is infected with lice, signifiers of "the parasitical nature of white freedom" (Morrison 57). The family's violent incestuousness marks its blood as dysgenically stained. Their property abuts the town's literal garbage dump and looks "like the playhouse of an insane child" (*TKAM* 194). Bob Ewell on the witness stand has the appearance of a "deaf-mute" (*TKAM* 198). Creating collateral damage at the site where externalized and internalized oppression meet, racism and constructions of disability collide. "One supposes," Morrison writes, "that if Africans all had three eyes or one ear, the significance of that difference from the smaller but conquering European invaders would also have been found to have meaning" (49). Not without companion meaning is the depiction of Bob Ewell, that little rooster of a man, as a "three-legged chicken or a square egg" (*TKAM* 287). The disconstructive significance of the Ewells within the larger presentation of disability in the novel is a subject to which I will return later in this inquiry.

Relentlessly engaged in field work to compile family pedigrees (largely those of poor, rural "tribes," a term widely applied in eugenic texts and *Mockingbird* alike), eugenic researchers were most drawn, in the late nineteenth and early twentieth century, to dysgenic white subjects like the Ewells. The biological inferiority of African Americans was already considered an irrefutable fact; a comforting conviction that pervasive social segregation and antimiscegenation laws would protect white America from black contagion made study of the latter less compelling than an inquiry into aspects of purported white degeneracy. Nicole Hahn Rafter recounts in *White Trash* that examinations of clans like the Jukes, the Ishmaels, and the Smoky Pilgrims were rife with lurid narratives of criminal, feebleminded, incestuous vagabonds who lurked throughout rural America and reproduced their kind in alarming numbers, leading to an increasingly dangerous, degenerate, and pervasive social underclass. As scientific inquiries, many of these studies were suspected at the time (and revealed with more certainty later) to be profoundly unscientific, deeply flawed methodologically, and driven by class bias—outing eugenics as an instrument of social Darwinism. The researchers effectively found what they came to find—a new model of biological determinism and scientifically constructed disability. As Rafter explains, the authors of these narratives invariably

> assume that the distribution of social power can be explained in hereditarian terms. The poor are destitute, the criminal wicked, and the feeble-minded retarded owing to unfortunate heredity; conversely, members of the middle-class are thrifty, law-abiding, and intellectually superior thanks to genetic virtue. After the early twentieth century rediscovery of Mendel's laws of inheritance, the authors used this model to map social worth. In their works heritable unit characteristics

become codes for social hierarchy. Genetic and social worth coincided exactly. (6–7)

But in their quest to find a biological basis for human value, eugenicists did not limit themselves to investigations of the degenerate poor. They engaged in a vigorous program to educate the public about the perfectability of the species and to identify the best and brightest that the American gene pool had to offer. Fittingly, they found a popular venue to pursue both impulses at an iconic American ritual—the annual county fair. County fairs served as rural meccas of both agricultural accomplishment and popular entertainment. Along the fairs' midways, spectators could gaze at spectacles of human prowess in the selective breeding of produce and livestock, while diverting themselves at sideshows that might display examples of *lusus naturae* every bit as wondrous as three-eared Africans and three-legged chickens. And beginning in 1920 at the Kansas State Fair, spectators would witness a new sort of exhibit that combined both these traditional presentations. This exhibit staged a competition not between pumpkins or pigs, but between human families, who would submit an "Abridged Record of Family Traits" for the review of eugenically minded doctors, psychologists, and scientists. Each family was judged on its presented quality of eugenic health and vied for prized recognition, medals that proclaimed, "Yea, I have a goodly heritage." This contest in human breeding, known as Fitter Families for Future Firesides, was the brainchild of Mary Watts and Florence Sherbon—not, as the good folks in Maycomb might have guessed, Alexandra Finch.[10]

Family geography in Maycomb County is mapped by long-standing contours of ascribed social worth; the farther we stray from the center of town, the less trustworthy and valued those ascriptions become. "Fine Folks" and "Old Families" enjoy the privileges of a proper noun, landed status, and knit neighborhoods; the relatively uncapitalized "common folk" occupy more uncertain physical and cultural terrain. The "enormous and confusing tribe" (*TKAM* 10) of Cunninghams live on the northern fringe of the county, where they intermingle with Coninghams and branch into honest dirt farmers, a delinquent class of "gangs," or a hybrid of both. The Ewell "tribe" (*TKAM* 147) lives beyond, near the town dump, in a degenerate, semi-human form that garners attention as both a persistent social burden and resident freak show. And on the furthest inhabited margin live the black people of Maycomb, reduced in much serious white thinking to a separate, subordinate species. Human value spreads not just horizontally along the land, but vertically along a eugenic-dysgenic axis.

The boundaries appear clear, as they usually do at first glance. In *Not Quite White*, Matt Wray suggests the uses of "boundary theory" in an examination of cultural issues like the one at play here in *Mockingbird*.[11] This theory "begins by asking how categories shape our perception of the world. . . . [T]o state that two things belong to different categories is to assert that they have nothing in common. To state that two things belong to the same category is to assert that they share a common identity" (7). Thus, the markers we place to define boundary placement "offer cognitive shortcuts . . . quick understanding without having to expend much thought" (Wray 8). Boundaries assume symbolic shape "to differentiate things that might otherwise appear similar and to render discontinuous what would otherwise be continuous" (9). Most particularly for my purpose here, he adds that "symbolic boundaries have a distinctly moral dimension. . . . Boundaries are normative in that they are routinely used to establish basic distinctions between good and bad people, distinctions used to determine who belongs where in social space" (16).

The process of dividing and arranging population tracks not simply along socioeconomic lines in Maycomb, but more significantly (in a disconstructive reading) across a sociobiological spectrum that adheres to fundamental eugenic principles. In the eugenic worldview, "good and bad" largely signified the absence or presence of heritable defect, and the quality of trait distribution governed social outcomes. In this sense, boundary-making is a disabling cultural enterprise.

Such identity markers are repeatedly linked to heritable "tribal traits" in Scout's earliest readings of her world. The Haverfords, whom Atticus unsuccessfully defends early in his career, bear "a name synonymous with jackass" (*TKAM* 5). Miss Caroline comes from Winston County and is suspected to be a carrier of the "peculiarities indigenous to that region" (*TKAM* 18). Scout's own uncanny ability to read at an early age suggests to Jem that his sister is not a Finch, but a Bullfinch (*TKAM* 19)—a "changeling" figure whose presence, in folklore, was intimately associated with disability and "often implied a closely related panic about neighboring peoples" (Silver 86–87).[12] Her effort to explain to Miss Caroline the behavior of Walter Cunningham—"he's a Cunningham" (*TKAM* 22)—seems perfectly satisfactory to Scout; it appears equally reasonable to shame Walter at the Finch dinner table because "he ain't company, Cal, he's just a Cunningham" (*TKAM* 27). Foot-washing Baptists, she learns, think "women are a sin by definition" (*TKAM* 50), just as women in the nineteenth and early twentieth century were widely viewed as *disabled* by definition, their "social position . . . treated as a medical problem that necessitated separate and special care" (Baynton 43).[13] Atticus appears "feeble," his partial blindness "the tribal curse of the Finches" (*TKAM* 102). Miss Dubose's verbal attack on the Finches' "moral degeneration" is an assault on "the family's mental hygiene" (*TKAM* 117), both popular catchphrases in eugenic texts.

One is sorely tempted, in fact, after we have encountered Aunt Alexandra, to conclude that Scout's extreme trait consciousness—which serves, in part to create new boundaries of difference within old ones—is itself inherited. "Cold and there," a compulsive trait monger, and high priestess of the religion known as What's Best for the Family, Alexandra bears an uncanny resemblance to Charles Benedict Davenport—a solitary, aloof man who in his role as head of the Eugenics Records Office in Cold Spring Harbor, New York, in the first decades of the twentieth century devoted himself to the collection and interpretation of data on human pedigrees—America's high priest in the eugenic movement's mission to ensure What's Best for Mankind.

Unlike the Finches, Davenport's father traced his Anglo-Saxon roots to within twenty years of the Battle of Hastings (Black 33). Heredity and worth were inextricably linked concepts for the younger Davenport; heritable traits influenced the entire human character. "Each 'family' will be seen to be stamped with a peculiar set of traits depending on the nature of its germ plasm," he wrote in *Heredity in Relation to Eugenics*. In his opinion, academic achievement, professional success, political prowess, artistic creativity, insanity, epilepsy, sexual licentiousness, suicide, and criminality were all predictable narratives told by bloodline (Black 73). So too were "participation in church activities . . . interest in world events or neighborhood gossip . . . modesty," the inclination to "hold a grudge," as well as the capacity for "optimism, patriotism, and car[ing] for the good opinion of others" (Black 106). Davenport and his staff, between 1904 and 1917, painstakingly gathered data from American families (organized into "family trait booklets"), the record of which "proved" these assertions. In all, the Eugenics Record Office compiled over fifty thousand pages of family data and index cards on more than five hundred thousand individuals, "each card offer[ing] lines for forty personal traits" (Black 105).

Even if Alexandra's research is less exhaustive, her famous maxims for evaluating the "streaks" in Maycomb's families seem eerily similar and rooted in her own version of pseudo-science.

> She never let a chance escape her to point out the shortcomings of other tribal groups to the greater glory of our own . . . the old citizens, the present generation of people who had lived side by side for years and years, were utterly predictable to one another; they took for granted attitudes, character shadings, even gestures, as having been repeated in each generation and refined by time. Thus the dicta No Crawford Minds His Own Business, Every Third Merriweather Is Morbid, The Truth Is Not in the Delafields, All the Bufords Walk Like That . . . (*TKAM* 147, 149)[14]

Alexandra's "royal prerogative" (her very name is imperial) relocates boundary-making in *Mockingbird* from outside the world of "Fine Folk" to its interior, as a kind of policing activity to enforce disabling distinctions among Maycomb's relatively privileged citizens and confine the limits of their cultural space. Born of the same belief in biological determinism that facilitates the formation of local boundaries separating races and classes, her activity shares the same viral characteristics—an attachment to a faith in stigmatized difference that is historically constructed and eugenically propelled.

But boundaries are not just formed and maintained; they may be transformed as well (Wray 14). Just as Scout learns to read against the grain of the dominant discourse surrounding Boo and Tom, she learns how unstable boundaries can be in Maycomb, the multiple ways in which they may be transgressed, and the normalizing power that is ultimately seen to attend disability.

At each margin of tribal fencing they erect and defend, Aunt Alexandra and like-minded people of Maycomb attempt to define what they are *not* as much as what they *are* in the interests of a time-honored hierarchy wobbling under the strain of economic hardship, racial tension, and uncertain personal identity. Yet, significantly, there are several examples of literal and symbolic boundaries crossed as the story progresses, most of which involve contact with a culturally (and biologically) discredited Otherness.

Fine Folks and common folks alike straddle familiar and alien spaces. Sam Levy and his family retain their privileged status though implicitly stigmatized by their Jewish identity. Dolphus Raymond lives with black people and fathers mixed children, but is not reduced to "trash" because "he owns all one side of the riverbank down there, and he's from a real old family to boot" (*TKAM* 183). Calpurnia lives a double life, moving with a sense of moral command in white and black worlds alike and "having command of two languages" (*TKAM* 143). Mayella Ewell violates taboo by kissing Tom Robinson. And it is one of the Cunninghams who holds out, albeit briefly, for Tom's acquittal.

But it is Scout who challenges boundaries most vigorously. Reassured by Atticus that her aunt's admonition to be mindful of her gentle Finch "breeding" is advice best forgotten, she realigns herself as common folk. She rejects Alexandra's identification of the Cunninghams as "trash." A "mutt" in Miss Dubose's eyes (*TKAM* 115), Scout remains loyal to Dill, who's a mere "stray dog"[15] to Francis (*TKAM* 94). She goes with Calpurnia to a black church and sits with the black spectators at Tom's trial. And she openly violates prescribed codes for female dress and behavior, contesting the closeted confinement of her "pink cotton penitentiary" (*TKAM* 155) to forge an unconventionally gendered identity. If these various transgressions do not obliterate boundaries, they blur them sufficiently to permit Scout, in particular, to see beyond the array of divisive biological determinants of which they are built. Consequently, the certainties of human makeup and destiny offered up by quack science prove illusory, like the notions of Old Families and Fine Folks. "There's just one kind of folks," Scout comes to believe, "[f]olks" (*TKAM* 259), human beings with a shared heritage of constructed imperfection.

   To Kill a Mockingbird literally begins after it ends, after Jem "waked up in the morning" (*TKAM* 323) with "his arm badly broken" (*TKAM* 3). One of many instances of narrative time travel in Lee's story, this particular example serves strikingly to reconstruct the events of the novel by foregrounding disability and investing it with a central significance from the start, a newly "awakened" understanding, which gathers meaning as the story unfolds. For Maycomb's usual disease is more than the pathology of racism; it is the social fear of widespread infection by exposure to difference, "fear itself" that has caused a community to erect and strive to maintain boundaries among its members, all of whom live under the shadow of one sort of disability or another and labor under an inherited burden of disqualifying biologically constructed Otherness.

   Folks become "just folks" not simply by daring to transgress boundaries, but by recognizing that disability itself freely violates barrier. Most prominently, the afflictions of the Finches persistently link them with the Others. Jem's permanently deformed left arm connects the family to Tom Robinson's. Atticus' "blindness" connects the Finches to the nearsighted Calpurnia, the Cunninghams' "blind spot," Boo's nearly "blind" gray eyes,[16] and the more symbolic lack of visual acuity that pervades the community.[17] And, the tribal "curse" of incest is one the best family in Maycomb implicitly shares with its worst. For if, as Laura Fine argues, "the most unacceptable double upon whom Scout projects her fears or desires is . . . Mayella Ewell" (74), it is in no small part because incest—the taboo lurking in Maycomb's moral center as well as at its most discredited periphery—suggests the two girls share a kind of figurative siblinghood.

   Eugenicists warned of the dual danger posed by people "of inferior blood" and by families "so interwoven in kinship with those still more defective that they are totally unfitted to become . . . useful citizens" (Black 58–59). And so from the eugenic perspective, the folks of Maycomb, from the Finches to the Ewells, more than faintly resemble one another because they are more disconstructively like than unlike. Maycomb's thoroughly mingled bloodlines cast all of its families to a dysgenic margin; paradoxically, then, deviance from the "normal" *is* the norm, and folks become folks (at least in part) because a shared kinship of disability becomes "the great leveler" and assumes normalizing power. "To kill a cripple" becomes a more generalized violence than Mr. Underwood may fully understand when penning his editorial—it is effectively an act of social self-destruction.

It is more than curious that the events of *To Kill a Mockingbird* and its literary creation both unfold against the historical backdrop of one of America's most disabling viruses—poliomyelitis. As young Scout learns a new and better way of reading her world as a child in the 1930s, a polio survivor, Franklin Roosevelt, assumes central responsibility for wrenching the paralyzing grip of "fear itself" from the economic landscape. And as Lee put the finishing touches to her work a half century ago, the fear of polio itself was beginning to abate in the American psyche, thanks to the breakthrough findings of Jonas Salk and Albert Sabin. It is Sabin's discovery of an attenuated vaccine, in particular, that I have been mindful of with this reconsideration of the book on the occasion of its fiftieth anniversary. Attenuation takes a living agent and alters it so that it becomes harmless or less virulent, but still recognizable to the immune system that is roused to combat it. The Sabin vaccine consisted of live polio virus that, when introduced into the bloodstream of children, empowered their immune systems to recognize and render polio powerless. *To Kill a Mockingbird* offers a vision of a world in which exposure to attenuated versions of disability can render the disabling viruses of race, class, and gender oppression (and their historically constructed narratives) powerless. Or, to put it otherwise, our vision of humanity is most encompassing and humane when we look at those disabled by history, science, and small-town mythology—cast to the margin, like people with disabilities everywhere—and see ourselves.

Notes

1. In her 1997 dissertation, Kathleen Anne Patterson offers a Goffmanesque interpretation that *Mockingbird* is a novel "depicting disability as one of many potentially stigmatizing conditions" (64), but she does not see disability itself as the historically constructed, foundational master key of difference in the text, as I will argue here. Patterson's insights, nonetheless, are consistently interesting; her reading of Boo Radley in the context of stigma theory is especially good and an interpretation which I largely share.

2. Later, Mr. Avery attributes the strange snowstorm to disobedient children.

3. As Levi-Strauss points out, "[T]he term 'gift' . . . has the dual meaning of 'present' and 'betrothal'" (63). In this sense, Boo's persistent gifting prefigures the symbolic "engagement" with Scout at the novel's end, when the two walk arm in arm. That engagement, in turn, suggests the natural kinship between their disconstructed identities.

4. In folding Jem's pants and putting the blanket over Scout's shoulders, Boo fills the role of the absent mother. In the more critical act of saving the children from Bob Ewell, he replaces Atticus, whose soothing mantra—"not time to worry yet"—betrays his naïveté about the danger Ewell poses. The mother-father dyad (like Scout's transgendered pose) adds hermaphroditic "monstrosity" to Boo's constructed disability.

5. This is the understanding in Maycomb, too, as Jem knows, because "around here, once you have a drop of Negro blood, that makes you all black" (*TKAM* 184).

6. When the children build the "Morphodite" during the snowstorm, they enact in the ritual of play a foreshadowed understanding of human origins and their implications.

Shaped to resemble Mr. Avery, the figure they construct is essentially earth, covered with just enough snow until "gradually Mr. Avery turned white" (*TKAM* 76). The uncontrasted *whiteness* of the snow Scout awakens to is terrifying ("I nearly died of fright" [*TKAM* 73]), recalling Morrison's observation that "whiteness, alone, is mute, meaningless, unfathomable, pointless, frozen, veiled, curtained, dreaded, senseless, implacable" (59).

7. Boo's whiteness is problematized in a way that suggests an even more layered affinity with Tom. The Radley Place "was once white" but is now "slate-gray" (*TKAM* 9), a merging of black and white. Physically revealed at the end of the story, Boo is "sickly white" (*TKAM* 310).

8. The events of *To Kill a Mockingbird* reach a climax in 1935. That same year, Shields reports, A. C. Lee joined many of his fellow state legislators in voting to enact involuntary sterilization into Alabama law.

9. From Old English "aewell" See A. D. Mills. "Ewell." *A Dictionary of English Place Names.* New York: Oxford U P, 2003. Encyclopedia.com. http://www.encyclopedia .com?doc/1O40-Ewell.html

10. Information on the phenomenon of "Fitter Family" contests is drawn from the Dolan DNA Learning Center website. See http://www.eugenicsarchive.org/eugenics/ topics_fs.pl?theme=8&search=&matches=

11. Earlier, far-ranging examinations of boundary themes in *To Kill a Mockingbird*— though they do not focus on disability as a master trope—are among the most valuable criticisms extant. See, in particular, Claudia Durst Johnson's book *Threatening Boundaries* (especially its chapter on "The Danger and Delight of Difference") and Laura Fine's essay "Structuring the Narrator's Rebellion," which appears in Alice Petry's more recent collection of *Mockingbird* criticism.

12. In European folk tales, children manifesting congenital disorders (mental and physical) were often assumed to be changelings, elfin beings emerging from the fairy world to inhabit a human space where "the psychologically alienated and the physically handicapped [were] conflated" (Silver 81). In "Fairies and the Folklore of Disability," Susan Schoon Eberly notes that children who failed to thrive or grow naturally were suspected to be changelings, and that "the different child who survives, perhaps with more mental than physical difference, offers a rational explanation for many of the solitary fairies . . . living quietly on the edges of society" (246). There is something of the changeling in both Dill ("I'm little, but I'm old" [*TKAM* 7]) and Boo, as well as Scout.

13. The encoded disability of the female body in Western literature extends most famously back to Aristotle's *Second Generation of Animals* and its characterization of women as, anatomically, "mutilated males."

14. When reminded by Atticus that the Finches have a long history of incestuous breeding habits, Alexandra dismisses this dysgenic "streak" as a genteel beauty mark ("that's where we got our small hands and feet" [*TKAM* 147]). Her eugenic doppelganger, Charles Davenport, made a similar distinction. In *Heredity in Relation to Eugenics*, Davenport generally "condemned the marriage of cousins as prohibited consanguinity," but "extolled the marriage of cousins among the elite as eugenically desired" (Black 74).

15. Harper Lee's mother, it is worth recalling, was Frances *Cunningham Finch* before marrying. The family surname also echoes in "Robert E. *Lee* Ewell." One is reminded of

Steinbeck's observation in *Of Mice and Men* that "the whole country is fulla mutts" (85). The image of the "mutt" serves as a useful metaphor, in fact as in fiction, for the concept of shared imperfection as normalizing counter-argument to pure breeding.

16. For a different and enlightening take on the way impaired "vision" serves as extended metaphor in the novel, see Laurie Champion's excellent essay, "'When You Finally See Them': The Unconquered Eye in *To Kill a Mockingbird*."

17. The Cunningham who holds out for Tom Robinson's acquittal does so because he's "a little disturbed in his mind" (*TKAM* 254). Linking the Cunninghams with the heroism of Boo, mental "disturbance" is recast as the equivalent of an advanced and elevated form of social consciousness and is consistent with Lee's broader strategy of investing shared disability with normalizing power.

Works Cited

Baynton, Douglas C. "Disability and the Justification of Inequality in American History." In *The New Disability History*. Ed. Paul K. Longmore and Laurie Umanski. New York: U New York P, 2001. (33–57)

Black, Edwin. *War Against the Weak*. New York: Four Walls Eight Windows, 2003.

Champion, Laurie. "'When You Finally See Them:' The Unconquered Eye in *To Kill a Mockingbird*." *Southern Quarterly* 37.2 (Winter 1999): 127–136.

Davis, Lennard. *Bending Over Backwards: Disability, Dismodernism, and Other Difficult Positions*. New York: U New York P, 2002.

Davenport, Charles B. *Heredity in Relation to Eugenics*. New York: Henry Holt and Company, 1911.

Early, Gerald. "The Madness in the American Haunted House." In *On Harper Lee: Essays and Reflections*. Ed. Alice Hall Petry. Knoxville: U Tennessee P, 2007. (93–103)

Eberly, Susan Schoon. "Fairies and the Folklore of Disability: Changelings, Hybrids, and the Solitary Fairy." In *The Good People: New Fairylore Essays*. Ed. Peter Narvaiez. Lexington: U Kentucky P, 1991. (227–250)

Fine, Laura. "Structuring the Narrator's Rebellion in *To Kill A Mockingbird*." In *On Harper Lee: Essays and Reflections*. Ed. Alice Hall Petry. Knoxville: U Tennessee P, 2007. (61–77)

Foucault, Michel. *Madness and Civilization*. 1961. New York: Random House, 1965.

Goffman, Erving. *Stigma: Notes on the Management of Spoiled Identity*. 1963. New York: Simon and Schuster, 1986.

Gould, Stephen J. *The Mismeasure of Man*. New York: W.W. Norton, 1981.

Hovett, Theodore R., and Grace Ann. "Fine Fancy Gentlemen and Yappy Folk." *Southern Quarterly* 40.1 (Fall 2001): 67–78.

Johnson, Claudia Durst. *To Kill a Mockingbird: Threatening Boundaries*. New York, Twayne, 1994.

Lee, Harper. *To Kill a Mockingbird*. 1960. New York: Harper Perennial Modern Classics, 2006.

Levi-Strauss, Claude. *The Elementary Structures of Kinship.* 1949. Trans. James Harle Bell, John Richard Von Sturmer, and Rodney Needham. Boston: Beacon Press, 1969.

Mitchell, David T., and Sharon L. Snyder. *Cultural Locations of Disability.* Chicago: U Chicago P, 2006.

———. *Narrative Prosthesis: Disability and the Dependencies of Discourse.* Ann Arbor: U Michigan P, 2000.

Morrison, Toni. *Playing in the Dark: Whiteness and the Literary Imagination.* 1990. New York: Vintage Books, 1993.

Patterson, Kathleen Anne. "Representations of Disability in Mid Twentieth-Century Fiction: From Metaphor to Social Construction." *Dissertation Abstracts International, Section A: The Humanities and Social Sciences.* 1998 June; 58 (12): 4655. University of California, Santa Barbara, 1997 Abstract no.DA9819467.

Quayson, Ato. *Aesthetic Nervousness: Disability and the Crisis of Representation.* New York: U Columbia P, 2007.

Rafter, Nicole. *White Trash: The Eugenic Family Studies, 1877–1919.* Boston: Northeastern U P, 1988.

Richards, Gary. "Harper Lee and the Destabilization of Hetero-sexuality." In *Harper Lee's "To Kill a Mockingbird."* Ed. Harold Bloom. New York: Chelsea House, 1996. (149–189)

Shields, Charles. *Mockingbird: A Portrait of Harper Lee.* New York: Henry Holt, 2006.

Siebers, Tobin. *Disability Theory.* Ann Arbor: U Michigan P, 2008.

Silver, Carole G. *Strange and Secret Peoples: Fairies and Victorian Consciousness.* New York: Oxford U P, 1999.

Steinbeck, John. *Of Mice and Men.* London: Penguin, 1994.

Wray, Matt. *Not Quite White: White Trash and the Boundaries of Whiteness.* Durham, NC: Duke U P, 2006.

CHAPTER 15

To Kill a Mockingbird: Perceptions of "the Other"

Alec Gilmore

William Wordsworth, in one of his major poems reflecting on his growing up,[1] recalls how one summer evening he found a small boat under a willow tree and on impulse decided to go off rowing down Lake Windermere. As he rowed in the moonlight, surrounded by the mountains, it seemed as if the boat was gliding along almost under its own power and, anxious to prove his skill to row in a straight line, he fixed his gaze "upon the summit of a craggy ridge/The horizon's utmost boundary" (ll.371–72) with nothing above but the stars and the grey sky, "When, from behind that craggy steep till then The horizon's bound, a huge peak, black and large, As if with voluntary power instinct Upreared its head" (ll.377–80).

Suddenly the mountains, the water and the skies, which had cradled and fascinated him from birth, created a deep anxiety. Stricken with fear, a mixture of awe, wonder, respect, and apprehension, Wordsworth turned about; yet the more he rowed, the more that "huge peak" seemed to pursue him "with measured motion" as he made his way back to the safety of the willow tree, abandoned the boat, and made for home. For days the author lived with an awareness "of unknown modes of being . . . a darkness . . . call it solitude or blank desertion" (373).

In that experience Wordsworth was the victim of an encounter with "the other," an unknown force able to disturb his equilibrium that he could neither control nor ignore. Deep down, he knew that that other called for respect. A little deeper down perhaps, or maybe deeper in a different way, it frightened him.

In the context of religion, Rudolph Otto[2] has defined such disturbing encounters with "the numinous" as a nonrational (not to be confused with irrational) mystery, which lies at the very heart of humanity. He called it *mysterium tremendum* to sharpen the strength of the emotion and the fear that goes with it. Similarly, critic C. S. Lewis comments (5) that it is unlike other fears and defines it not so much as the fear of a reality (like confrontation with a wild animal) but as the fear of the uncanny (like a ghost). But then to the *mysterium tremendum* Otto adds *et fascinans*, the overwhelming experience from which you cannot escape, like confrontation with a mighty spirit. The consequences are profound because you never know what such a spirit might do or how to respond to it, and hence you find yourself living with the need to keep your distance. Though unable to handle or control it, you cannot deny it or leave it alone either.

Against a backdrop of Otto's philosophical or theological musings, "otherness" emerges as an essential component of our common humanity, which from infancy calls for a natural caution, suspicion, fear, and anxiety when confronted by the other. It may be in our genes or something we imbibe with our mother's milk, but it is an important and necessary part of growing up until we learn to discover who is or is not to be trusted. In this process, the other morphs from anyone not in our family to anyone not in our street, town, country, tribe, race, or the like, or to anyone who does not share our faith, interests, likes, and dislikes.

Starting in a different place and using narrative as her method, Harper Lee, in her only published novel, explores the experience of otherness in a variety of guises. At one level, *To Kill a Mockingbird* is a human story of racial prejudice in a fairly limited, not to say small-minded, community relating to a particular place and time ("a tired old town" in the 1930s); at another it is a communal expression of Wordsworth's personal experience of fear and fascination. In order to dig into this latter experience the first step is to identify the other.

Identifying the Other

Identifying the other varies from person to person and from place to place and is by definition self-centered. To the white, the other is black; to the black, the other is white; and so on, in a multitude of less sharply defined, but no less significant, shades of grey, such as the educated and the uneducated, the rich and the poor, the clean and the dirty, the courteous and the rude, and so on. All are expressions of an "exclusive other," which is one of the most popular and familiar expressions of otherness. It is a product of the "them and us" syndrome, a label we pin on people we don't like, are afraid of or suspicious of; unfortunately we are all party to it, sometimes as victims and sometimes as perpetrators.

For the most part, otherness can be kept in check by various balances and counterbalances and ironically can even form the foundation for a healthy, positive, and creative way of life. Without the checks and balances, however, such exclusivity too easily becomes set in stone with negative results for all parties. In an extreme form or in the hands of lobby groups or manipulators, it may even become little more than a deceptive creation or crude invention. To Kill a Mockingbird focuses on both kinds of exclusivity—the one in the main story (Tom Robinson) and the other in the meta-narrative (Boo Radley).

In the main story, where the predominant theme is race and color, the exclusive other cuts both ways—the white excluding the black and the black excluding the white. So when Calpurnia takes Scout and Jem to *her* church, for example, she and the children are rebuffed by Lula, a member of the congregation, who says to Calpurnia, "I wants to know why you bringin' white chillun to nigger church. . . . You ain't got no business bringin' white chillun here—they got their church, we got our'n. It is our church, ain't it, Miss Cal?" (*TKAM* 135–136).

In the meta-narrative, which is almost a commentary on the main story, we see the damage caused by otherness extreme and unchecked. Not altogether unlike Wordsworth, three children (all under twelve and moved by a mix of fear and fascination) let loose their imaginations on something strange or unusual: perhaps not of great consequence but quite beyond their experience and understanding. Almost before they know what they are doing, and certainly before other people know what they are up to, they allow their imaginations to distort what is there, either for their amusement or to bolster their fear and uncertainties. These fears are complicated by the background provided by the environment and folklore they have grown up with. They find their scary perceptions escalate to the point where they find themselves creating something that is not really there at all. In their case, the consequences may turn out to be relatively unimportant. However, in the hands of a manipulator or lobby group the same experience may prove disastrous.

Both the narrative and the meta-narrative are then backed by a chorus of others. Each character tells us something about the way we treat not only the others we keep on the outside but also the others we allow inside our circle, though not without taking care to establish our distance from them with phrases such as, "Of course, *we* are not like *them*" or "Some people would do this, but *we* don't." Together, the chorus demonstrates that there is no single brand of otherness. There is a touch of the exclusive other in us all, often a part of ourselves of which we may not even be aware but which we need to confront head on. Once understood and wisely handled, this exclusive other can help us establish the "togetherness of the others" that creates the harmony of community life, but to fully appreciate that, step two is necessary. We must struggle to appreciate the other in us all.

The Other in Us All

Jem sums up his own feelings toward the end when he says,

> There's four kinds of folks in the world. There's the ordinary kind, like us and the neighbors. There's the kind like the Cunninghams out in the woods, the kind like the Ewells down at the dump, and the Negroes. . . . The thing about it is, our kind of folks don't like the Cunninghams, the Cunninghams don't like the Ewells, and the Ewells hate and despise the colored folks. (*TKAM* 258)

Scouts adds to this, "Naw, Jem, I think there's just one kind of folks. Folks" (*TKAM* 259).

To Kill a Mockingbird suggests the issues are not quite so simple. Otherness is not confined to education, social class, or lifestyle, and there are many other forms every bit as prevalent, powerful, and destructive as those of race, color or eccentric behavior. Every community has its own collection of others, some more obvious and troublesome than others.

Miss Caroline, the newly arrived teacher in Maycomb, might be described as the *inevitable other*. She is the product of what her previous life has made her and quite unaware of the hazards she faces as soon as she steps outside her own familiar environment. In her case, the focus is education but might just as readily be a host of other factors.

Given Miss Caroline's divergent background, the whole of Maycomb is other to Miss Caroline, a fact exemplified on the one hand by a bright Scout, whose father is "interfering with her reading" by teaching her at home (*TKAM* 19), and on the other by a Walter Cunningham, who turns up without lunch and refuses to go and buy some even when Miss Caroline offers to lend him money. Most interesting is the fact that when Miss Caroline goes berserk at the sight of a cootie in Burris Ewell's hair, her class begins to see her as the other as well (*TKAM* 28–30) and the extent of her otherness is confirmed as she struggles to cope with the fact that Burris has no intention of coming back the following day anyway.

Miss Maudie is a variation on the inevitable other, perhaps better described as the *characteristic other*. She would be other in almost any fairly small, traditional and close community. Otherness is her driving force. It makes her who she is and enables other people to identify her. She cherishes her otherness and takes a pride in it. She hates her house and spends most of her time in her garden, which she loves, along with "everything that grew in God's earth including the weeds" (*TKAM* 47). When her house is burnt down and most of her possessions destroyed, Miss Maudie still takes a lively and almost totally detached view of possessions compared to the interest she still has in Jem and Scout's affairs (*TKAM* 83).

At the same time, however, she is not averse to distinguishing herself in such a way as to make the other person the "other," as if to use their otherness to define her own. She and Nathan Radley, for example, may both be Baptists, but she is quick to point out that they are different sorts of Baptists (*TKAM* 49–50).[3] She is also "not Miss Stephanie"—a more traditional, churchy sort of person, a gossip and a busybody,[4] and one of the main sources for stories about Boo Radley—and is dismissive of what she considers Miss Stephanie's negative attitudes.[5] Miss Maudie may not actually reject the other, but she does assert that the other is not Miss Maudie.

In Dolphus Raymond and Mrs. Dubose, we have a couple of *self-created others*, similar in their isolation but very different from each other and in the reasons that determine their otherness. Dolphus Raymond helps us to understand why some people choose to be other to the point of deliberately creating an "other image" for themselves,[6] whereas in the case of Mrs. Dubose, otherness is a device to cover the root of her problems, which only comes out after her death.

During a break in the trial of Tom Robinson, Dill notices Dolphus sitting apart with the Negroes, looking somewhat out of place and behaving strangely.[7] Jem explains that Dolphus comes from a real old family and owns all one side of the river bank but also has a reputation for being a drunkard (which he isn't) and (some people say) has a colored woman and several mixed children. These details result in Dolphus being identified with the colored folks, and Jem adds, "He likes 'em better 'an he likes us, I reckon" (*TKAM* 182–183). Later Dolphus explains to the children that the image people have of him is one he has deliberately created because "It helps folks if they can latch on to a reason. . . . It ain't honest but it's mighty helpful to folks [because] you see they could never, never understand that I live like I do because that's the way I want to live" (*TKAM* 227–229).

Mrs. Dubose similarly seems to choose awkwardness and hostility to present herself as "a lady with a difference." Neighborhood opinion is unanimous that she is "the meanest old woman who ever lived" (*TKAM* 39), and in the eyes of the children, she is no more than one step away from Boo Radley. However, whereas Boo Radley worries Scout and Jem by his absence, Mrs. Dubose irritates them by her presence. Fearsome, objectionable, and sitting in a wheelchair on her front porch, she consistently launches verbal abuse at Scout and Jem whenever they go by. Jem will not go near without Atticus (*TKAM* 39), and when Atticus requires him to read to her for two hours every afternoon for a month, as a penance for chopping the tops off every camellia bush in her front yard, Jem finds it a very harsh punishment indeed (*TKAM* 122).

Her negative feelings, however, are revealed as not entirely reciprocal because one of the last things Mrs. Dubose does before she dies is to place "a white, waxy, perfect camellia" in a candy box and send it to Jem. Jem is angry and confused by this act, not understanding the meaning of the gesture, but Atticus explains to him that it is the old lady's way of telling him that everything is all right. Her self-created image of awkwardness and hostility was her way of concealing the fact that she was a morphine addict. Atticus then explains that he wanted Jem to read to her to discover what real courage is. "She was a great lady," says Atticus. "She was the bravest person I ever knew" (*TKAM* 127–128).

The Other of a Different Order

Perhaps it takes an "other" to recognize an "other," for in Atticus we truly meet an "other" of a different order. What makes Atticus different is complex. Some of this is reflected in aphorisms (or Atticisms[8]), which tell us something about him—his character, principles, and values.

Early on, when Scout is having difficulty with her teacher and classmates, Atticus says, "You never really understand a person until you consider things from his point of view—until you climb into his skin and walk around in it" (*TKAM* 33),[9] an approach that Atticus spells out to Jem in detail toward the end when Jem is worried because Bob Ewell tells Atticus he is going to get him (*TKAM* 249). To Atticus we owe the phrase that "it's a sin to kill a mockingbird," though it falls to Miss Maudie to explain to the children afterward what he means by the statement (*TKAM* 103).

Equally important is Atticus' shrewd understanding of human nature, amply demonstrated when Scout's recognition of Mr. Cunningham saves Atticus from a mob, and he points out that it can take "an eight-year-old child to bring 'em to their senses" (*TKAM* 174–176, 179), or later when he explains to Jem that in that Maycomb jury, you can see what happens when something comes between "twelve reasonable men in everyday life" and "reason" (*TKAM* 251–252).[10]

For Atticus, living with oneself is a precondition of living with God; they might almost be synonymous. Asked why he insists on defending Tom Robinson, he says he couldn't go to church and worship God if he didn't. Told by Scout that most people think he is wrong, Atticus says that they are entitled to their opinions but "before I can live with other folks I've got to live with myself. The one thing that doesn't abide by majority rule is a person's conscience" (*TKAM* 86, 120).

No wonder the locals find him puzzling if not irritating. Even in his own family, he is something of a loner and an enigma (*TKAM* 94). He is a problem not only for his sister but also for his children. "Atticus," says Scout to Miss Maudie, "can't do anything" (*TKAM* 104).

> He is not like other dads . . . too old . . . unable to engage in rough
> and tumble . . . gives Jem a gun but won't teach him to shoot . . .
> never does anything interesting . . . doesn't hunt, play poker, fish,
> drink or smoke . . . just works in an office, sits, and reads . . . wears
> glasses and is half blind in one eye. (*TKAM* 102–103)

But then again (on the principle that it takes one to recognize one), Miss Maudie provides a useful corrective by providing a picture of a dad to be proud of (*TKAM* 104, 111),[11] though not perhaps without a Freudian slip when she lets it out that Atticus is not at all like other people.[12] With Atticus, "what you see is what you get" and (in a phrase which Scout later recalls) "he's the same in the court-room as he is in the public streets" (*TKAM* 226).

In his toughest test, toward the end of the novel, when initial evidence (based on Scout's report) suggests that Jem was responsible for the death of Bob Ewell and therefore the case would have to come before the county court, Sheriff Heck Tate has other evidence to show that Bob Ewell fell on his knife and killed himself. Atticus suspects Tate of a cover-up and, despite Jem being his own son, insists that everything must come out in the open. He does not want Jem starting out with something like this over his head, adding, "If this thing's hushed up it will be a simple denial to Jem of the way I've tried to raise him" (*TKAM* 312 ff).

Such a man inevitably amuses some, puzzles others, and probably angers as many as he pleases. He has a natural, if unintended, flair to keep the tongues wagging; is clearly not everybody's cup of tea; is possibly not the sort of man you would want to meet up with in a bar; and is unlikely ever to be the soul of a party. He doesn't easily build close relations with anyone and has few friends, associates, and supporters, almost as if people respect him but don't like him. Yet Atticus risks his reputation if not his life in order to be himself, with all that that entails for himself and for his family, and few will doubt that he is unique, his own man, *sui generis*.

What motivates him is a matter for speculation. Unlike Browning's Pippa,[13] Atticus would probably never say, "God's in his heaven, All's right with the world!" but he always seems to have a kind of hunch that all was well—the kind of hunch we all need in childhood if we are to mature as we grow. He never doubts who he is, where he belongs, and whom he belongs to, and these traits are more than enough to give him sufficient confidence to face life for himself and with plenty left over for others. In any community he would be a *distinctive other.*

The Distinctive Other

What enables Atticus to develop his hunch is never spelled out, but the seeds may be found in relationships within his own family, particularly with his sister, Alexandra.

Atticus is other to Alexandra. Alexandra is other to Atticus.[14] On family traditions, standards, values, and social graces they are poles apart, and it is only as they come to terms with their own personal backgrounds and problems, in a particular situation and in the interests of others (in their case, the rearing of children), that each (the distinctive and the exclusive) morphs to create a *balancing other,*[15] rather like the "sail and keel" in marriage or the "good guy/bad guy" in management.

Life and relationships for a balancing other are never entirely smooth, sometimes creating harmony, sometimes strife (as siblings who have struggled to find their own niche in a family know only too well), but it is in the balancing other that we see the potential for a new world. To Alexandra, her family is special—and different—so when Atticus has opened Scout's eyes to a different view of the Cunninghams and Scout tells Aunt Alexandra that she is proposing to invite Walter to tea and even to stay the night, not surprisingly, she is firmly rebuffed. "Why not, auntie?" she asks, "they're good folks." Alexandra has no wish to challenge the fact that they are "good folks" but replies, "They're not our kind of folks." But then we hear Atticus telling Scout that "most of this Old Family stuff's foolishness because everybody's family's just as old as everybody else's," and that includes "colored folks and Englishmen," thereby essentially demolishing the one thing that makes them different from the Cunninghams, the Ewells, and the rest and thus destroying one of the myths that props up not only Alexandra but so many others like her (*TKAM* 255–259).

With that sharp division, rearing children is bound to be a bone of contention, as Atticus accepts Scout as something of a tomboy while Aunt Alexandra is committed to making her a lady (*TKAM* 257).[16] So when Atticus feels obliged to give Scout and Jem a lecture to make them aware that they are "not from run-of-the mill people [but] the product of several generations' gentle breeding," Scout immediately hears Alexandra rather than Atticus in the lecture, and by the time he has finished neither Scout nor Jem has any doubt that their father was simply repeating what his sister had asked him to say, a view confirmed when he ends the conversation telling them not to worry about anything. "When I heard that," says Scout, "I knew he had come back to us" (*TKAM* 151–152).

Further tensions come to light over Calpurnia. When Alexandra is not getting what she wants with Scout, for example, she tells Atticus Calpurnia must go. He has a daughter to think of, and Alexandra feels that while she is around, Calpurnia is no longer needed. But Atticus will not hear of it. Alexandra gets in only two words to object and then she is silenced immediately and the matter is considered closed (*TKAM* 155–156). The balanced others may not have reached agreement and probably never will, but they have come to terms with each other, learned to respect each other and to live together. Each knows and recognizes what the other will and will not do. They also know they both have to live in Maycomb.

There still remains however one crucial difference between them. Whereas one balanced other (Alexandra) is still most at home among the exclusives,[17] the other (Atticus) has one other facet to his character that distinguishes him from most. He cannot countenance the killing of a mockingbird, and with it goes a distinctive yen for that other whom so far we have not mentioned and who needs help most of all—the *victimized other*, of which there are three classic examples: the rejected, the ignored, and the not needed.

The Victimized Other

Tom Robinson—to all intents and purposes a quiet, unassuming fellow but a fall guy and a scapegoat—is rejected, caught in the crossfire of more powerful forces and prejudice, and the fact that we know so little about him tells its own story.[18] For Atticus, Tom is one of many. Atticus has to do what he does in order to help.

Mayella Ewell is ignored. When Atticus asks her in court if she has any friends, Mayella seems not to know what he means, almost as if he were making fun of her. Scout then reflects what she knows Atticus is feeling when she says Mayella "must have been the loneliest person in the world"; not so much rejected as ignored, and as sad as "what Jem called a mixed child" (*TKAM* 218).[19]

Dill is just not needed, and he knows it and feels it (*TKAM* 158). He scarcely counts in the role of life, the victim of an indifference that is the antithesis of love. He arrives and departs very much like a summer holiday, has ideas and drive but is barely taken seriously. He knows his face will be forgotten once he closes the door behind him. Nobody except Jem and Scout seem to notice him at all, though (like father, like daughter) Scout understands— she *knows* she is needed and that Dill isn't.[20] Dill's contact with Atticus is minimal, though Dill clearly regards him with respect if not fear. Thus, when Dill turns up unexpectedly in Maycomb after running away from home, the way Atticus calmly accepts the situation, deals with the essentials, and leaves the judgments to others, is a fair reflection of how he relates to anybody and everybody (*TKAM* 158–160).

Tom, Mayella, and Dill are not natural others. Unlike Atticus and the rest, they have done nothing to merit otherness. Victims of the attitudes of others, they have each had otherness thrust upon them.[21] Yet as we see Atticus in action with the victims we begin to see Atticus, the distinctive other, as "the other for all others."

Though very much one of the society to which he belongs, Atticus almost seems to have come from another world and has found no personal difficulty maintaining the values of that other world come what may. Atticus launches no drive or campaign to promote his philosophy, but those closest to him (a few) find him an inspiration. More general reactions vary from admiration to puzzlement, from appreciation to anger, and by the end of the story, it is questionable whether anything really has changed as a result of his presence. Perhaps that was because change depended not on him but on the Maycomb community. It was up to them to write the sequel and for us, the readers, to imagine what it might be, either in their situation or in a similar one of our own world. Before we can do that, however, there is yet one more other.

The Corporate Other

The *corporate other* is not dissimilar from all the other forms except that it finds expression in groups and communities rather than individuals and therefore can be more insidious. At its heart is the fundamental nature of the otherness we started with: a suspicion, fear, anxiety relating to the unknown (*mysterium*) coupled with a desire to preserve one's identity and linked with an inability to achieve detachment and closure (*fascinans*). In Maycomb the focus is race and color. In other places and other times it may be religion, politics, or gender, possibly even language or dress.

At one level, it is what leads children in the playground to gang up against one who presents no threat but who is slightly out of the norm. At another level, it may lead to more serious attacks (or defense), ranging from minor skirmishes to wars and rumors of war between races, tribes, and nation states; it can and does surface anywhere.[22]

In Maycomb, both sides subscribe to a corporate otherness and both seem to accept it. History may explain how it came about, but it takes more than history to tell us how and why it persists. In one sense, nobody in Maycomb is responsible for it. It is bigger and more far-reaching than any of them. In another sense everybody in Maycomb is responsible. So how *does* corporate otherness persist and *why*?

The idea that some group (such as the Ku Klux Klan) is actively promoting it in Maycomb seems unlikely, and there is no evidence for it in Lee's novel. What seems more likely is that Maycomb residents are all victims in different ways of something that has been there for as long as they can remember. They have grown up with it and learned to live with it. Perhaps, as with our growth from childhood to maturity, what began as a perfectly reasonable suspicion or anxiety has taken over. Eventually, this emotion hardens with age to the point that it becomes little more than a deceptive creation or crude invention that nobody has the courage to challenge. Instead it is in the interests of some people to preserve it, and most individuals prefer not to think about its negative consequences too closely.

Harper Lee makes no attempt to get involved in such issues, and it probably would not be very helpful if she did. Instead she offers a meta-narrative in which she uses the eyes of three children to help us to see a very similar situation in a slightly different context; she relies on the sensitive reader to spot the connections and reflect on them. In this way, while alerting us to the potential damage in all forms of otherness and particularly to the dangers associated with corporate otherness, she concludes her novel with a faint hint that once we can view all others with a more perceptive eye, we may begin to see that, at least in some cases, it is through embracing the other that we find our own deliverance; hence, we move on to Boo Radley.

The Tale of Boo Radley

The tale of Boo Radley addresses the brand of otherness for which there is virtually no evidence but which can readily root and blossom if there is a seed or a doubt, a bit of mystery or imagination, and somebody on hand to exploit it.

Boo Radley is the *nonexistent other*. There is indeed a person with that name and you can "find him" in Maycomb, but of the real Boo Radley and his family, Harper Lee tells us little or nothing. We never meet him until the end, and when we do he is totally different from what we have been led to expect. Yet in Boo's story, we can observe the story of so many others, individual and corporate, in all parts of the world.

The reactions of three children to the nonexistent other are not unlike those of society in general, possibly a reflection of the attitude of many in Maycomb to those of a different race, color, or way of life, and (some would say) a reflection of ourselves in similar situations. It starts (as noted before) when three children, an overdose of imagination, and a modicum of maturity are let loose on something strange or unusual (*mysterium*), of no great consequence and quite beyond their experience and understanding. Not surprisingly, they cannot let it lie (*fascinans*), at least not without trying to examine it and discover its reality for themselves.

Initially, Jem and Scout are hardly aware of Boo. He was "just there." He always had been. Sometimes they wondered if he was real, but mostly they saw him as part of the furniture, treated him with respect, and kept their distance. All they knew depended on stories, myths, and the innuendoes that surrounded him, or what they had gleaned from comments and gossip, and most of it merely washed over them and they paid no attention to it. Boo barely encroaches on their lives, and when he does, there are always others around to offer assurance, security, and protection. There is, however, just enough "strangeness" to breed suspicion.[23]

This is how the nonexistent other first claims our attention.[24] Individuals, families, tribes, races, dogmas, ideologies, and the like can live for years if not generations surrounded by all kinds of others that they know are there but that scarcely impinge on their consciousness. Then one day something happens.

In this case, the catalyst was the arrival of Dill, a year younger than Scout, a "visitor" from another world.[25] When boredom sets in at the end of a long summer vacation, Dill sells Jem and Scout the idea of taking on Boo Radley. From that moment, Scout and Jem's world turns on its axis as Boo Radley becomes a phantom, symbol, or icon of the other and suddenly possesses a power over the children, which they find hard to ignore. What they do may ring familiar bells for anyone who has lived through a similar situation.

First comes a dare. Three children play "chicken" with the "other," testing and teasing themselves as to who has the courage to go and touch the Radleys' house or knock at the door (*TKAM* 15–16).

Next, fantasy feeds on "mysterious messages," as stories,[26] handed down from year to year, are combined with presents found in a tree adjoining the Radley home, suggesting that Boo may be playing games with them (*TKAM* 37–38, 69–70).

Then, play-acting occurs as they dramatize the other; their sense of fear and anxiety find expression in humor as they make fun of the whole idea (*TKAM* 43–45), followed by careful planning to get Boo to come out of his hiding place (*TKAM* 52).

At each stage, boldness and the lack of response feed suspicion, matched by increasing confidence and risk taking, until even the adults join in after a shot is fired in the Radley garden one night, and the story goes round that Boo's older brother had shot a Negro. These occurrences and the rumors they generate thereby confirm precisely the sort of thing that everybody wants to believe.

Hard facts may still be difficult to come by, but slowly there is an increasing awareness and a growing suspicion of this nonexistent other, possibly enough to cause alarm (in a childlike way), as the children dream about him to the point where he looms larger and larger on their radar. Like Wordsworth's peak, fear (*mysterium*) is balanced by a fatal, almost irresistible attraction (*fascinans*).

Adult attitudes vary. Nobody seems to doubt that Boo Radley is real. Some actually claim to know the real story.[27] Some claim to have seen him (*TKAM* 48). Some adopt a healthy indifference. Some just don't see it as a problem. Some go into denial. Some wage a war against it. Only a few, Scout and Jem especially, want an explanation.

Miss Maudie's view is simply that Boo Radley stays in the house because he doesn't want to come out (*TKAM* 49). She knew him as a boy and testifies he was fine as a youngster. Everything people say about him is "three-fourths colored folks and one-fourth Stephanie Crawford,"[28] and Miss Maudie has no time for such rumors. She reasons that nobody knows what some people have to endure, and nobody knows what goes on behind closed doors (*TKAM* 51).

Similarly Atticus, wise and detached as ever, puts the whole incident in proportion, tells them to "stop tormenting that man," to stop their games, and to keep well away from the house until they are invited (*TKAM* 54–55).

Without any hard evidence, it is a story that runs only on fear and suspicion, and serves only those who want to relieve their boredom or those who find it stimulating to have an enemy. So it is that something "nonexistent" can assume reality.

Conclusion

As the story closes, the details of narrative and meta-narrative become secondary. By the middle of October little in Maycomb has changed,[29] and by the end of the month, life for Scout and Jem has resumed the familiar routine of school, play, and study. (*TKAM* 277, 287). For the reader, however, the story may only just be beginning. The tale of Boo Radley may come to an end but not without a hint of a positive note.

Boo, it appears, was a much misunderstood character, a caring person who goes about his business unobtrusively, making advances and offering openings but leaving others to respond. He it was who made overtures to the children with gifts,[30] but they had no understanding of what was going on, found it impossible to believe it was Boo, and (blinded by neighborhood legend and folklore) found themselves unable to share their anxieties with the adults around them.

Yet, when Jem lost his breeches, making a hasty exit from Radley territory, it was Boo who repaired them and left them in an orderly fashion for Jem to collect at his own convenience (*TKAM* 66). On that cold night when Miss Maudie's house was burned to the ground, Boo provided a blanket for Scout (*TKAM* 81), and he was the one on hand when she needed someone to protect her after the Halloween party (*TKAM* 309–310). At no point, however, had the children seen him, not even on the night of the fire (*TKAM* 80–82). As Jem points out, all Scout had to do was to turn round, but she was too busy looking at the fire to notice (*TKAM* 82). After the Halloween party, standing there in Boo's presence with Atticus and Mr. Tate, Scout finds there is still something of the mysterious about him that makes it difficult for her to acknowledge him.

Asked by the sheriff what happened, she says, "Mr. Ewell was tryin' to squeeze me to death, I reckon . . . then somebody yanked Mr. Ewell down. . . . Somebody was staggerin' around and pantin' and—coughing fit to die." Asked who she thought it was, with Boo standing straight in front of her, she still cannot say his name. About all she can do is to point and say, "Why there he is, Mr. Tate, he can tell you his name" (*TKAM* 309). Her description that follows is poignant as she finally acknowledges Boo's presence:

> He had been leaning against the wall when I came into the room, his arms folded across his chest. As I pointed he brought his arms down and pressed the palms of his hands against the wall. They were white hands, sickly white hands that had never seen the sun. . . .
>
> I looked from his hands to his sand-stained khaki pants . . . up his thin frame to his torn shirt. His face was white as his hands. . . . His cheeks were thin to hollowness; his mouth was wide; there were shallow, almost delicate indentations at his temples, and his grey eyes were so colorless I thought he was blind. His hair was dead and thin. . . .
>
> When I pointed to him his palms slipped slightly . . . and he hooked his thumbs in his belt. A strange small spasm shook him . . . but as I gazed at him in wonder the tension slowly drained from his face. His lips parted into a timid smile, and our neighbour's image blurred with my sudden tears.
>
> "Hey, Boo," I said. (*TKAM* 310)

Readers familiar with the Bible[31] (or Handel's *Messiah*[32]) may be reminded of other parallels to Lee's portrait of Radley. In addition, readers familiar with religious art may recall associations with portraiture. This is not to suggest that Boo is Jesus or even a Christ figure, but simply to note that occasionally, and not least among the rejected, despised, and dispossessed others, one comes across a character who so closely resembles the one at the heart of the Christian tradition, and when it happens, nobody is more surprised than we are, except perhaps the person themselves. Atticus is the only one who knows the story of life is never all failure and that there is much more to it than what regularly passes for success.

Closing

We began with Otto's *mysterium tremendum et fascinans* and noted how scholars of the history of religion have sometimes regarded this as humanity's searching after God, a response to a limited understanding of life with a mixture of fear, suspicion, and fascination. If there is any connection between Otto and Harper Lee, it is not so much in the characters as in the quest. Biblical images of early encounters with God are scarcely concealed below the surface, beginning with God telling Moses, "You will see my back, but not my face";[33] continuing in Isaiah's description of the suffering servant;[34] coming to a climax with the women weeping at the cross;[35] and finding the ultimate expression in the stone that the builders rejected.[36]

Perhaps Harper Lee is telling us more than she realized as she offers us a text that acts as a tool for dealing with our fears and uncertainties and gives us a fresh way of looking at them. If so, one way to get the most out of *To Kill a Mockingbird* is to identify the principal characters (Boo, Atticus, Tom, Mayella, or the like) in our own experience, and instead of "playing games" with them or fantasizing about them, learning to see what we are doing to the other, to hear what the others are trying to tell us, and to spot what it is that we are missing.

Notes

1. William Wordsworth was an English romantic poet (1770–1850) and poet laureate (1843–1850). "The Prelude," his magnum opus, is a semi-autobiographical work, one section of which deals with Childhood and School-time. Born in Cockermouth, he grew up with an intense love and appreciation of nature, especially in the Lake District where he lived most of his life.

2. Rudolph Otto (1869–1937) was a German Lutheran theologian and a specialist in comparative religion.

3. Unlike Nathan Radley, for example, Miss Maudie is not "a foot-washing Baptist . . . footwashers believe anything that's pleasure is a sin," and though they may use the same Bible, she says sometimes "the Bible in the hand of one man is worse than the whiskey bottle" in the hand of another" (*TKAM* 50).

4. Her "nose quivered with curiosity" (*TKAM* 245).

5. Her retort to Miss Stephanie's story about Boo Radley gazing through her window, for example, is hardly understanding and sympathetic (*TKAM* 51).

6. An explanation he believes only children could understand (*TKAM* 228).

7. He is drinking through two straws out of a brown paper bag, reputed to be concealing "a Coca-Cola bottle full of whiskey" when in fact it turns out to be nothing more than Coca-Cola (*TKAM* 182–183, 227).

8. For a selection see classiclit.about.com/od/finchatticus/a/aa_atticusquote.htm.

9. For corroborative evidence, witness the way Atticus receives Walter Cunningham into his house (though an unexpected guest) and how within minutes "he and Atticus talked together like two men" (*TKAM* 27).

10. At this point, there is a reflection in the meta-narrative as Atticus explains to Jem that his failure to understand is because he has not yet faced a situation in life that has interfered with his reasoning process, yet, in a sense Jem has, without being aware of it, in his treatment of Boo Radley, in that the selfsame "neighborhood legend" that had come between "twelve reasonable men . . . and reason" had enabled Jem and his friends to behave as they did. (*TKAM* 251–252).

11. When Scout and Jem are struggling with the animosity of the community following the trial, she explains that "there are some men in the world who are born to do our unpleasant jobs for us. Your father's one of them," she adds, and despite the current climate she goes on to say that there are many people in Maycomb who value his presence, including the judge, the sheriff, and many colored folks too (*TKAM* 245–246).

12. A view reinforced by an unsolicited testimonial from Dolphus Raymond during the trial when he says to Scout, "You're pa's not a run-of the-mill man" (*TKAM* 229).

13. Robert Browning, *Pippa Passes*, part 1, line 221.

14. The polarization is such that Scout wonders whether they ever grew up in the same family and even speculates that perhaps Alexandra had been swapped with someone else at birth (*TKAM* 88, 149).

15. Sometimes described as the "parking lot" theory, based on the idea that when you see a car parked very oddly in a car park, you don't have to assume that the driver was either an idiot or an incompetent driver; the chances are that was the only available spot when he arrived. Similarly, a second child in a family may well turn out different from the expected because the first has claimed her territory.

16. An approach shared with brother Jack, who takes Atticus to task for his leniency in dealing with her (*TKAM* 99–101). Jack chides Scout for bad language whereas Atticus sees it as little more than a stage in growing up (*TKAM* 89–90). Jem's assessment (to Scout) is that Alexandra's "not used to girls, leastways, not girls like you" (*TKAM* 257).

17. Toward the end, when normality is being restored, "Alexandra and her Missionary Circle" were still "fighting the good fight all over the house" (*TKAM* 260 ff).

18. All we have is Scout's judgment, after watching him closely during the trial, that he is "a respectable Negro" (*TKAM* 219).

19. "White people wouldn't have anything to do with her because she lived among pigs; Negroes wouldn't have anything to do with her because she was white" (*TKAM* 218). See Jem's other remark that "they're just in-betweens, don't belong anywhere" (*TKAM* 183).

20. "As Dill explained," she says, "I found myself wondering what life would be if Jem were different . . . what I would do if Atticus did not feel the need of my presence, help and advice. . . . Even Calpurnia couldn't get along unless I was there. They needed me" (*TKAM* 162).

21. Otherness is not unlike greatness, of which Shakespeare wrote, "Some men are born great, some achieve greatness, and some have greatness thrust upon them (*Twelfth Night*, act 2, scene 5).

22. Most recently, on the international front, some would cite the cold war, weapons of mass destruction, or the war on terror. Others would strongly disagree and that, in part, is what makes the corporate other so potentially dangerous.

23. Rather than pass the Radley Place, "a negro would cut across to the sidewalk opposite and whistle as he walked" (*TKAM* 9), and Cecil Jacobs would walk "a total of one mile per school day going by the back street an' all the way around by town to get home" rather than pass close by (*TKAM* 39).

24. In a predominantly white British community in the 1960s, when race and color were still only coming over the horizon, a child went home and told his parents he had found a new friend. "Is he black or white," says mum. "I don't know," replies the child, "I'll go and ask him."

25. "A pocket Merlin whose head teemed with eccentric plans, strange longings, and quaint fancies" (*TKAM* 9).

26. For example, observe the belief that the nuts that fall in the school playground from a tree in the Radley's garden are poisonous.

27. According to "neighborhood legend," Boo in his teens had got involved in some high-spirited activity with a gang of others and been brought before the local judge charged with "disorderly conduct, disturbing the peace, assault and battery, and using abusive and profane language in the presence and hearing of a female." Thanks to his father's reputation and relationship with the judge, Boo had escaped the worst of punishments on the grounds that his father "would see to it that Arthur gave no more trouble." After this he was not seen again for fifteen years. Subsequently, at the age of thirty-three it was alleged that he had driven a pair of scissors into his father's leg and shown no sign of remorse, though there seemed to be little evidence to substantiate the story (*TKAM* 10–13).

28. Miss Stephanie claims that one night she woke up and found him looking in her window (*TKAM* 13–14, 51).

29. There are three exceptions. Bob Ewell was somewhat chastened, Judge Taylor had been shot at, and Link Deas (Tom Robinson's employer) had offered a job to Helen, Tom's widow, and was providing strong support against the innuendoes of Bob Ewell.

30. These gifts range from "chewing gum minus their outer wrappers" (*TKAM* 37–38) to "a ball of gray twine" (*TKAM* 66) and included a medal and "two small images carved in soap" (*TKAM* 67–68).

31. Isaiah 53, especially verses 2–3 and 7.

32. Especially the chorus, "He was despised."

33. Exodus 33:23, *Good News Bible* (GNB).

34. Isaiah 52:13–53:12. This passage is often thought to be a foretaste of the crucifixion. Notice the detailed description of Boo. He has his back to the wall, a "thin frame" with a "torn shirt", white hands and face, cheeks "thin to hollowness," "grey eyes so colorless [Scout] thought he was blind," hair "dead and thin"—but as tension slowly drained from his face, he managed a timid smile that moved an onlooker to tears (*TKAM* 310).

35. Luke 23:28.

36. Acts 4:11, GNB.

Works Cited

Lee, Harper. *To Kill a Mockingbird.* 1960. New York: Harper Perennial Modern Classics, 2006.

Lewis, C. S. *The Problem of Pain.* London: Geoffrey Bless, 1940.

Otto, Rudolph. *The Idea of the Holy.* Trans. John W Harvey. Oxford: Oxford U P, 1923.

Wordsworth, William. "The Prelude." In William Wordsworth, *The Complete Poetical Works.* London: Macmillan, 1888. (book 1, lines 357–400).

Related Readings and Publications

Althouse, Ann. "Reconstructing Atticus Finch? A Response to Steven Lubet." *Michigan Law Review* 97.6 (May 1999): 1363–69.

Atkinson, Robert. "Comment on Steven Lubet's 'Reconstructing Atticus Finch.'" *Michigan Law Review* 97.6 (May 1999): 1370–72.

——. "Liberating Lawyers: Divergent Paths in *Intruder in the Dust* and *To Kill a Mockingbird*." *Duke Law Journal* 49.3 (1999): 601–748.

Baecker, Diane. "Telling It in Black and White: The Importance of the Africanist Presence in *To Kill a Mockingbird*." *Southern Quarterly: A Journal of the Arts in the South* 36.3 (Spring 1998): 124–32.

Baines, Lawrence. "From Page to Screen: When a Novel Is Interpreted to Film, What Gets Lost in Translation?" *Journal of Adolescent & Adult Literacy* 39.8 (May 1996): 612–22.

Bakerman, Jane S. "Maycomb Revisited: *To Kill a Mockingbird*, Novel and Screen Play." *Indiana English* 8.1–3 (1974): 18–28.

Barra, Allen. "What *To Kill a Mockingbird* Isn't." *Wall Street Journal*, 24 June 2010: Arts and Entertainment. http://online.wsj.com/article/SB10001424052748703561604575283354059763326.html

"Being Atticus Finch: The Professional Role of Empathy in *To Kill a Mockingbird*." *Harvard Law Review* 117.5 (March 2004): 1682–1702.

Bernard, Catherine. *Understanding "To Kill a Mockingbird*." San Diego: Lucent Books, 2003.

Blackall, Jean. "Valorizing the Commonplace: Harper Lee's Response to Jane Austen." In *On Harper Lee: Essays and Reflections*. Ed. Alice Hall Petry. Nashville: U Tennessee P, 2007. (19–34)

Bloom, Harold. *Modern Critical Interpretations: "To Kill a Mockingbird."* Philadelphia: Chelsea House Publisher, 1999.

———. *To Kill a Mockingbird.* Bloom's Guides. Philadelphia: Chelsea House Publishing, 2003.

Bowers, Kristen. *"To Kill a Mockingbird" Literature Guide.* Secondary Solutions Teachers Guides. San Dimas, CA: Secondary Solutions, 2007.

Bragg, Rick. "The Book That Changed My Life." *Reader's Digest,* May 2010: 152–61.

Cauthen, Cramer R. "The Gift Refused: The Southern Lawyer in *To Kill a Mockingbird, The Client,* and *Cape Fear.*" *Studies in Popular Culture* 19.2 (October 1996): 257–75.

Champion, Laurie. "Lee's *To Kill a Mockingbird.*" *Explicator* 61.4 (2003): 234–36.

———. "'When You Finally See Them': The Unconquered Eye in *To Kill a Mockingbird.*" *Southern Quarterly* 37.2 (1999): 127–36.

Chappell, Charles M. "The Unity of *To Kill a Mockingbird.*" *Alabama Review* 42.1 (1989): 32–48.

Chura, Patrick. "Prolepsis and Anachronism: Emmett Till and the Historicity of *To Kill a Mockingbird.*" *Southern Literary Journal* 32.2 (2000): 1–26.

Clausen, Andrew. *"To Kill a Mockingbird" Study Guide.* Eau Claire, WI: Progeny Press, 1994.

Collins, Mary. *"To Kill a Mockingbird" LitPlan Teacher Pack.* Berlin, MD: Teacher's Pet Publications, 2007.

Crespino, Joseph "The Strange Career of Atticus Finch." *Southern Cultures* 6.2 (Summer 2000): 9–29.

Crowe, Chris. "Atticus, David, and Raymond: Role Models for YA Males." *The English Journal* 88.6 (July 1999): 119–22.

Dare, Tim. "Lawyers, Ethics, and *To Kill a Mockingbird.*" *Philosophy and Literature* 25.1 (2001): 127–41.

Dave, R. A. "Harper Lee's Tragic Vision." In *Indian Studies in American Fiction.* Ed. M. K. Naik, S. K. Desai, S. Mokashi-Punekar. Delhi: MacMillan Company of India, 1974.

Downton, Susie. "Defending *To Kill a Mockingbird.*" *The English Journal* 89.3 (March 1998): 9.

Elizabeth, Mary, and Kathy Kifer. *"To Kill a Mockingbird": A Teaching Guide.* Eugene, OR: Garlic Press, 2002.

Failinger, Marie A. "Gentleman as Hero: Atticus Finch and the Lonely Path." *Journal of Law and Religion* 10.2 (1993–1994): 303–9.

Fine, Laura. "Structuring the Narrator's Rebellion in *To Kill a Mockingbird.*" In *On Harper Lee: Essays and Reflections.* Ed. Alice Hall Petry. Nashville: U Tennessee P, 2007. (61–77)

Foote, Horton. *"To Kill a Mockingbird": The Screen Play and Related Readings.* Literature Connections. Evanston, IL: McDougal Littell, 1997.

Friedland, Joyce. *To Kill a Mockingbird: A Study Guide.* Novel-Ties. New York: Learning Links, 1983.

Gibbons, Louel C. *"To Kill a Mockingbird" in the Classroom: Walking in Someone Else's Shoes.* NCTE High School Literature. Urbana, IL: National Council of Teachers of English, 2009.

Greaber, Mary Michael. *Literature Teaching Guide for "To Kill a Mockingbird."* Ikon Literature Teaching Guides. Winona, MN: St. Mary's College Press, 1968.

Haggerty, Andrew. *Harper Lee: "To Kill a Mockingbird."* Writers and Their Works. New York: Benchmark Books, 2009.

Hartley, Mary, and Tony Buzan. *To Kill A Mockingbird.* Literature Made Easy series. Hauppauge, NY: Barron's Educational Series, 1999.

Heath, Samuel D. G. *"To Kill a Mockingbird": A Critique on Behalf of Children.* New York: iUniverse, 2007.

Henderson, R. *"To Kill a Mockingbird." Library Journal,* 15 May 1960: n. p.

Hicks, Granville. "Three at the Outset." *Saturday Review* XLIII (23 July 1960): 30.

Hovet, Theodore, and Grace-Ann Hovet. "'Fine Fancy Gentlemen' and 'Yappy Folk': Contending Voices in *To Kill a Mockingbird." Southern Quarterly: A Journal of the Arts in the South* 40 (Fall 2001): 67–78.

Inge, M. Thomas. "To Kill a Prejudice: Racial Relations and the Lynch Mob in Twain, Faulkner, and Harper Lee." In *Southern Ethnicities.* Ed. Youli Theodosiadou. Thessaloniki, Greece: Kornelia Sfakianaki. 61–74.

Johnson, Claudia. "The Secret Courts of Men's Hearts: Code and Law in Harper Lee's *To Kill a Mockingbird." Studies in American Fiction* 19.2 (Autumn 1991): 129–39.

Johnson, Claudia Durst. *"To Kill a Mockingbird": Threatening Boundaries.* Twayne's Masterwork Studies Series. New York: Twayne Publishers, 1994.

———. *Understanding "To Kill a Mockingbird": A Student Casebook to Issues, Sources, and Historical Documents.* Literature in Context. Westport, CT: Greenwood, 1994.

Jolley, Susan Arpajian. "Integrating Poetry and *To Kill a Mockingbird." The English Journal* 92.2 (November 2002): 34–40.

Jones, Carolyn. "Atticus Finch and the Mad Dog." *Southern Quarterly: A Journal of the Arts in the South* 34 (Summer 1996): 4.

Keershan, Charles. "Harper Lee's Novel Achievement: With *To Kill a Mockingbird,* Published 50 Years Ago, Lee Gave America a Story for the Ages. Just Don't Ask Her About It." *Smithsonian,* June 2010: 82–91.

King, Sandra Ray. "May, a Courtroom in Maycomb." *Callaloo* 24.1 (Winter 2001): 106–7.

Lee, Harper. *To Kill a Mockingbird.* 1960. New York: Harper Perennial Modern Classics, 2002.

LeMay, Harding. "Children Play; Adults Betray." *New York Herald Tribune,* 10 July 1960: n. p.

Liu, Guohzi. "On the Bi-Circular Structure in *To Kill a Mockingbird." Foreign Literature Studies* 119 (2006): 130–36.

Lubet, Steven. "Reconstructing Atticus Finch." *Michigan Law Review* 97.6 (May 1999): 1339–62.

———. "Reply to Comments on 'Reconstructing Atticus Finch.'" *Michigan Law Review* 97.6 (May 1999): 1382–84.

Madden, Kerry. *Harper Lee (Up Close).* New York: Viking, 2009.

Mancini, Candice, ed. *Racism in Harper Lee's "To Kill a Mockingbird."* Detroit: The Gale Group, 2008.

May, Jill. "Censors as Critics: *To Kill a Mockingbird* as a Case Study." In *Cross Culturalism in Children's Literature: Selected Papers from the Children's Literature Association.* Ed. Susan R. Gannon. Ottawa, Canada: Carleton U P, 1987. (91–95)

McCarty, Lisa. *To Kill a Mockingbird.* Focus on Reading Study Guides. Irvine, CA: Saddleback Educational Publishing, 2006.

Metcalf, R. *York Notes on Harper Lee's "To Kill a Mockingbird."* London: Longman, 1997.

Metress, Christopher. "The Rise and Fall of Atticus Finch." *The Chattahoochee Review* 24.1 (September 2003): 95–102.

Milton, Joyce. *To Kill a Mockingbird.* Barron's Book Notes. Hauppauge, NY: Barron's Educational Series, 1984.

Murphy, Mary McDonagh. *Scout, Atticus, and Boo: A Celebration of Fifty Years of* To Kill a Mockingbird. New York: Harper, 2010.

Noble, Donald, ed. To Kill a Mockingbird: *Critical Insights.* New York: Salem Press, 2009.

O'Neill, Terry, ed. *Readings on "To Kill a Mockingbird."* San Diego: Greenhaven, 2000.

Palmer, R. Barton. *Harper Lee's "To Kill a Mockingbird": The Relationship between Text and Film.* London: Metheun Drama, 2008.

Petry, Alice Hall, ed. *On Harper Lee: Essays and Reflections.* Nashville: U Tennessee P, 1994.

Robbins, Mari Lu. *A Guide for Using "To Kill a Mockingbird" in the Classroom.* Westminster, CA: Teacher Created Resources, 2004.

Saney, Isaac. "The Case against *To Kill a Mockingbird.*" *Race & Class* 45.1 (July–September 2003): 99–105.

Santos, Marlisa. "Stand Up, Your Father's Passing: Atticus Finch as Hero Archetype." In *The Hero's Journey.* Ed. Harold Bloom. New York: Bloom's Literary Criticism, 2009.

Schuster, Edgar H. "Discovering Theme and Structure to the Novel." *The English Journal* 52.7 (October 1963): 506–11.

Sergel, Christopher. *Harper Lee's "To Kill a Mockingbird": A Full Length Play.* Chicago: Dramatic Publishing Company, 1970.

Shackleford, Dean. "The Female Voice in *To Kill a Mockingbird*: Narrative Strategies in Film and Novel." *Mississippi Quarterly: The Journal of Southern Cultures* 50.1 (Winter 1996–1997): 101–13.

Shields, Charles. *Mockingbird: A Portrait of Harper Lee.* New York: Henry Holt, 2006.

Simon, William H. "Moral Icons: A Comment on Steven Lubet's 'Reconstructing Atticus Finch.'" *Michigan Law Review* 97.6 (1999): 1376–77.

Stefanovici, Smaranda. "Gender Roles and Femininity in Harper Lee's *To Kill a Mockingbird.*" Gender Studies 1.7 (2008): 71–78.

Stephens, Robert O. "The Law and the Code in Harper Lee's *To Kill a Mockingbird. Southern Cultures* 1.2 (1995): 215–27.

Suhor, Charles and Larry Bell. "Preparing to Teach *To Kill a Mockingbird.*" *English Journal* 86.4 (1997): 1–16.

Tavernier-Courbin, Jacqueline. "Humor and Humanity in *To Kill a Mockingbird.*" In *On Harper Lee: Essays and Reflections.* Ed. Alice Hall Petry. Nashville: U Tennessee P, 2007. (41–60)

Taylor, Art. "Do the Right Thing: Harper Lee and *To Kill a Mockingbird." Mystery Scene* 101 (Fall 2007): 23–28.

Ward, L. "*To Kill a Mockingbird* (book review)." *Commonwealth*, 9 December 1960: n. p.

Ware, Michele. "'Just a Lady': Gender and Power in Harper Lee's *To Kill a Mockingbird.* In *Women in Literature: Reading through the Lens of Gender.* Ed. Jerilyn Fisher and Ellen S. Silber. Westport CT: Greenwood, 2003.

White, Brian. "The Case for Studying Character(s) in the Literature Classroom." *Journal of Language and Literacy Education* 2:2 (2006): 1–21.

Zorn, Eric. "Language of Mockingbird Still Sings After 50 Years: Harper Lee's Thoughtful Writing Underscores the Message of the Classic Story of Courage." *Chicago Tribune*, 10 July 2010: Section 1, 13.

Index

About the Editor and Contributors

Editor

Michael J. Meyer is Professor Emeritus of English at DePaul University in Chicago. Meyer is the present bibliographer for Steinbeck studies, having published *The Hayashi Steinbeck Bibliography (1982–1996)* in 1998 (Scarecrow) and a follow-up volume (1996–2006) in 2008. In addition to his bibliographic work, Meyer's essays have appeared in the *Steinbeck Quarterly,* the *Steinbeck Review,* and the *Steinbeck Newsletter,* and he has contributed chapters to numerous monographs and books, including serving as editor for *Cain Sign: The Betrayal of Brotherhood in the Works of John Steinbeck* (Mellen, 2000). He is presently the bibliographer for the *Steinbeck Review* and serves on its editorial board. Other publications include *A John Steinbeck Encyclopedia* (Greenwood, 2006), on which he served as co-editor with Brian Railsback.

Since 1994, Meyer has been an editor for Rodopi Press's series Perspectives in Modern Literature where his seven volumes include *Literature and the Grotesque* (1995), *Literature and Music* (2002), and *Literature and the Law* (2003). As senior editor of Rodopi's new series entitled *Dialogues,* he has supervised volumes where classic canonical texts are examined on the basis of controversial issues and are discussed in parallel studies prepared by recent PhDs as well as by more experienced scholars. His most recent books are *The Essential Criticism of "Of Mice and Men"* (Scarecrow, 2009), which reviews the novel's critical reception over seven decades, and *"The Grapes of Wrath": A Re-Consideration* (Rodopi, 2009).

Contributors

Derek Blair worked for over eighteen years in television news and video production. The twice Emmy-nominated producer earned his undergraduate degree in communications studies from the University of Windsor. He has recently graduated from Madonna University's College of Education, Livonia, Michigan, with certification in communication arts and English.

Lisa Detweiler Miller was born in the Philadelphia area. She received her BA from Juniata College and MA from Carnegie Mellon University. She is currently pursuing her PhD at West Virginia University in Morgantown, West Virginia, where she lives with her husband. Her research interests include nineteenth- and early twentieth-century American literature with a strong focus on Southern literature. She is most drawn to critical race theory, performance theory, and pedagogy.

Cecilia Donohue is a professor and chairperson in the Department of Language and Literature at Madonna University in Livonia, Michigan. Author of *Robert Penn Warren's Novels: Feminine and Feminist Discourse*, Cecilia has recently edited a forthcoming volume of essays on Sandra Cisneros's *Woman Hollering Creek*. Cecilia's scholarly interests include twentieth-century Southern women authors, John Steinbeck, film translations of novels, sports fiction, and popular culture. She has authored entries on American literature and culture for *The Literary Encyclopedia* and Salem Press. Her current research is focused on Steinbeck's *East of Eden* and *Journal of a Novel*, as well as on the fiction of Anne Tyler.

Ann Engar is an assistant professor and Presidential Teaching Scholar at the University of Utah, where she directs and teaches in the Pre-Law LEAP Program and teaches for the Honors College. She received her PhD in English from University of Washington. A senior bibliographer for the Modern Language Association, Ann is the author of over sixty articles, many on women writers and their works.

Robert C. Evans has taught at Auburn University Montgomery (AUM) since 1982, earning his PhD at Princeton University in 1984. He has received various academic honors, including fellowships at the Folger, Huntington, and Newberry Libraries and from the National Endowment for the Humanities, the

American Council of Learned Societies, and the Mellon Foundation. He is the author or editor of more than twenty-five books and nearly two hundred essays. At AUM he has been distinguished research professor, distinguished teaching professor, and university alumni professor. In 1989 he was chosen as Professor of the Year for the state by the Council for the Advancement and Support of Education.

Alec Gilmore is a Baptist minister in the United Kingdom, a lecturer in biblical studies, and a Senior Research Fellow at the International Baptist Theological Seminary in Prague, where he specializes in the Old Testament, preaching, and hermeneutics. His most recent book is *A Concise Dictionary of Bible Origins and Interpretation* (T & T Clark, Continuum, 2007). Interest in Steinbeck arose from frequent visits to San Francisco with research opportunities at San José State and Stanford universities. He contributed a paper ("Did Steinbeck Have a Suffering Servant?") at the Steinbeck Centennial Conference in 2002 and wrote a chapter ("Steinbeck's Multi-layered Use of the Biblical Image") in *"The Grapes of Wrath": A Reconsideration*, ed. Michael J. Meyer (Rodopi, 2009).

Malcolm Gladwell has been a staff writer with the *New Yorker* magazine since 1996. His 1999 profile of Ron Popeil won a National Magazine Award, and in 2005 he was named one of *Time* magazine's 100 Most Influential People. He is the author of four books: *The Tipping Point: How Little Things Make a Big Difference* (Back Bay Books, 2000); *Blink: The Power of Thinking without Thinking* (Back Bay, 2005); *Outliers: The Story of Success* (Little Brown, 2008)—all of which were number one *New York Times* bestsellers—and the bestselling anthology *What The Dog Saw* (Little Brown, 2009). From 1987 to 1996, he was a reporter with the *Washington Post*, where he covered business and science, and then served as the newspaper's New York City bureau chief. He graduated from the University of Toronto, Trinity College, with a degree in history. He was born in England, grew up in rural Ontario, and now lives in New York City.

Christian Z. Goering is an assistant professor of secondary English and literacy education at the University of Arkansas, where he coordinates the English education program and directs the Northwest Arkansas Writing Project. He received a PhD in curriculum and instruction from Kansas State University in 2007 and currently serves on the executive board of the Arkansas Council of Teachers of English Language Arts. He provides educational outreach through his website dedicated to literacy and the teaching of literature through music at www.littunes.com.

James B. Kelley is an associate professor of English at Mississippi State University–Meridian, where he teaches literature, theory, and writing. He has published reference book entries and articles on various subjects in modern literature and culture as well as a book on the African American writer Langston Hughes.

Hugh McElaney is an instructor in the Department of English at Fitchburg State University in Fitchburg, Massachusetts, where he teaches "Literature and Disability." His essay on Louisa May Alcott's disabling treatment of the male body, "Alcott's Freaking of Boyhood," appeared in *Children's Literature* 34 (2006). He lives with his wife in Princeton, Massachusetts.

Carl F. Miller teaches twentieth-century British and American literature at the University of Alabama in Tuscaloosa, where he lives adjacent to Harper Lee Drive. He received his doctorate from the University of Florida and has recently published other articles on the impact of the Cold War on the graphic novel and the utopian dimensions of Michael Jackson's *Captain EO*. He is currently completing a book manuscript on popular expressions of modernism.

Katie Rose Guest Pryal is a lecturer in the Department of English and Comparative Literature and an adjunct assistant professor of law at University of North Carolina at Chapel Hill. She earned her law degree from the University of North Carolina School of Law and her doctorate in English from the University of North Carolina at Greensboro, specializing in rhetoric and composition. Her book manuscript, *Pragmatism and the Rhetoric of Affirmative Action* examines the intransigence of the affirmative action debate and suggests ways to find common ground. Her current book, *A Short Guide to Writing about Law* (Pearson 2010), teaches scholars how to incorporate legal sources into their research and writing.

Jochem Riesthuis is a scholar of German and English literature with a PhD in comparative literature from the University of Chicago. With a primary interest in the twentieth century, he has published on authors like Ralph Ellison, Anthony Burgess, John Dos Passos, Richard Wright, and Stefan Heym, as well as on Klaus Mann's *Mephisto* and Ann Petry's *The Street*. His work centers on the intersection of politics, identity and language. Currently he is a lecturer of English with Media and Entertainment Management at Stenden University, Leeuwarden, The Netherlands.

Angela Shaw-Thornburg is an assistant professor of English at South Carolina State University, where she teaches and writes on American and African American literature. She also serves as the co-editor of *Plenum: The South Carolina State University Journal of Interdisciplinary Studies.*

Cindy M. Williams is a graduate assistant at the University of Arkansas where she is pursuing a PhD in curriculum and instruction, English education. She has taught secondary English for fourteen years and postsecondary education and composition courses for seven years. She serves as co-director of inservice for the Northwest Arkansas Writing Project and became a teacher consultant in 2008.

Jeffrey B. Wood is a member of the Illinois Bar and a corporate attorney with a financial services institution in the Chicago area. He graduated with honors from the College of William and Mary and received his JD from Northwestern University School of Law. His research and speaking engagements cover a wide variety of topics, including law, literature, ethics, and public policy.

Cover Artist

David Kellam Brown is a freelance artist/illustrator living in Plano, Texas. His former career was as a system software designer in the telecom industry, but for the past six years, Brown has concentrated on producing fine art and illustration, teaching drawing and painting at a four-year arts college, and working on his MFA in illustration at the Academy of Art University in San Francisco. Brown has won several awards at local, national, and Internet art shows and is a Juried Member of EBSQ and a Signature Member of the Texas Visual Arts Association.